ENCYCLOPAEDIA OF EMINENT THINKERS

VOLUME-XXI: SIR SYED AHMED KHAN

Volumes by the same author

The Political Thought of ***Veer Savarkar***
The Political Thought of ***M.A. Jinnah***
The Political Thought of ***Mohammad Iqbal***
The Political Thought of ***K.B. Hedgewar***
The Political Thought of ***M.S. Golwalkar***
The Political Thought of ***Lokmanya Bal Gangadhar Tilak***
The Political Thought of ***Pandit Deendayal Upadhyaya***
The Political Thought of ***Gopal Krishna Gokhale***
The Political Thought of ***Maulana Abul Kalam Azad***
The Political Thought of ***Sir Syed Ahmed Khan***

About the Author

Dr. Jai Narain Sharma (*b.* 1951) is Professor and Chairman of the Department of Gandhian Studies, Panjab University, Chandigarh. He is also Hon. Director of Gandhi Bhawan; member of Board of Studies, Nagpur University, Nagpur and Mahatma Gandhi Kashi Vidyapith, Varanasi; member of Research Degree Committee of the Department of Political Science, H.P. University, Shimla: General Secretary of Indian Soviety of Gandhian Studies; and member on the Presidium of the Alliance for Sarvodaya. He regularly writes for leading newspapers, and has published more than hundred research papers in professional journals of repute. Dr. Sharma has many books to his credit including *"Gandhi's View of Political Power"*, *"Economics of Defence: A Study of SAARC Countries"*, *"Economic Thought of Mahatma Gandhi"*, *"Human Resource Management"*, *"Alternative Economics: Economics of Mahatma Gandhi and Globalisation"*, *"Power, Politics and Corruption: A Gandhian Solution"* and *"Research Methodology: The Discipline and its Dimensions.*

ENCYCLOPAEDIA OF EMINENT THINKERS

VOLUME-TWENTY ONE

THE POLITICAL THOUGHT OF SIR SYED AHMED KHAN

Dr. Jai Narain Sharma
Professor and Chairman
Department of Gandhian Studies
Panjab University, Chandigarh

CONCEPT PUBLISHING COMPANY, NEW DELHI-110 059

Cataloging in Publication Data—DK
Courtesy: D.K. Agencies (P) Ltd. docinfo@dkagencies.com

Encyclopaedia of eminent thinkers.
p. cm. — (Gandhian studies and peace research series ; 11)
Vols. 11- lack series statement.
In Indian context.
Includes bibliographical references.
Includes indexes.
Contents: v. 21. The political thought of Sir Syed Ahmed Khan / Jai Narain Sharma.
ISBN 10: 8180695816

1. Statesmen—India. 2. Political science—India. 3. India—Politics and government. I. Sharma, Jai Narain, 1951- II. Pasricha, ashu, 1967- III. Series: Gandhian studies and peace research series ; 11.

DDC 954.035 22

ISBN -13: 978-81-7022-684-0 (Series)
ISBN -10: 81-7022-684-8 (Series)
ISBN -13: 978-81-8069-581-0 (Vol. XXI)
ISBN -10: 81-8069-581-6 (Vol. XXI)

First Published 2009

Published and Printed by
Ashok Kumar Mittal
Concept Publishing Company
A/15-16, Commercial Block, Mohan Garden
New Delhi-110059 (India)
Phones: 25351460, 25351794
Fax: 091-11-25357103
E-mail: publishing@conceptpub.com

DEDICATED
TO
THE SACRED MEMORY
OF MY
MATERNAL UNCLE
(Late) PANDIT SHRINIVAS SHARMA

PREFACE

It is because the thought of Sir Syed Ahmed Khan stands out as an important landmark in the development of Muslim thought in the South Asian subcontinent that there is perennial interest in him, and also the need for reassessment. Yet in his own time, he was one of the most controversial figures on the British Indian landscape, and he has been the centre of fierce passions, both among his contemporaries and among more recent historians.

During his lifetime, Sir Syed Ahmed was regarded as an educational reformer by the small class of English-educated Muslims and as a religious heretic by the orthodox 'Ulema', while Victorian England saw him as a Messiah who could end the age-old Muslim resistance in Hindustan and lead the Muslims into rationalism and enlightened Imperial submissiveness.

More lately, the complexities of Syed Ahmed's life and attitudes have been subordinated to the requirements of nationalist ideology in India and Pakistan. Indian historians tend to see him as a communalist and separatist who first propounded the 'two-nation' idea. On the other hand, Pakistani historians tend to see him as the prophet of a nation and the first spokesman for a Muslim homeland.

He has been all things to all men, for he is one of the truly great 19th century figures. He is like a mountain, with many facets and angles, and because he wrote and spoke so much, there are diverse elements in the legacy of this Muslim leader. Men of all shades of religious and political opinion claimed him as the originator of their particular schools of thought. Nevertheless, he was a man who must be seen and judged in the context of his own time and contemporaries, and as the main link between the decaying feudalism of pre-British Mughal Hindustan and the renaissance of modern Muslim India. Over the years, Syed Ahmed's legacy has had a profound influence upon the thought of Muslim India.

Even from the brief sketch, it can be seen that Sir Syed's career and writings had many facets; he was much more complex than is often appreciated, even by his supporters. But it is precisely this which makes an investigation of the literary origins of the legend of Sir Syed Ahmed so important. He considered his theological work as an integral part of his overall endeavour. I think that his life exemplifies that change of ideas, rather than being a mere epiphenomenon or ideological superstructure of changes in the economic, social and political field, is in fact related to all of them by way of mutual interaction. The present study deliberately confines itself to the Political ideas of Sir Syed Ahmed Khan.

My work has benefited from the advice and suggestions of Professor R.N. Pal, former Pro-Vice Chancellor, Panjab University, Patiala; Dr. K.S. Bharti, Head, Department of Gandhian Thought, Nagpur University, Nagpur; Dr. A.D. Mishra, Deputy Director, National Gandhi Museum, New Delhi; Dr. R.P Diwedi, Head, Department of Gandhian Thought, Mahatma Gandhi Kashi Vidyapith, Varanasi; Professor B.R. Duggar and Dr. Anil Dhar, Jain Vishwabharati Institute, Deemed University, Ladnun; Professor Raj Singh, Department of Sociology, H.A.U. Hissar; Professor Rakesh Dutta and Dr. (Ms) Meena Dutta, Department of Defence and Strategic Analysis, Panjab University, Chandigarh.

I am deeply indebted to my colleagues in the department—Dr. M.L. Sharma and Dr. Ashu Pasricha—who were good enough to read through the draft of the book, and from whose many penetrating criticisms and constructive suggestions I have benefited more than I can express.

There are many other teacher colleagues and students who have contributed in so many ways and I express my thanks to them.

To my wife Rashmi, I owe the deepest debt for her emotional support, her unfailing encouragement and her indispensable contribution towards providing congenial environment in which I could complete this work.

Thanks are also due to my publisher Shri Ashok Kumar Mittal for the keen interest he has shown in this project.

Chandigarh **JAI NARAIN SHARMA**

CONTENTS

Encyclopaedia of Eminent Thinkers Series

Vol. I. The Political Thought of Mahatma Gandhi/ *K.S. Bharti*
Vol. II. The Political Thought of Nehru/ *K.S. Bharti*
Vol. III. The Political Thought of Rabindra Nath Tagore/ *K.S. Bharti*
Vol. IV. The Political Thought of Radhakrishnan/ *K.S. Bharti*
Vol. V. The Political Thought of Vinoba/ *K.S. Bharti*
Vol. VI. The Political Thought of Aurobindo/ *K.S. Bharti*
Vol. VII. The Political Thought of Jayaprakash Narayan/ *K.S. Bharti*
Vol. VIII. The Political Thought of Vivekananda/ *K.S. Bharti*
Vol. IX. The Political Thought of Ambedkar/ *K.S. Bharti*
Vol. X. The Political Thought of M.N. Roy/ *K.S. Bharti*
Vol. XI. The Political Thought of Dadabhai Naoroji/ *Ashu Pasricha*
Vol. XII. The Political Thought of Veer Savarkar/ *Jai Narain Sharma*
Vol. XIII. The Political Thought of M.A. Jinnah/ *Jai Narain Sharma*
Vol. XIV. The Political Thought of Tej Bahadur Sapru/ *Ashu Pasricha*
Vol. XV. The Political Thought of C. Rajagopalachari/ *Ashu Pasricha*
Vol. XVI. The Political Thought of Subhas Chandra Bose/ *Ashu Pasricha*
Vol. XVII. The Political Thought of Mohammad Iqbal/ *Jai Narain Sharma*
Vol. XVIII. The Political Thought of K.B. Hedgewar/ *Jai Narain Sharma*
Vol. XIX. The Political Thought of Bhagat Singh/ *Ashu Pasricha*
Vol. XX. The Political Thought of M.S. Golwalkar/ *Jai Narain Sharma*
Vol. XXI. The Political Thought of Sir Syed Ahmed Khan/ *Jai Narain Sharma*
Vol. XXII. The Political Thought of Mahadev Govind Ranade/ *Ashu Pasricha*
Vol. XXIII. The Political Thought of Pandit Deendayal Upadhyaya/ *Jai Narain Sharma*
Vol. XXIV. The Political Thought of Lokmanya Bal Gangadhar Tilak/ *Jai Narain Sharma*
Vol. XXV. The Political Thought of Annie Besant/ *Ashu Pasricha*

Forthcoming

The Political Thought of C.R. Das/ *Ashu Pasricha*
The Political Thought of Gopal Krishna Gokhale/ *Jai Narain Sharma*
The Political Thought of Lala Lajpat Rai/ *Ashu Pasricha*
The Political Thought of Maulana Abul Kalam Azad/ *Jai Narain Sharma*
The Political Thought of Sir Pherozeshah Mehta/ *Ashu Pasricha*

1

LIFE AND ACTIVITIES

Syed Ahmed Khan was born in Delhi, on October 17, 1817. His paternal and maternal ancestors were men of mark under the Moghul empire. His great-great-grandfather, Syed Hadi, was a native of Herat, who afterwards settled in Hindustan. His grandson, Syed Ahmed's grandfather, during the reign of Alamgir II, was given the titles of Jowahid Ali Khan and Jowadud Dowla, commander of 1000 foot and 500 horsemen, each of the latter having two or three horses. Syed Ahmed Khan's father, Syed Mohomad Takki, was a recluse, deeply religious, who on his father's death, declined all the titles from the Emperor, though offered those of his father.[1]

Syed Ahmed's maternal grandfather was Khwajeh Fariduddin Ahmed, a man of great ability, who went to Calcutta about the year 1791, and accompanied the embassy sent in 1799 by Lord Wellesley to Persia as *attachi.* On his return to Calcutta he was appointed Political Officer at the Court of Ava, where he stayed some years, returned to Calcutta, and revisited his native city after a prolonged absence. Once more, in the reign of Akbar II, we find him in Calcutta. Soon afterwards Syed Ahmed Khan's father was offered the prime-ministership by the Emperor; but he thanked his Majesty for his favour, and respectfully conveyed that his father-in-law at Calcutta was the best man for the post. Akbar acted upon his advice, sent for Khwajeh Fariduddin, and made him Prime Minister, with the title of Nawab Dabir ud Dowla Amin ul Mulk Khwajeh Fariduddin Khan Bahadur Masleh Jang. The Emperor, although a ruler but in name, clung with Eastern tenacity to the empty pomp of a Court, and titles were still of as great value in his and his courtiers' estimation as they had been in the palmy days of the Moghul empire. General Ochterlony was at this time the British Resident at Delhi, and he and the Prime Minister and Syed Ahmed Khan's father were close allies. The General visited them at all hours of the day and night.

The Syeds had an interesting relic of those days in the shape of a photograph of a picture taken by the Court painter, the original being now in the possession of the artist's descendants at Delhi. In this, amongst the crowd of princes and nobles who are represented standing in two lines in front of the Emperor, are the figures of General Ochterlony and the Prime Minister side by side. The General is in full dress, cocked-hat on head, leaning on the *jarib,* or "staff of honour," given to him by the Emperor. The Prime Minister has also the *jarib* in his hand. The scene is the famous *Diwan-i-Aam* or "general audience-hall" in the palace at Delhi, and the Emperor is depicted seated on the celebrated peacock throne.

When Syed Ahmed was about six years old, one day he ran from the women's apartments to his grandfather's room, but when General Ochterlony sitting with him, he turned to go back. But he saw was called back, and told to speak to the General, who took him on his knee, and after a little while, the young Syed quietly asked him why he wore feathers in his hat (the General had come back from the Court and was in full dress), and had so many gold buttons on his coat. The General was much amused at the youngster's curiosity, which remained ungratified.[2] General Ochterlony soon after this in 1825, died of a broken heart at his supersession by Metcalfe. Khwajeh Fariduddin did not long survive him, as he died in the following year. Syed Ahmed's father, Syed Mohomad Takki, was the most intimate of the Emperor's friends, and the only one permitted to sit in his presence. Etiquette prevented anyone from sitting ; so the Emperor, who sat on a small square platform with his legs crossed, would quietly let one foot hang down, and Syed Mohomad Takki would seat himself on the ground on the pretence of shampooing it; etiquette and convenience were thus mutually served. When a youth, Syed Ahmed used to be constantly in the palace, and often received robes of honour from the Emperor. One morning, when he should have been at Court to receive one of these marks of royal favour, he overslept himself. His horse, an old

Deccani one, thirty years old, but still full of spirit, was brought to the door, and the Syed rode slowly—being afraid of its running away—to the palace. The official whose duty was to give out the robes of honour in which the recipients appeared before the Emperor, told him to be quick, put on his robe. Syed Ahmed hurriedly went towards him but found that the Emperor had risen from the throne and had entered the species of sedan-chair in which he used to be carried about the palace. Syed Ahmed's name, as was the custom, was called out by the chamberlain, and the Emperor mentioned his being late to the Syed's father, who was standing by him. The Emperor was not displeased, though after proceeding a short distance, he stopped in the picture-chamber and sent for Syed Ahmed. After he came, he took him by the hand, and asked him why he was late. Syed replied that he had got late as he overslept and was afraid of his house running away with him. The courtiers were aghast by his coverage when he spoke the truth, and hinted to him the necessity of saying something complimentary to the Emperor but Syed Ahmed insisted that it was nothing but the truth, and that he could give no other answer. The child was the father of the man. The Emperor laughed heartily, and himself gave to Syed the usual necklace of pearls, and the jewel of honour. The respect and esteem in which Syed Ahmed's father was held by the courtiers was extended by the Emperor's graciousness to his son.

On Khwajeh Fariduddin's death, Mohomad Takki Khan, as was the custom, went on the third day after the death to Court to receive the usual *khilat,* or robe of honour, which was given by the Emperor to denote that the time for mourning was over. Shah Alam was then on the throne, but the empire was in ruins. The Emperor sent his chamberlain to Mohomad Takki with a message to the effect that he would be presented with the usual khilat the next day in Durbar. Syed Ahmed's father sent back the message, that "as there is no army, and no place to fight, what is the use of the titles (his father-in-law's) to me?"[3]

On his father's death in 1836, Syed Ahmed, who was then nineteen years old, was invested by Bahadur Shah, the last Emperor of Delhi, with his grandfather's titles, and with the additional one of Arif Jang, or Master of War. The only time that he was engaged in war—i.e. in the Mutiny—he certainly did his best to do credit to his title. Syed Ahmed was at first educated at home by his mother, who up to his twelfth year used to make him repeat to her at night what he had learnt during the day. He learnt no English. In January 1837 he stopped his education, and, greatly against the inclination of his relatives, entered the British service as Shiristehdar of the Criminal Department in the Sadr Amin's office at Delhi. In February 1839, he was transferred to Agra as Naib Munshi or deputy reader in the office of the Commissioner of that Division, Mr. (afterwards Sir) Robert Hamilton. In December 1841, he became Munsif or Sub-judge of Fatehpur Sikri, Akbar's capital for ten years, now famous for its ruins, and was transferred to Delhi in January 1846.

He did not know English, but was otherwise a man of letters, and produced several works. His 'Archaeological History of the Ruins of Delhi' won him a Fellowship of the Royal Asiatic Society. He was so enamoured of the British that Indians to him were 'animals' compared with Englishmen. During the Revolt of 1857-58, he chose to support the British, and in doing so invited the wrath of his co-religionists. For his services, he won high praises, and substantial material reward from the Government. A Lieutenant-Governor of the North-Western Provinces said of him: 'No man ever gave nobler proofs of conspicuous courage and loyalty to the British Government than were given by him in 1857: no language that I could use would be worthy of the devotion he showed.'[4] He was granted a special pension of Rs. 200 per month, which was to continue throughout the eldest son, and he also received symbolic rewards in kind. In 1869, he has awarded the Third Class of the Star of India reward. In the same year he was given a sum of £ 250 per annum for two years 'in consideration of the services during the Mutiny'.

Sir Syed's loyalty to the British was to the extent of criticising the Government for not using the Hindu-Muslim differences to ensure the loyalty of the Indian army. In his 'Causes of the Mutiny', he observed, that the English army system in India has always been faulty, and one great fault was the paucity of English troops. When Nadir Shah conquered Khorasan and became master of the two kingdoms of Persia and Afghanistan, he invariably kept the two armies at equal strength. The one consisted, or rather was composed of Persians and Kuzul Bashis, and the other was composed of Afghans. When the Persian army attempted to rise, the Afghan army was at hand to quell the rebellion, and *vice versa*. The English did not follow this precedent in India. The sepoy army was no doubt faithful in its day and served the Government well, but how could Government feel certain that it would never act contrary to its orders? Government certainly did put the two antagonistic races into the same regiment, but constant intercourse had done its work, and the two races in regiment had almost become one. It is but natural and to be expected, that a feeling of friendship and brotherhood must spring up between the men of a regiment, constantly brought together as they are. They consider themselves as one body; and thus it was that the difference which exists between Hindus and Mohammedans had, in these regiments, been almost entirely smoothed away. If a portion of the regiment was engaged in anything; all the rest joined. If separate regiments of Hindus and separate regiments of Mohammedans had been raised, this feeling of brotherhood could not have arisen.'[5]

Sir John (afterwards Lord) Lawrence, who took an active part in putting down the Revolt, and who was later appointed Viceroy of India, said almost the same thing as Sir Syed: 'Among the defects of the pre-Mutiny army, unquestionably the worst, and the one that operated most fatally against us, was the brotherhood and homogeneity of Bengal army, and for this purpose the remedy is counterpoise; firstly, the great counterpoise of the Europeans, and secondly, of the native races.'[6] A Royal Commission, known as the Peel Commission, was appointed to make suggestions how the policy should be given effect to, and in 1861, the army was reorganized. Various communal groups were so arranged that they retained their tribal or communal loyalties and at the same time balanced the characteristics and influence of one another.

Sir Syed's suggestion fitted in with a series of such suggestions which had earlier emanated from eminent British rulers. Monstuart Elphinstone, a Governor of Bombay, suggested on May 14, 1859: 'Divide el Impera was the old Roman motto and it should be ours.' Earlier, in 1843, the Governor-General, Lord Ellenborough, had given warning to London (in a dispatch to the Duke of Wellington) and suggested the use of communalism to preserve imperialist rule: 'I cannot close my eyes to the belief that that race (Mohammedan) is hostile to us and our true policy is to reconcile the Hindus.'[7]

It will be interesting to contrast how later political development necessitated passing the reconciliation to Muslims. The Secretary of State for India, Lord Olivier, said in a letter to *The Times* (London) dated July 10, 1926: ' No one with any close acquaintance of Indian affairs will be prepared to deny that on the predominant bias in British officials in India in favour of the Muslim community, partly on the ground of closer sympathy but more largely as a make-weight against Hindu nationalism.'[8]

For, many years, far-sighted Englishmen had been warning the British rulers that Indian unity would prove disastrous to their rule. Sir John Seeley, writing in *The Expansion of England,* observed that 'so long as the populations have not formed the habit of criticizing their Government, whatever it be, and of rebelling against it, the government of India from England is possible, and there is nothing miraculous about it. But if the state of things should alter, if by any chance the population should be welded not into a single nationality, then I do not say we ought to begin to fear for our dominion; I say we ought to cease at once to hope it.'[9]

Therefore, naturally, Sir Syed's suggestion was received by the British rulers with gratitude. He was not popular, however, with Muslims of the old conservative school. His attitude in favour of the British and the British system of education antagonised many learned doctors of Islam. He received numerous anonymous letters in which the writers said they had sworn on the Koran to take his life. But threats did not change the course of his life. He was an ardent religious reformer, and naturally his reforms came seriously into conflict with the prevalent Muslim conservatism. His interpretation of Islam was thoroughly compatible with progress—progress that the British connection with India was ushering in. In his journal *Tahzib-al-Akhlaq,* he vigorously attacked the social conservatism which rejected any advance or change, and the type of religion which upheld this.

He organised, in 1864, the Translation Society, later renamed as the Aligarh Scientific Society. Mainly Muslim Government servants, and some English officials, were members of the society. Brick by brick he built the edifice of the co-operation of the Muslim aristocracy with the British and its liking for English education. When his high school at Aligarh was being raised to a second-grade college, the Viceroy, Lord Lytton, was invited and presented an address, in which the founders of the institution expressed these sentiments. The aims of the college are to educate our fellow countrymen in order that they may be able to appreciate the benevolence of the British; to make the Muslims of India worthy and useful subjects of the British Crown; to inspire them with loyalty which flows not from a servile submission to a foreign rule but from a sincere appreciation of the benevolence of a good government…these are the aims of the founders of the college.'[10]

About the time the Aligarh Muslim College took birth, India had mildly begun to express her self, especially in Bengal and Maharashtra. Sir Syed's utterances caused hopes to be entertained that in him this nationalism could find sagacity and leadership of a high order. He once said: 'Remember that Hindus and Mussalmans are religious words; otherwise Hindus, Mussalmans and even Christians who inhabit this country, all constitute one nation. Now the time is gone when only on account of difference in religion the inhabitants of a country should be regarded as of two different nations.' At another time he said, addressing a gathering of Hindus in the Punjab: 'The word " Hindu" that you have used for yourself is in my opinion not correct, because that is not in my view the name of a religion. Every inhabitant of Hindustan can call himself a Hindu. I am, therefore, sorry, that you do not regard me as a Hindu although I too am an inhabitant of Hindustan.' Hindus, too, looked upon him as a national leader, and presented him with addresses of welcome.[11]

His sense of self-respect was painfully hurt when discrimination was observed between Europeans and Indians. On the occasion of the Durbar at Agra, he walked out because in the seating arrangement the chairs for Europeans were placed on the platform and those for Indians down below. In the *Tahzib-al-Akhlaq,* he wrote: 'No nation can acquire honour and respect so long as it does not attain equality with the ruling race and does not participate in the Government of its own country. Other nations can have no respect for Mussalmans and Hindus for their holding the position of clerks or other similar petty posits. Rather, that Government also cannot be looked upon with respect which does not give to its subjects due respect. Respect will be commanded only when my countrymen will be holding positions equal to those of the ruling race.'[12]

In 1877, he associated himself with the agitation started by Surendranath Banerjea's Indian Association demanding equal opportunities and facilities for Indians to enter the Indian Civil Service. (His association was limited to the speech he made at a public meeting at Aligarh over which he presided in response request of Banerjea, while the latter was in that city during his tour of Northern India).

Sir Syed Ahmed Khan was initially a votary of Hindu-Muslim unity but on his own terms. He was an ardent supporter and promoter of Urdu written in Persian script. Till the last days of his life, Sir Syed opposed the introduction of Hindi in Devanagari script in the United Provinces (now Uttar Pradesh), the very citadel of Hindi. In 1867, Hindus demanded that the Urdu language and the Persian script, as far as possible, be discontinued and that Hindi written in Devanagari script should be adopted in its place. Sir Syed opposed it tooth and nail and went to the extent of saying that Hindu-Muslim unity and co-operation were impossible ideals. He described his feelings in the following words:

"When all this was going on in Benares, I was talking to Mr. Shakespeare (then Commissioner of Benares) about Muslim education. He was astonished when he heard my views and told me that it was the first time he had ever heard me talk in terms of advancement of the Muslims alone rather than in terms of the welfare of the Indian people as a whole. I replied that I was convinced that the two communities were incapable of putting their heart and soul into anything requiring mutual effort, and even though the opposition was not yet as serious as it might be, I thought that would increase ... I assured him that anyone who lived long enough would see the truth of my prediction.."[13]

It would be interesting to quote the distinguished Pakistani scholar, Abdul Haque who, speaking on the role of Urdu in the context of the birth of Pakistan, said in Karachi on February 15, 1961:

"Pakistan was not created by Jinnah; nor was it created by Iqbal. It was Urdu that created it. For, the fundamental reason for the discord between Hindus and Muslims was the Urdu language. The entire two-nation theory and all other difficulties of this nature issued solely from Urdu".[14]

Too much importance has been given to Sir Syed Ahmed Khan's occasional expressions of Hindu-Muslim unity. The fact is that from the very beginning, he was a staunch communalist and remained so upto his last. It is incorrect, as many other writers have alluded, that, before the birth of Congress, the Syed was the nationalist and that he became a communalist only at the behest of the British. The rules of the Mohammedan Anglo-Oriental College, Aligarh, set up by the Syed (1875) of which he was the life-secretary, provided that only the Muslims could be its members and that funds were to be raised from the Muslims and other people of the Book only, namely, Christians and Jews. Others (meaning Hindus) were not to be approached. He raised objections to every book which, according to him, touched the Muslim psyche. At one place he objected to a book which referred to places like 'Mecca' or the Jama Masjid of Delhi, without a complimentary epithet.[15] He jeered at the national agitation for emancipation and called it as 'no more than the cries of Jackals and crows'. The Syed dreamt of re-establishing the lost Muslim power in India with British help and, therefore, his ambition soared higher and higher.

Thus, the Muslims of foreign origin became the self-styled leaders of the Muslim community and were accepted as such by the British. In a letter to the British Government, Sir Syed Ahmed Khan prayed for nomination of only the upper class Muslims, because:

"You will see that it is one of the necessary conditions of sitting at the same table with the Viceroy, that the person concerned should have high social status in the country. Will the members of the noble families in our country like it that a person of lower class or lower status, even if he has taken a B.A. or M.A. degree and possesses the necessary ability, should govern them and dispose of their wealth, property and honour."[16]

A close associate of Sir Syed and the one who carried Syed's mission in U.K., Sir Ameer Ali wrote in his 'A cry from Indian Mohammedan':

"The waves of adversity, which have one after another passed over the Mohammedans of India, have left the great majority of the leading families stranded and a large portion completely wrecked... The destruction of Muhammedan aristocracy has proved as injurious to the interests of the community as to those of the state."[17]

Having so said, Ameer Ali questioned:

"Was it necessary to deprive them (Muslim aristocrats) of influence and wealth and reduce them to their present impoverished and subordinate condition? Was it necessary to ruin them by taking away the lands and giving them to their Hindu bailiffs ?"[18]

In fact, all the alleged sufferings and deprivations of the Muslim aristocracy were based on a study of the situation in Bengal, but the data and the information compiled was applied to whole of India. Besides, neither this aristocracy nor their supporters in the British government had any concern for the fate of the Muslim masses.

About the Congress, Sir Syed said:

"I consider the experiment which the Indian National Congress wants to make is fraught with dangers and suffering for all the nationalities of India, especially for the Muslims. The Muslims are in a minority but they are highly united minority. Traditionally, they are prone to take the sword in hand when the majority oppresses them. If this happens, it will bring about disasters greater than the ones which came in the wake of the happenings of 1857... The Congress cannot rationally prove its claim to represent the opinions, ideals and aspirations of the Muslims."[19]

However, there were also Muslim intellectuals like M.A. Jinnah, Badruddin Tyabji, Rahmatullah Sayani, who strongly pleaded that though the Indian Muslims followed a different religion from the Hindus, the political and economic needs and aspirations of the two communities were the same. In later periods, the number of such worthy people declined; most of them fell to the communal tantrum.

Altaf Husain Hali, author of *Hayat-i Jawed,* the outstanding biography of Syed Ahmed Khan, wrote in 1901:

"The biography of this extraordinary man is not the kind of work that can be duly effected just by one or two authors.... Sir Syed's achievements will be more and more appreciated, the circumstances of his life will be more closely scrutinised, numerous people will take up the pen to write his biography and for centuries to come the praises of this hero will be sung in Hindustan."[20]

Hali was prescient. Today, we can count about fifteen biographies and monographies, more than fifty articles in English and over a hundred in Urdu journals, dealing with Sir Syed's life and achievement. In addition there are chapters dealing with or passages commenting upon him in a number of books.

In an attempt to single out the most significant lines of interpretation that have been taken in writing about Sir Syed, it is intended to provide an essential background as well as an introduction to the present study. The writings concerning Sir Syed can be divided into two main groups: one viewing him, above all, as a leader of Indian Muslims, and the other as an Islamic thinker.

Within this group we discern a number of different images of Sir Syed. It is not always easy to keep each neatly separate from the other; yet they are sufficiently distinct to warrant certain formulations.

The image of Sir Syed as an important loyal and liberal "Native of our (British) Indian Empire" appeared while he was still gaining importance. John Macdonald, then editor of *The Pioneer* of Allahabad, gave Sir Syed this label. In a collection of brief biographies, he called him a leader of "the Mahomedan Liberals" who "are English in everything—the essential elements of their religion excepted," and "seem to be the most emphatic in their approval of the Asian Protectorate, and the annexation of Cyprus."[21] G.F.I. Graham's outlook on Syed Ahmed Khan in the first full-scale biography of him was not essentially different. The biography aimed to provide "a stimulant to the rising generation of our Indian gentry" by presenting an example of "how a native gentleman of high and distinguished family, but poor, educated only up to his nineteenth year, has raised himself, without the great advantage of a knowledge of English, to become, as he now is, the foremost Mohammedan of his day in India. Graham regarded Syed Ahmed Khan's establishment of Aligarh College as "the crowning of his work," and stressed how Sir Syed was furthering the well-being of the British Empire by doing "his utmost to bring about a good feeling between rulers and the ruled, by making them a united brotherhood, working hand in hand for the good of our great empire."

John Strachery (1823-1907)—like G.F.I. Graham, a long standing friend of Sir Syed—in characterizing Syed Ahmed Khan, gave prominence to exactly the same aspect of his achievement. Assessments by Theodore Beck (1859-99) and Theodore Morison (1863-1936), principals of Aligarh College during 1884-99 and 1899-1905 respectively, and those in the *Census of India* follow the same line; in addition, James Kennedy, Magistrate and Collector in Aligarh in the late 1880s and 1890s, stressed Sir Syed's open mindedness towards western culture and learning as an important element preparing and complementing his new insights in politics. Hugh George Rawlinson, in as late as 1930, portrayed Sir Syed as "the finest and most representative Mahommedan in the annals of British India."[23]

D.N. Bannerjea, the well-known Congress leader, and other writers with similar political leanings, presented Syed Ahmed Khan as an Indian Muslim leader who had made an outstanding contribution to the social and cultural cohesion of the country, especially by working for the cause of Hindu-Muslim understanding. Syed Ahmed Khan is not seen by him as a nationalist in the strict political sense of the word, i.e. as someone advocating for his country a separate national government. Bannerjea sees him as one of the great nation-builders of India.[24]

A few decades later, in significantly altered political circumstances, Asoka Mehta and Achyut Patwardhan, as also Rajendra Prasad declared Syed Ahmed Khan to have been a "nationalist" in his early days, i.e. till 1880s. The word "nationalist" certainly carried with it a new undertone. Rajendra Prasad wrote that Sir Syed "was a nationalist and a believer in the Hindus and Musulmans constituting one nation which he called the Hindu nation on account of both being inhabitants of Hindustan. He, therefore, in his earlier days, spoke and wrote like a nationalist and was regarded as a national leader by both Hindus and Musalmans." In his belief that British rule was for the good of the people of India, "he was at one with others of the time, including those who helped in founding the Indian National Congress, with whom he shared his political aspirations." Sir Syed's change of stand and "keeping away" from "the national movement which found its expression in the Indian National Congress" is explained by these writers, as well as by Saiyid Tufail Ahmed Manglori, as being the influence of English principals at Aligarh College, and above all that of Theodore Beck.[25]

A number of post-partition books, all of them published in India, have viewed Syed Ahmed Khan in terms of Hindu-Muslim unity. His differences with the Congress Party are judged to have been based "on considerations of political expediency alone." "Communal ideas never took any roots in his mind, states Shan Muhammad, and Mushir U. Haq strongly defends the view that Sir Syed was an "Indian nationalist," that he was in fact "as nationalistic as the Congress."

In sharp contrast to this is the image of Syed Ahmed Khan as the political leader working to build the Muslim community into a political entity separate from the Hindu community. This "separate" policy is seen as having been pursued within the British Indian Empire. According to this view, the word "nation," when applied by Sir Syed to the Muslim community or to any comparable group, stressed a separate Muslim entity generating a political will—but within the framework of the Empire.

Theodore Beck, who has been held responsible for having turned Sir Syed against Congress or even for having made him an anti-Hindu communalist, attributed the view that India consisted of diverse "nations" (in the sense just defined) to Sir Syed. Beck stressed that in the mind of Sir Syed—as well as his own—"parliamentary government is unsuited to a country containing two or more nations, tending to oppress the numerically weaker and to provoke it to rebellion."[26]

Whereas the term "nation" as used in Beck's writings certainly bore politically separatist overtones, this may not be so with other writers, or at least it may be difficult to determine the strictly political implications of its use. Whereas Valentine Chirol and Sir Reginald Coupland characterize Sir Syed's political attitude as simply "communal," I.H. Qureshi and Abdul Hamid put a stronger accent on the separatist character of his policy. Qureshi, for instance, states:

"Having been brought up initially in the traditions of the House of Shah Wali-u'llah, he was not unaware of the struggle of the Muslims throughout the ages to maintain their separate entity. This was the reason why he almost invariably thought of the Hindus and Muslims as separate entities. Even where he preached the need of unity, he spoke of two communities separately, without whose equal progress India as a whole could not prosper. In a situation when the question of the departure of the British from the subcontinent was unlikely to arise for a considerable time to come, there was no point in raising theoretical problems, but the context of Syed Ahmed Khan's writings shows that he believed in the Muslims being a nation; once or twice he went out of his way to say that all the inhabitants of the subcontinent formed a single nation; but then he also repeated the observation of the Qur'an that all human beings were a single nation."[27]

M.S. Jain projects another image, when he writes that Syed Ahmed Khan's "concept of the Muslims and their role in the future set-up of the country would never have been fulfilled by adopting the attitude of the (Congress) nationalists. He was first and foremost a Musalman; and a Muslim's point of view was essentially different from an Indian's point of view.... The Pakistanis rightly claim him as one of the fathers of their country (Pakistan)."[28]

In various publications since the middle of the 1940s, there emerges, with great clarity, the image of Syed Ahmed Khan as the progenitor of a Muslim nation on the subcontinent, a fully self-governing nation that, finally, found its expression and embodiment in the independent Republic of Pakistan. In stating this view authors like S. Abdul Latif, Sachin Sen, and Abd-ur-Rafi' Khan have in mind Sir Syed's political and educational activities. B.A. Dar, in addition, stresses the great importance of Syed Ahmed Khan's outlook on Islam for the ideological needs of Pakistan in the 1950s. Abd-al-Haqq, popularly known among the Muslims of the subcontinent as *Baba-i* Urdu (Father of Urdu), repeatedly underlined Sir Syed's unique contribution to the creation of the Muslim *qaum* (community or nation) and *qaumiyat* (communal or national consciousness). In a language borrowed from mystical lyrical writing, he says:

"Farhad did not love Shirin and Nal did not love Daman as much as he loved his *qaum.* Whether sleeping or waking, standing or sitting, this and this alone was his devotional exercise (wird). It is no exaggeration to say that he had reached the (mystical) stage of annihilation in the *qaum (fana' fi 'l-qaum ka darjah).* The Syed changed the very notion of *qaum.* Before him *qaum* had meant Syed, Shaikh, Mughal, Pathan. The Syed made it synonymous with nation and created among Muslims the concept of *qaumiyat* (national consciousness; nationalism).[29]

'Abd-al-Haqq concludes: "If one studies his life in depth then it will become clear that the *pir mard* (grand old man) in fact laid the first brick in the foundation of the stronghold of Pakistan."

But, perhaps the most systematic exponent of the "Muslim nationalist" line of interpretation is Hafeez Malik, who, although he regards Syed Ahmed Khan's cooperation with the British as a corner-stone in his activity, feels still that this loyalty was consciously not more than "an act of policy".

Foremost in Sir Syed's mind was a preoccupation with the Muslim "nation," (which, in Malik's translation throughout, is *qaum*, the ambiguous term in Sir Syed's speeches and writings). In his 1968 article Malik even speaks of Syed Ahmed Khan's "separatist Muslim nationalism" already evinced in the latter's *History of the Bijnor Rebellion of 1858*. And in 1970 Malik writes: "In judging his policies one must constantly remind oneself that Sir Syed was a Muslim nationalist first, and an Indian second." Malik traces the origin of the present State of Pakistan back to Syed Ahmed Khan's Aligarh Movement. The spiritual progeny of the Aligarh Movement was the All-India Muslim League which passed the Pakistan Resolution in Lahore demanding the partition of India.

From the 1930s onwards, a few commentators and historians examined Syed Ahmed Khan's career and achievement in terms of class interest and class conflict, and made an attempt to understand the development and character of his policies and thought (as well as that of his movement) in the context of economic and social changes affecting Indian society during his life. They portrayed him as a defender of Muslim upper or middle class interests.

Jawaharlal Nehru, for example, saw Sir Syed as standing for the interest of the Muslim feudal landlord class.[31] In W.C. Smith's view, on the other hand, he and his college catered to the new middle class produced by the second phase of British imperialism in India, a phase which "was accompanied by the infiltration of British liberal culture."[32] Consequently, states Smith, Sir Syed's Islamic modernism was nothing but "the working out of a liberal Islam compatible with the nineteenth century West, similar to it in general outlook and, especially, in harmony with its science, its business method, and its humanitarianism." Following Nehru's line, a number of historians in favour of the Congress (K.M. Panikkar, 1895-1963 and Ram Gopal, for instance), explain Sir Syed's opposition to it in the 1880s and 1890s as being the result of his belonging to the Muslim upper class.

Begum Ruknuddin Hassaan relates Sir Syed's educational efforts to his preoccupation with the Muslim upper class and S. Abid Husayn clearly makes Syed Ahmed Khan's interest in his own class, i.e. the "aristocracy and gentry of Northern India," the decisive and overriding factor determining all aspects of his activity and thought.

Francis Robinson, by following closely "the very changes in and development of Sir Syed's ideas has the merit of introducing a more differentiated view of Syed Ahmed Khan's political ideas and activities. He concludes that in the years after 1857, he "was much more concerned about the way in which the government policies were affecting the interests of the Urdu speaking elite of which Muslims were only part" than he was "about relations between government and Muslims." Robinson maintains that only by the end of the 1860s did Syed Ahmed Khan begin to regard and treat Muslims as a Political and Cultural entity, making it his overriding aim to enable them to exert in the future the power in Indian affairs that they had wielded in the past. In the 1860s, this had been his objective for the Urdu-speaking elite as a whole; it was now his aim for its Muslim members alone.

Finally, a number of authors, among those who portray him as primarily a leader of Muslims, see him as the man who, above all others, helped the Muslims in India to emerge again, revitalized and respected after a general decline (during the late Mughal period and the aftermath of the Mutiny and Rebellion of 1857). Various writings have emphasized different areas of Syed Ahmed Khan's thought and activity—social and political, educational and cultural—in which this revival occurred. But all agree that his prime achievement was a revival of Muslim morale and prestige in British India, and that to him goes the credit for having re-established the dynamism of the Muslims in India as a social and political force. S.M. Ikram, the Pakistani historian writing in 1950 under the pseudonym A.H. Albiruni, gave this line of interpretation (which was shared, incidentally, by Hindus like Nehru and K.M. Panikkar), which was perhaps the most comprehensive expression, adding to it a significant national dimension:

"Syed Ahmed filled the big void created in the life of the Muslim community by the disappearance of the Muslim rule. But he did more. His long life, spanning almost a century, bridged the gulf between Medieval and Modern India. Himself, a relic of the palmy days of the Great Mughals, he ushered in a new era. He gave the Indian Muslims a new cohesion, a new policy; new educational ideals, a new prose, a new approach to their individual and national problems, and built up an organisation which could carry on his work. Before him there was all disintegration and decay. He rallied together the Indian Muslims and became the first prophet of their new nationhood."[33]

There are others who share this view of Sir Syed. However, they tend, particularly, to underline the cultural and educational component. Among the earliest to do so was the Lebanese Christian writer Jurji Zaidan, who saw Syed Ahmed Khan's main achievement as having been the weaning away of his co-religionists from cultural opposition to the west, and demonstrating to them that modern western science was not hurtful to their religion. Similarly, an anonymous Muslim writing in the *Indian Review* (Madras), considered Syed Ahmed Khan's educational activities to have been his most important contribution. Through them "he wished to raise his co-religionists to a position of social efficiency, moral worth, spiritual greatness and political power."

The doctoral thesis by Begum Ruknuddin Hassaan is the first monograph written on the educational work of Sir Syed and the educational movement he generated. She says that if, with A.H. Hali, one were to label Syed Ahmed Khan as "a great educationist ... the word educationist must be used in a very wide sense," because he looked upon education "as a means of reform.... He restored Muslim self-respect and yet succeeded in effecting British-Muslim rapprochement. "

Sir Syed's image as the reformer of Urdu writing and the initiator of the modern epoch in Urdu literature should also be mentioned here. Maulana Shibli Nu'mani (1857-1914), the distinguished historian and theologian, argued in as early as 1898, that Urdu literature is one of the areas of Indian Muslim life most deeply affected by Sir Syed's "reformation and reform (islah)." Shibli calls Ghalib the founder and Syed Ahmed Khan the "imam and mujaddid" of modern Urdu prose writing. He regards this as the latter's main contribution to Urdu literature—first, to have led Urdu writing out of the confines of subjects like love and gallantry and widened its compass considerably by writing on the most diverse subjects in Urdu; second, to have brought to his own writing a clarity, purity of style and charm—the hallmark of good prose writing; and finally, to have successfully presented English thought—by its creative transference, rather than a slavish translation into Urdu. Hali Ram Babu Saksena, and Hamid Hasan Qadiri, among others, confirmed Shibli's assessment. The latter, in his pioneering work on the history of Urdu prose writing, points out Sir Syed's literary mastery, as shown in some of his essays in *Tahdhib al-akhla.* S.M. Abdullah thus sums up Syed Ahmed Khan's achievement in the field of Urdu literature:

"It was through the initiative of Syed Ahmed that the element of "sincerity" was introduced into Urdu literature and conventionalism was rejected. His writings generated a spirit of freedom, gave birth to a craving for inquiry and search for truth and stimulated a desire for progress. Not only was the substance of literature transmuted, its form and style also underwent a profound change."[34]

Altaf Husain Hali's (1837-1914) assessment put forward in Hayat-i Jawed (1901), and his biography on Sir Syed is the most comprehensive. Hali's view of Sir Syed is basically that of the revitalizer of the Muslim community. However, Hali is so comprehensive that his interpretation reaches well into the second section of the introductory exposition, where Sir Syed is viewed as the inaugurator of a new, modernized Islam.

Hali writes in the awareness of a western-educated Muslim middle class growing in India. He presents Syed Ahmed Khan as the 19th century hero of the Muslim community in India, as the man who was able—after the trauma of 1857—to restore to it a self-respect and an honour within British India. Sir Syed is the exemplar for the rising Indian Muslim generation.

His life and work are, more than that of anyone else, relevant to the peculiar situation of having to live under foreign, non-Muslim rule. Since the Muslim no longer rule India by physical power, they have to conquer the hearts of their rulers and compatriots in order to gain honour and respect. To further this aim they need a new solution and outlook. It is here, according to Hali, that Sir Syed can give a unique lead. Was not this, he asks, the basic principle of Sir Syed's life and teaching—*Qaum aur watan ki mohabbat ko jano* (consider the love of your community and homeland to be a part and parcel of your faith).

It was for this that Syed Ahmed Khan concentrated on laying the foundations of a "this-worldly" progress of the Muslim community. He viewed education (including the learning of English and the acquisition of western knowledge and acceptable western values) as the basic means for improvement. All his other activities were rooted in this one basic desire—to restore Islam in India to its pristine dignity and prestige.

After presenting this overall view of Sir Syed, Hali sets out to describe his various services to country, community and religion. He denotes Sir Syed's work by the western term "reformation," calling him a reformer. He explains:

"Although the basic objective of Syed Ahmed Khan was the adjustment of the social condition of the Muslims, it remains true nevertheless that the Muslims always considered their religion the guide in matters of *din* and *dunya*. They have never accepted anything—*dini* or *dunyawi*—until it proved to be acceptable from the point of view of religion. For all these reasons Syed Ahmed Khan had to remain constantly engaged in religious discussions."

Hali knows that there have been many reformers in Islamic history. But for him the vital difference between earlier reformers and Syed Ahmed Khan is that whilst they advocated particular reforms, stressing the need for a reformation only of certain items or aspects of Islamic teaching, Syed Ahmed Khan attempted a comprehensive reform of Islamic teaching. This is not to say that Sir Syed's teaching was radically new. In fact, Hali writes: "We find very few singular reforms of Sir Syed, the roots of which could not be found in the writings of former critical scholars of the Islamic community (*muhaqqiqin-i ahl-i Islam*)."[35]

Hali depicts Sir Syed as always having adamantly refused to act as the leader of a new faction in Islam. "The sole aim of his reformation was simply to remove the obstacles in the way of 'this-worldly' progress of Muslims and to reject the criticism of the Christian nations that Islam cannot go together with progress and moral refinement."

REFERENCES

1. Graham, G.F.I., *The Life and Work of Sir Syed Ahmed Khan* (London: Oxford University Press), 1974, p. 2.
2. *Ibid.*, p. 3.
3. *Ibid.*, p. 4.
4. *Ibid.*, p. 19.
5. Khan, Sir Syed Ahmed, *Asbab-i-Baghavat-i-Hind* (Agra: Matba-i-Mufidi), 1859.
6. Ram Gopal, *Indian Muslim* (Bombay: Asia Publishing House), 1959, p. 46.
7. *Ibid.*
8. *Ibid.*
9. *Ibid.*, pp. 46-47.
10. *Ibid.*, p. 48.
11. *Ibid.*
12. Rajendra Prasad, *India Divided* (Bombay: Hind Kitabs), 1946, p. 53.
13. Hali, Altaf Hussain, *Hayat-i-Jawed* (Delhi: Idarah-i-Adabiyat-i-Delhi), 1979, p. 199.

14. *Hindustan Times*, New Delhi, 28-07-1994.
15. Lal Bahadur, *The Muslim League, Its History, Activities and Achievements* (Agra: Agra Book Stores), 1954, p. 23.
16. Sharma, T. L., *Hindu Muslim Relations*, 1913-1925 (Delhi: B.R. Publishing Corporation), 1987, p. 17.
17. *Ibid.*
18. *Ibid.*, p. 18.
19. Karunakaran, *Indian Political Thought 1832-1921* (New Delhi: Peacock), 1976, p. 129.
20. Hali, Altaf Hussain, *Hayat-i-Jawed, op: cit.*, p. 54.
21. Escott, T.H.S. (ed.), *The Pillars of the Empire* (London: Chapman & Hall), 1879, pp. 165-70.
22. Graham, G.F.I., *The Life and Work of Sir Syed Ahmed Khan, op. cit.*, Preface.
23. Troll, Christian, W., *Sayyid Ahmad Khan: A Reinterpretation of Muslim Theology* (New Delhi: Vikas), 1978, pp. 4-5.
24. Bannerjea, D.N., *India's Nation Builder* (London: Headley), 1919, pp. 104-105.
25. Rajendra Prasad, *India Divided, op. cit.*, pp. 93-94.
26. Beck, Theodore, *Essays on Indian Topics* (Allahabad: Pioneer Press), 1888, p. 81.
27. Hamid, Abdul, *Muslim Separatism in India* (Lahore: OUP), 1967, p. 25.
28. Jain, M.S., *The Aligrah Movement* (Agra: Sri Ram Mehra), 1965, p. 123.
29. Dar, B.A., *Religious Thoughts of Syed Ahmed Khan* (Lahore: Institute of Islamic Culture), 1961, p. vi.
30. Malik, Hafeez, *Muslim Nationalism in India and Pakistan* (Washington D.C: Public Affairs Press), 1963, pp. 220-230.
31. Nehru, Jawaharlal, *An Autobiography* (London: The Bodley Head), 1949, pp. 463-464.
32. Smith, W.C., *Modern Islam in India* (London: V. Golanez), 1946, pp. 19-26.
33. Albiruni, A.H., Makers of Pakistan and Modern Muslim India (Lahore: Ashraf), 1950, p. 60.
34. Abdullah, S.M., *Spirit and Substance of Urdu Prose* (Lahore: Ashraf), 1940, p. 32.
35. Hali, Altaf Hussain, *Hayat-i-Jawed, op. cit.*, p. 508.

2

IDEOLOGY AND PERCEPTION

Sir Syed was born and grew up in the house of his maternal grandfather, Khwdjah Farld al-din Ahmed Khan (1747-1828), the scion of an illustrious family of Mughal aristocrats. Khwdjah Farid held the high position of wazir at the Mughal court, and acted as ambassador to Iran and Burma for the East India Company's government in Calcutta. A well-known teacher, he held the post of Superintendent of Calcutta Madrasa for some time. He was also a renowned mathematician and astronomer, a line of interest continued by his younger son, Khwajah Zain al-'Abidin.

In the religious outlook of Sir Syeed's family, one discerns a strong Sufi trend. Two of the seven brothers of Farid al-din were in fact outspoken dervishes. The famous Khwdjah Najib al-din (d. 1843), then popularly known as Shah Fida Husain, was an adept of the Rasulshahis, a recent branch of the Suhrawardi *silsilah* (Sufi order). Najib al-din strongly adhered to the doctrine of *wahdat al-wujud* (unity of being), and taught the *Fusus al-hikam,* the *al-Futuhat al-Makkiyah,* and other works by Muhyi al-din Ibn al-'Arabi (A.D. 1165-1240). Khwajah Ala al-din (d. 1855), on the other hand, was *murid* (disciple), and *khalifah* (successor) of the famous Naqshbandi Shaikh, Shah Mubammad Afaq (d. 1835), a direct descendant of Shaikh Ahmed Sirhindi and a close adherent of the *Mujaddidi silsilah.* Syed Ahmed Khan wrote of Ald al-din, "Although he had married he spent his whole life in *goshah nashini* (religious retirement), in remembering God *(dhikr adhkar),* in renunciation *(zuhd),* and acts of self-mortification *(mujahidah).*"[1]

Khwajah Farid al-din who, Sir Syed tells us, took a special interest in the education of his grandchildren, was disposed towards Sufism, and in his later years became known in the city for the earnestness of his spiritual endeavour.[2]

As Sir Syed himself testifies, it was his mother 'Aziz al-nisa Begam, the daughter of Khwajah Farid al-din, who made a lasting impact on him'. He regarded her all his life as an example in the practice of the fundamental religious virtue of *tawakkul* (complete reliance and trust in God). She stressed the moral—and above all—the social injunctions of religion. She was remarkably independent, despite prevailing religious customs, taking a permanent stand against superstitious beliefs and practices—for instance, the vows and offerings made with a view to obtain certain favours, and exorcism by means of amulets and the like. In 1892 Sir Syed wrote:

"At this moment when my religious ideas are based on true and accurate principles I cannot name any among the many beliefs of my mother that could be qualified as *shirk* (associationism) or *bid'at* (innovation) except one. She held fast to the belief of '*ibadat-i badani,* i.e. that a dead person will receive reward in return for having the Qur'an recited and alms given (on his behalf) or in return for having the Fatihah read over the deceased (for forty days after his death) and for having distributed alms and food (on his behalf)."[3]

Sir Syed stresses the close connection between Khwajah Farid al-din's family and Shah 'Abd al-'Aziz (1746-1824), the son of Shah Wali Allah (c. 1702-63). 'Aziz al-nisa, however, gave allegiance *(bai'at)* to the other outstanding religious personality of her day, the *Naqshbandi Mujaddidi* Shaikh Shah Ghulam 'Ali (Shah 'Abd Allah, d. 1824), and adhered to his teaching. Shah Ghulam 'Ali took a line more strict than that of Shah 'Abd al-'Aziz on superstitious practices such as vows, offerings and amulets. In accordance with the teaching of her pir, 'Aziz al-nisa seems to have been against all forms of "mediation," advocating the soul's direct contact with God. "God alone should be approached in everything, then He will do what He pleases to do,"[4] she used to say.

Sir Syed's father, Saiyid Muhammad Mir Muttaqi (d. 1838), who married 'Aziz al-nisa in 1810, was connected from his mother's side with the family of the *Naqshbandi Mujaddidi Mir* Dard

(1721-85). He too had given his allegiance to Shah Ghulam Ali. There was close, daily contact between the family, and the *khdnqdh* of Ghularn Ali. Hall wrote that:

"From early childhood onwards consideration for men of God and holy people took firm root in Sir Syed. Quite often he went together with his father in the presence of Shah Ghulam 'Ali. In this way he experienced personally the (special) character of the Shah Sahib's belief."[5]

The biographical facts of Syed Ahmed Khan's early life and the character of his early theological writing point to three schools of religious thought and practice as being the main influence on his outlook and thought—the *Naqshbandiyah Mujaddidiyah,* Shah Wali Allah and his school of religious thought, and the *Mujahidin* movement.

The living tradition of Sufism which made its impact on Syed Ahmed Khan since early childhood can be characterized by the stress on a truly personal religion, and a streak of religious radicalism and independence evinced especially in the connection with the Rasulshahis. Yet more important is the presence of the *Naqshbandi Mujaddidi* tradition in the lives of his parents, and throughout his own. Shah Ghulam 'Ali was the leading *Mujaddidi* Shaikh in Delhi and his *khanqah* had become a centre of spiritual and theological teaching, well known in other parts of the Islamic world.

The *Mujaddidi* branch of the *Naqshbandi order* is named after Shaikh Ahmed Sirhindi *Mujaddid-i alf-i thani,* who was initiated into this order of Sufis in 1599-1600 by Khwajah Muhammad al-Baqi bi Allah in Delhi. Among the various writings of Shah Ghulam 'Ali (Shah 'Abdallah), his collection of letters, *Makatib-i sharifah,* gives a vivid picture of the preoccupations of his teaching. Of the 123 letters, twelve, for instance, deal with Shaikh Ahmed Sirhindi. They express and defend his teaching against critics like 'Abd al-Haqq Dihlawi (1551-1642), a contemporary of Sirhindi who is mentioned repeatedly.

The general trend of the letters, even where they deal with doctrinal matters, is more towards Sufi practice than towards theory. Sufism is entirely brought back into normal daily life, in complete imitation of the Prophet and his Companions, i.e. a life strictly according to the sunnat-i habib-i Khuda. "What is darwishi?" Ghulam 'Ali asks. "To believe in full accordance with one another in perfect and unceasing following of the Friend of God and to look all together into one direction."[6]

In short, the Mujaddidi spiritual tradition represented by Shah Ghulam 'Ali, had the following salient features [7]:

> The via purgative does not proceed by harsh, ascetic exercises but by strict and earnest moral striving.
> Refinement of inner attitudes and purification of the heart are placed foremost.
> In ascetic practices one wants to follow a path of moderation.

It stressed the inner aspect of Sufi practices, taking a critical stand against mobilizing emotional, and aesthetic expressions such as music, dancing, publicly and collectively performing *dhikr* (recollection of God's presence), not to speak of painting. Instead, silent contemplation (*muraqabah*) and contemplation of the Shaikh in one's imagination (*tasauwur-i shaikh*) were advocated as a means of conforming to the Prophet's sunnah and of meeting God as he did. In this sense, the intellectual element gained, as compared to the emotional. Personal intercourse with the spiritual guide (*suhbat-i murshid*) was more important than a regular participation in the "circle".

Utmost care is taken in the effort to conform to the Sharia law in its Sunnite (ideally Hanafite) form. One, therefore, lives on good terms with the ulama. In fact, many ulama, as prominent members of the family of Shah Wall Allah, for instance, are themselves adepts of this order.

Yet, there seems to be less interest in the details of fiqh among the Shaikhs of the khanqah, as compared to men like Shah 'Abd al-Aziz, whose fatwas were of importance. Shah Ghulam 'Ali dwells on inculcating the right moral and spiritual attitude rather than on legal points. The esoteric aspect of following the Prophet receives greater attention in the teaching of the Shaikh than in the circles of non-Sufi ulama.

The second great influence on Syed Ahmed Khan were the writings of Shah Wall Allah Dihlawi, and his teachings as they were carried on by his descendants in Delhi.

Shah Wall Allah's achievement was his attempt at a new synthesis of all religious sciences of Islam, as they had developed throughout Islamic history. Abdel Hamid writes: "The central challenge facing Shah Wall Allah was, as he himself expressed it, the need for a restatement of the Islamic religious sciences, Iqamat 'ulum al-din. This he endeavoured to achieve through his all-suffusing principle of tatbiq."[8] By emphasizing the method of tatbiq (harmonization) in his own, original way, Shah Wall Allah smoothened out differences among theologians, philosophers and traditionalists. In Sufi thought he tried to harmonize the two schools of wahdat alwujud (unity of being; Ibn al-'Arabi) and wahdat al-shuhud (unity of appearance; Ahmed Sirhindi); in fiqh the differences between the four madhahib; and finally, he tried to clarify the difference between the Sunnite and Shi'ite traditions, by researching upon the origins of the dispute.

Another remarkable feature of Shah Wali Allah's thought is his sense of history and his awareness of the development of Islamic thought. In his treatment of the problems of taqlid (blind following) and ijtihad (independent judgement) for example, he offers a competent historical account of the development of these two principles of Islamic thought.

His interest in proving the relevance of the Sharia law is another aspect of his work that impressed Sir Syed. On the one hand, Shah Wall Allah worked out a method of developing and adapting the Shari'a by practising *ijtihad* through a selective reference to all four schools of jurisprudence. On the other hand, he introduced into his exposition of the Shari'a, two principal, additional elements—*al-masalih* (salutary purposes in terms of human welfare) and *al-fitrah* (human nature). To quote 'Abdel Hamid again:

"The emphasis on the salutary purposes in terms of human welfare of the Shari'a and on the scholar's capacity to exercise his own *ijtihad* to achieve these salutary purposes in particular circumstances enabled Shah Waliullah to depict the Shari'a as having an inherent flexibility. Thus, some commentators have found a modernist quality in Shah Waliullah's thinking."[9]

Last, though not the least, a fundamentalist streak is discernible throughout Shah Wali Allah's work. "Fundamentalist" in the sense that his "writings reflect clearly his profound belief in only the Qur'an and the *sunnah* as the sole significant sources of the Islamic Shari'a ... Even *ijma* or *qiyas,* or any other source, must be subjected to and guided by these two sources, i.e. Qur'an and *sunnah,* in the final analysis.

The third school of religious thought and practice that throughout his life deeply impressed Syed Ahmed Khan is that of Saiyid Ahmed Shahid of Ra'e Bareli (1796-1831), and of one of his earliest disciples, Maulana Shah Muhammad Isma'il Shahid (1779-1831), a member of the house of Shah Wall Allah. The movement initiated by Saiyid Ahmed Shahid is commonly known as the *Mujahidin* movement. It has found literary expression, above all, in Muhammad Isma'il's (1781-1831) writings, to which Sir Syed referred throughout his life.

There are certain characteristics of the religious outlook of the two men. They want to assert pure *tauhid* (unity) and believe this to be achieved only by a radical return to the "Islam of the days of the Prophet." Accordingly, they emphasize the importance of the Qur'an and *sunnah* as a criterion of thought and conduct, and are consistently against innovation. The most serious threat to *tauhid* in India comes from Hindu practices that have crept into the life and thought of Indian Muslims. Thus to a very large extent, the fight against innovation turns out to be a fight against borrowing from Hinduism, or, as they saw it, superstitious degradations shared with Hinduism.

No change or adjustment in the traditional structure of religion was envisaged in the contemporary situation. Yet, Shah Isma'l's writings are pervaded with a keen sense of the difference between Islam as practised in the Muslim India of the day, and "pure" Islam as in the days of the Prophet. The five pillars of Islam—assertion of unity, ritual prayer, fasting, alms tax and pilgrimage—are interpreted strictly and insisted upon in their pristine form of implementation.

As its title suggests, *Tariqah-i Muhammadiyah* discloses the Still character of the movement. Reform of Sufi ideas and practices of *piri-muridi* master-disciple relationship and *dhikr* for instance and a puritanical return to the practice of the prophet are envisaged to bring about an ideal exoteric and esoteric Islam, understood and enacted as *Tariqah-i Muhammaidiyah.* There is a noticeable shift in moral teaching towards more this-worldly outlook and a stress on the reform of Islamic life in society. Muhammad Hedayatullah writes: "The moral teaching of Saiyid Ahmed (Shahid) was more in relation to this-worldly values than to the world hereafter." Rahman thinks that "the result of this trend among the more enlightened strata of society was an orientation towards a positive attitude to this world and its moral, social and economic problems than towards eschatological issues."[10]

The two reformers Saiyid Ahmed Shahid and Shah Isma'l have very little to say about the system of Muslim law. A relevant passage in Sirat al-mustaqim explicitly states the rejection of all four orthodox schools of Muslim jurisprudence "which meant positively," comments Hedayatullah, "that he (Saiyid Ahmed Shahid) declared himself a *ghair muqallid* (non-conformist). Rejection of taqlid means, in its positive aspect, the acceptance of ijtihad."[11]

Early Religious Writings

Sir Syed's religious thought in his early period, is contained in the following works:

(a) jila' al-qulub bi dhikr al-Mahbub (polishing of the Hearts by Remembering the Beloved), 1841.

(b) Tuhfah-i Hasan (The Gift to Hasan), 1844. Nur al-Hasan was Sir Syed's teacher in Agra in the early 1894s.

(c) Tadhkirah-i ahl-i Dihli (Biography of the People of Delhi, contained in the fourth chapter of the first edition of Athar al-sanadid), 1846.

(d) Kalimat al-Haqq (The True Discourse), 1949.

(e) Rah-i sunnah dar radd-i bid'ah (The Path of the sunnah in Rejection of Innovation), 1850.

(f) Namiqah dar bayan-i mas' alha-i tasuwar-i sheikh (A Letter Explaining the teaching of tasuwur-i shaikh), 1852. This meant visualizing interiorly the image of one's Shaikh and thus achieving unity with him and with his nearness to God.

(g) Aghaz-i tarjumah-i Kimiya-i sa'ddah (Beginning of the translation of al-Ghazali's famous The Elixir of Happiness), 1853.

The religious works listed here are only a fraction of total literary output during this period. Any fame that Syed Ahmed Khan achieved as a scholar in and outside India before 1857 was really because of his historical writings, especially the two editions of Athar al-sanadid and that of the A'in-i Akbari.

Very few of the numerous collected and published letters of Syed Ahmed Khan belong to this period, and none deal with his religious thought and work. Besides, contemporary comment on his thought is not known. But one can have later reflections of Sir Syed upon his outlook during these early years, in a number of Reviews. In them, Sir Syed looks back to the time when he wrote the tract to which they are attached. He indicates the circumstances that occasioned its writing and mentions the doctrines because of which he changed his views. In June 1878, he reflects upon his theological position as a hole, viewing its development from an unreflecting, traditional position to a Wahhabi-like outlook, and from there to the resent position which he describes as mu'taziliyat. These reflections in the Reviews are, however, of a rather random and summary nature, being his interpretations at a much later stage of his thought.

Jila' al-qulub, the first piece of religious writing by Syed Ahmed Khan, is a maulud writing (a biography of the Prophet) he recited at the customary monthly gatherings, commemorating the birth of Muhammad). Apart from a short Persian poem in praise of the Prophet at the beginning, and one in Arabic at the end, it is written throughout in idiomatic Urdu prose. Syed Ahmed Khan declares at the end of it to have title use of a maulud *risalah* entitled S*urur al-mahzun* (The Joy of the Afflicted), and to have taken a few items from Maddrij al-nubuwah (Degrees of Prophethood), the copious biography of the Prophet by 'Abd al-Haqq Dihlawi (1551-1642). He further states that a certain Maulana Nur al-Hasan corrected and improved upon his tract.

In 1878, he explained why he wrote the risalah. He wanted to produce "a short risalah in the form of a factual account of the Prophet's life that would omit all unreliable material."[12] This endeavour has an interesting parallel in *Ihya* al-qulub (Quickening of the Hearts), the risalah (in Urdu) by 'Abd al-Jalil ibn 'Abd al-Mujib, published only about ten years later. The introduction to this work suggests motives that might possibly have moved Syed Ahmed Khan to compose the Jila' al-qulub.

'Abd al-Jalil in his risalah criticizes his contemporaries for spending "day and night in listening to erotic tales of 'ashiqi and ma'shuqi, stories that incite them to disobedience to the Shari'a and make them rebellious against it." Furthermore, he states:

"Everywhere the Christians tell of the miracles and the superiority of Jesus, Peace be upon him, and they defame our Prophet. Although it is right to recognise His (Jesus') greatness yet the greatness of our Prophet is something different—but the common man is not aware of it and in some people's mind there originates a devilish insinuation (waswas). This sinner (the humble author) has abridged the full story of the Prophet and produced it in this risalah so that our brother Muslims in their spare time may come together and recite this sweet story for themselves or to other people. Thus, listening to this dear story the mind may be refreshed and the faith strengthened and the longing may be born in everyone's heart to follow the sunnah and to flee from shirk and bid'at."[13]

There emerges from this text a concern among Indian Muslims at this time, to produce "reformed" maulud writings, considered a means to bring people back to the undiluted sunnah of the Prophet, and to lure them away from innovations to the veneration and imitation of Muhammad. The text further suggests that this endeavour was occasioned by an awareness, among leading Muslims in India, of the impact of Christian preaching on broad sections of the population. Particularly since many Protestant missionaries were influenced by the Evangelical movement, and handed out copies not only of the Bible, but also of the Gospels by different Evangelists, thus presenting the life of Jesus as exemplary. It seems that the preachers, concentrating on the person and life of Jesus of Nazareth, and the message of the Bible, effected a new concern for the central place held by Muhammad and the Qur'an in the religion of Islam.

Syed Ahmed Khan's teacher and friend in Agra, Maulana Nur al-Hasan (d. 1868), during the late 1830s and early 1840s actively engaged in a controversy with Carl Gottlieb Pfander (d. 1869), the apologist and missionary working in Agra since 1835. As elaborated in the next chapter, Syed Ahmed Khan from this period onwards was not only aware of the missionary challenge to the religion of Islam, but also concerned about appropriate ways to counteract it.

Maulana Nur al-Hasan, mentioned above, encouraged Syed Ahmed Khan to translate into Urdu, the tenth and twelfth chapters of Tuhfah-i Ithna 'Ashariyah, Shah 'Abd al-'Aziz's scholarly work on the Shi'a. The tenth chapter answers the abuse levelled against the Companions and Hazrat 'A' ishah (one of the Prophet's wives) and the twelfth deals with the Shi'a terms tawalla and tabarra (meaning love, and the enmity of one's neighbour on religious grounds, respectively).

The remaining theological writings of the period 1841-53 belong to the time when Syed Ahmed Khan was a munsif (judge) in Delhi (1846-55). During these eight years he became increasingly acquainted with western culture. A comparison between the first edition of Athar al-sanadid (1846) and the second revised one (1852) gives an idea of the extent to which his intellectual outlook had changed during this period. However, at the same time Syed Ahmed Khan had deepened his traditional religious education under the guidance of renowned teachers at the Jami'ah Masjid and the then internationally renowned khanqah of Shah Ghulam 'Ali and his successors. It is in this context that Syed Ahmed Khan wrote Kalimat al-haqq and Rah-i sunnat.

Kalimat al-haqq, published in 1849, deals with piri-muridi. A clear structure and a direct and idiomatic style of writing mark this tract. The author aims at a wide audience, the oratorial ring betraying his close connection with traditional ulama and Sufi's at this time. The first part discusses the notion of pir, coming to the conclusion that the Prophet is the one valid pir, and that therefore all organized Sufi life must be strictly directed to following the Prophet alone, by adhering closely to the Qur'an and sunnah. The second part on muridi discusses mainly the concept and practice of bai'at.

In his Review of Rah-i sunnat (1850) in 1879, Sir Syed tells us that in its basic approach the treatise follows al-haqq al-sarih fi ahkam al-mayyit wa'l-darih (Elucidation of the Plain Truth Concerning the Rules About the Dead and the Tombs)[14], Shah Muhammad Isma'il's tract in Persian. A comparison of the two works shows that Syed Ahmed Khan has adopted Shah Isma'il's analysis of the term bid'ah, and some of is exemplifications. Yet the introduction and the second half of the work are mainly Sir Syed's own composition. There is the same lucid Urdu prose, and the effort to reach a wider readership, as in Kalimat al-haqq. The immediate cause for writing this tract was an interesting exchange of views Syed Ahmed Khan had (in one of the meetings at the house of Sadr al-sudar Maulana Muhammad Sadr al-din Azurdah) over the licitness of eating mangoes. Sir Syed had defended his views, saying that to eat mangoes—though not a blameworthy action—was a matter of doubt, since the Prophet had not decided upon it explicitly, having himself never eaten them. "I swear by God in whose hands rests my life," stated Syed Ahmed Khan, "if a person does not eat a mango for the reason that the Prophet did not eat it then the angels will kiss his feet at his (death) bed." In 1879, he recalls, "This I had said with utter conviction and much fervour. The Maulana listened to it and remained silent. It was at this period of noisy and tumultuous Wahhabism that after the discussion just recorded I wrote this tract."[15]

In 1853 the Sufi 'alim Haji Imdad Allah of Thana Bhavan (1815-99) on a visit to Delhi, asked Syed Ahmed Khan to translate into Urdu the Kimiya-i sa'adah, al-Ghazali's work in Persian the incomplete translation survives.

A year earlier, a few Naqshbandi elders, perhaps disturbed by Syed Ahmed Khan's earlier condemnation of the practice of tasauwur-i shaikh (the practice of visualizing within, the image of one's spiritual guide, thus achieving union with him), had urged him to write on its defence. Accordingly, Sir Syed wrote a *namiqah* in

Persian, in which he endeavours to show the tasauwur-i shaikh being an apt and lawful means to develop the love of God in an adept. To corroborate his view he states that Shah Isma'il, despite what he wrote in *Sirat al-mustaqim,* did not cease practising *tasauwur-i shaikh* till his death.

Main Themes of Early Writings

Two main themes emerge from Syed Ahmed Khan's early religious writings—his endeavour to bring the Prophet back into the mainstream of religious life of individuals and society, and his desire to unmask all innovations in the lives of Indian Muslims which could be attributed to their non-Muslim environment.

The Practice of the Prophet as the Straight Path

It is a commonplace that Muhammad, soon after or even before his death, became for his community the model of a life wholly pleasing to God—a pure and perfect human being worthy of praise and reverence, the Friend and Beloved of God whom everyman must imitate.

In Syed Ahmed Khan's early writings the two strands of obedience to the prescriptions of the Shail'a law and of love and veneration for the Prophet as the living embodiment of this law on earth—are welded into a whole, thus giving another powerful dimension to the religious outlook of the *tariqah-i Muhammadiyah.*

The introductory and final lines of Sir Syed's *Jila' al-qulub* convey not only the religious outlook of the believer taking part in a *maulud* gathering, but also the atmosphere marking such a liturgical occasion. The faithful believer of that period would regard these gatherings (as did Sir Syed) as not facultative customs but as part and parcel of the officially prescribed rite. He would, further, even believe in a "liturgical presence" of the holy soul of the Prophet.

In his *Review (1878)* of *Jila' al-qulub* Sir Syed states that his motive in composing this *risalah* was to produce a more reliable text. In it, his account of Muhammad's life is more sober, succinct, and factual, when compared to the source he indicates.

Innovation as Deviation from the Straight Path

The argument Syed Ahmed Khan had in Mufti Sadr al-din's majlis shows the kind of questions disturbing Sir Syed's conscience in the early 1850s. What he was later to call his "leaning towards Wahhabism," was basically his search for the authentic practice of the Prophet, and his determination to imitate it. Along with many contemporaries at that time, he became more and more aware of the gulf between Islam (as he conceived of it in its original purity) and the then state of Islamic practice in India. A natural result of this was his effort to define the concept of *bid'ah,* and to measure contemporary Islamic practice by what the great schools of Islamic law would regard as the *sunnah of* the Prophet.

In his introduction to *Rah-i sunnat,* Syed Ahmed Khan criticizes the religious life of the Muslims of his day. Their practice and beliefs, he felt, were so mixed with innovation, that it was just enough to remind them of the true concept *sunnah,* to be cried down as Wahhabi or Mu'tazilite. But since to be a good Muslim and to reach salvation it was essential to avoid innovation, its exact meaning needed clarification. In *Kalimat al-haqq,* Syed Ahmed Khan had defined *bid'ah* in vague terms as "something new". But here, in making use of Shah Isma'il's detailed exposition, he distinguished three main types. The first was:

The belief, spoken word, state of heart, worship, custom transaction that is new. New, that is to say: neither the thing itself nor anything else similar to it existed at the time of the Messenger of God and, neither the thing itself nor anything similar to it existed at the time of the Companions and the Followers of the Companions and the Followers of the Followers. If any person does such a thing because he regards it as harmful (on that Day) or if any person practises something because he regards it as an essential element or a condition or necessary part of a certain (act of) worship or of a transaction *(mu'dmalat),* then this is called "pure" innovation *(that bid'at).*[16]

Shah Isma'il defines this as *bid'at-i asliyah* (genuine innovation).

The second kind of innovation took place with changes in the order of things as prescribed in detail in the law. It referred to things and matters in themselves praiseworthy, but necessary for the action concerned to be counted valid, example, prescriptions regarding the positions of the during ritual prayer. This Shah Isma'il defines as bid'at-i *wasifyah* (descriptive innovation).

The third kind of innovation concerned religious matters or practices neither explicitly prescribed nor forbidden—things which did not belong to the distinctive marks of Islam. These became innovation because the effort spent on their practice was the same as that on putting into practice the distinctive marks of Islam. Shah Isma'il defines this as *bid'at-i hukmi* (virtual innovation).

Mohammad Talbi, in his historical analysis of the term bid'ah, states in his conclusion, *"on ne denoncait pas toujours la meme chose, mais on utilisait toujours le mime terme."*[17] Which then are the main items Syed Ahmed Khan condemns as *bid'at* in the three definitions of the term?

Under genuine innovation, for instance, falls Ibn al-'Arabi's theory (with its ensuing practical attitudes) of *wahadat al-wujud if* (unity of being); reasoning about the nature of God, predestination and free will and the "vision of God"; discussions about ambiguous verses of the Qur'an and ambiguous Traditions; the reading of books produced by the *madhhab* of theosophy and philosophy; all these things must be regarded as having developed against the true *sunnah.* Further innovations are the practice of ascetic and spiritual exercises as those taught by the Sufis (in so far as they have developed against the *sunnah,* the employment of charms and related magical practices; the prescription of *khatm* prayers; the use of music and musical instruments in the *majlis,* the practice of reading the *marthiyas,* pious lamentations and recitations; and various popular rites at the tombs, 'urs festivals and dance. All this is genuine innovation because it has been added to the law of Muhammad.[18]

The second form—qualitative innovation—is an act meritorious in itself, such as cooking food in honour of Imam Husain, and feeding the hungry from it on a fixed day (on special occasions like the month of Muharram for instance). Because to fix a day, a month or any time for a religious practice is the function of the shar' only.

The same act would fall under the third category, i.e. virtual innovation, if the person performing it would do so without believing thereby to gain special merit. In other words, it is enough to behave as if one was believing the action to be meritorious, in order to make it an act of virtual innovation.

Syed Ahmed Khan seems especially aware of innovations which militate against the Islamic teaching of brotherhood and equality of believers. Besides extravagant weddings, such innovations staged for reasons of social prestige the wilful interpretation and eclectic practice of the Shari'a by Maulwis and dervishes (for instance, by fixing time for visiting and receiving people, by performing ritual prayer in the mosque of one's pir, and by practicing celibacy).

Since these practices are performed as if they were prescribed, they are to be condemned as "Virtual" innovation. As a contrast Sir Syed points to the example of the Prophet and his Companions, laying stress on their unpretentious conduct.

The faithful believer who becomes aware of these innovations looks afresh at the religious life of his fellow Muslims, being critically aware of the many Hindu practices that intruded into the lives of Muslims. Sir Syed becomes aware, in other words, of his specifically Muslim identity.

A crucial question arises at this point: how is one to distinguish between good and evil innovation? The distinction was made, Syed Ahmed Khan explains, since the earliest days of Islam. if good innovation is taken to mean what Sir Syed would call sunnat-i hukmiyah, i.e. something not explicitly stated in the Qur'an and Tradition, but follows from it by the application of straightforward qiyas, then there can be no objection.

But usually "good innovation" refers to a practice which though not mentioned in the Qur'an and Tradition, is regarded as meritorious—as musafahah for instance (the greeting after the afternoon prayer), or halqah (gathering around the tomb with the recitation of the Qur'an). Syed Ahmed Khan condemns a distinction between this kind of innovation and an evil one. Because if a practice is good and meritorious, it is not an innovation in any sense, but contained implicitly or explicitly in Qur'an and Tradition, i.e. in the shar'. Neither reason ('aql) nor experience (tajribah), independent of the shar', can be a criterion for the goodness of an action, but only the text of the shar'. To support his argument, Sir Syed quotes here from al-Ghazali.[19]

There are, of course, shar'i practices not mentioned explicitly in the Qur'an and Tradition. Such practices are sunnah, if they have been established by the 'ulama-i mujtahidin to be shar'i. Only the 'ulama'-i mujtahidin can, by critically employing analogical reasoning to Qur'an and Tradition establish practices to be implicitly contained in the shar'. But are the 'ualma'-i *mujtahidin* merely the four founders of the great legal schools—Abu Hanifah - Malik b. Anas, al-Shafi'i, Ahmed b. Muhammad b. Hanbal—or later fuqaha' as well? Syed Ahmed Khan is not clear on this point in Rah-i sunnat. In any case, only the 'ulama'-i mujtahidin constitute actively ijmae.' Only those practices are ijma'i, that have been consciously deduced by the ulama from the text of Qur'an and Tradition. Only those which Muslims have adopted "because of their Islam," and not simply *qua* custom and habit.

Certain practices of the Prophet or the "three generations" are peculiar to them and have never been ratified by the ijma'-i ummah and the qiyas of the mujahhids. Other practices that became a habit during the first three generations (and were considered sacrosanct) are lawful, but they have to be practised without exaggeration.

Sir Syed's explanations do not clarify the function and competence of an alim today—whether or not he was entitled to apply qiyas beyond a decision of one of the four schools. He seems to confine himself to fighting fanatical excesses. He even warns the reader against overestimating the importance of the four imams, as compared to a direct, personal following of the Qur'an and sunnah. He expresses his disgust over a fanatical blind following of Abfi Ijanifah, for example. He attacks those who consider the taqlid (blind following) of the a'immah-i mujtahidin as part and parcel of their faith and who add to their shahadah: wa akhtartu madhhaba al-Hanafi wa al-Shafi wa al-Maliki wa al-Hanbali (And I have chosen the Hanafi and Shafi'i and Maliki and Hanbali schools). He declares this attitude towards taqlid as shirk (associationism).

It can be concluded that Syed Ahmed Khan was rooted firmly in the religious tradition of Indian Islam. The upbringing and early education in his remarkable family and, later on, his personal religious studies in the intellectually vivid atmosphere of pre-1857 Delhi contributed to a genuine concern for the purity and strength of Islamic belief and practice in India. This led to his active participation in contemporary religious debate, and the endeavour for reform. His later works in the field of theology were therefore not produced for want of other, more effective means to achieve his (allegedly) secular aims. They grew out of a long-existing commitment to, and an, ever-widening knowledge of, the theological tradition of Islam.

Syed Ahmed Khan's early writings reflect and express the important strands in contemporary Indian Muslim thought as they were being nourished by the continuing life of the Naqshbandiyah Mujaddidiyah tradition, by the influence of Shah Wali Allah's works and teachings, and by the movement of the Mujahiddin. Perhaps the most remarkable feature of these writings is the fusion of the Sufi and 'alim tradition, of tariqah and Shari'a—a trend that had started much earlier, but which has found a remarkable expression in Kalimat al-haqq (1849).

In his determination to "go back" to "pure" Islam, the young Syed is acutely aware of differences between Muslim religious practice of the India of his day, and that of the period of the "first three generations." A little later this awareness was to be sharpened further by the challenges he perceived by the western presence in India. This is thus an important clement in the evolution of his later theological position.

Sir Syed was a deeply committed man, who did not adopt a fanatic position. Even during his "Wahhabi" period at the end of the 1840s and the beginning of the 1850s, he takes up a comparatively tolerant, almost reconciling position. He shares the religious aspirations of the Mujahidin—at least as far as returning "to the sources," the fight against innovation and the endeavour towards religio-social reform is concerned. But significantly, in the directly political injunctions of the Shari'a—for example, jihad and khilafah, matters about which Shah Isma'il had written in detail—evidence suggests that Sir Syed did not commit himself publicly, or that he was opposed to Indian "Wahhabi" views and efforts in this field.

Finally, although he strongly criticizes the blind following of four schools in *fiqh* and advocates a return to the practice of the "first three generations"—much in the spirit of older Hanbali reformers—he does not advocate during this period ijtihad. Independent judgement is possible disregard of the teaching of the imams of the four great legal schools.[20]

REFERENCES

1. Khan, Sir Syed Ahmed, *Sirat-i-Faridiyah* (Agra: Matba-i-Mufidi), 1886 (Translation by Chr. Schackle), p. 638.
2. *Ibid.*, p. 674.
3. *Ibid.*, p. 689.
4. *Ibid.*, p. 687.
5. Hali, Altaf Hussain, *Hayat-i-Jawed, op. cit.*, p. 67.
6. Troll, Christian W., *Sayyid Ahmad Khan: A Reinterpretation of Muslim Theology, op. cit.*, p. 31.
7. *Ibid.*
8. *Ibid.*, p. 33.
9. *Ibid.*, p. 34.
10. Rahman, Fazlur, *Islam* (New York: Doubleday & Co.), 1968, p. 258.
11. Hedayatullah, Mohammad, *Sayyid Ahmad Khan: A Study of the Religious Reform Movement of Sayyid Ahmad Khan of Rae Bareli* (Lahore: Ashraf), 1970, p. 144.
12. Khan, Sir Syed Ahmed, *Tusanif-i-Ahmadiyah* (Aligarh: Institute Press), 1883, p. 19.
13. Troll, Christian W., *Sayyid Ahmad Khan: A Reinterpretation of Muslim Theology, op. cit.*, p. 38.
14. Khan, Sir Syed Ahmed, *Tusanif-i-Ahmadiyah, op. cit.*, p. 427.
15. Troll, Christian W., *Sayyid Ahmad Khan: A Reinterpretation of Muslim Theology, op. cit.*, p. 41.
16. Panipati, M. Ismail, *Maqalat-i-Sir Sayyid* (Lahore: Majlis-i-taraqqi-i-adab), 1972, Vol. V, pp. 371-372.
17. *Ibid.*, pp. 43-77.
18. Khan, Sir Syed Ahmed, *Tusanif-i-Ahmadiyah, op. cit.*, p. 108.
19. *Ibid.*, p. 123.
20. Khan, Sir Syed Ahmed, *Tusanif-i-Ahmadiyah, op. cit.*, p. 57.

3

MUSLIM COMMUNITY AS A DISTINCT AND SEPARATE FORCE

The factors which contributed to the growth of Muslim community as a distinct and separate force in Indian life in the nineteenth century are many. It is not possible to discuss all of them. So I have picked up the following points to throw some light on the subject: (1) Impact of Faraizi and Wahabi Movements; (2) Deoband and Aligarh: Centres of Muslim Learning; (3) Muslim Associations in Bengal; (4) Role of the Muslim Writers; and (5) Concluding Remarks. Let me now serially take up these points.

1. Impact of Faraizi and Wahabi Movements

The rapid expansion of British dominion in India during the period 1757-1818 brought a great change in Indian life. The Muslims could not forget that they had just lost their Empire to the British and could not reconcile themselves with the British rule. But the Hindus found no difficulty to make a satisfactory adjustment with the British rule. They easily took up English in place of Persian and "participated in trade, industry and banking along with their British principals."[1] As the Hindus became conversant with English language they were easily employed "in mercantile houses as well as in administrative services." In this way the Muslims lagged behind the Hindus. This uneven growth of these two communities helped the British to successfully apply the 'divide et impera' policy.[2]

To emancipate the Muslims from this bondage and degradation several Muslim theologians launched socio-religious reform movements in the beginning of the 19th century, more precisely called the Faraizi and the Wahabi movements. From 1818 to 1870 vast areas of India were affected by these movements, particularly by the Wahhabi movement. Mainly religious in character, directed towards purifying Islam and India by removing un-Islamic, influences from it, these came to acquire with the inclusion of economic and political programme, a mixed movement, socio-economic and political. In the agrarian sphere these movements stood for defending the socio-economic interests of the peasants against the zamindars and European indigo planters. In the religious sphere it strengthened the processes of Islamization. Pan-Islamic ideas had been infused into the body-politic of the Muslims by the Faraizis-Wahhabis. In the political sphere these movements were directed against the British rule. They considered the British India as dar-ul-harb (country of war or enmity). So they wanted to convert it to dar-ul-Islam (land of Islam or safety). The Wahhabis took up arms and fought battles against the British. The British had to suppress them by an armed intervention."[3]

There was no doubt that these movements helped much to remove the depression in which the Muslims had fallen, especially in political and economic spheres. Being politically defeated, the Muslim leaders at first took shelter in the canopy of religion to protect the interests of the Muslims. They failed to explain the problems of political defeat of the Muslims in terms of concrete political realities and hard facts of life. Their interpretations only lulled those questions which agitated the minds of the Muslims during this time, and they diverted their thought from the real situation to another direction. So, the Faraizi-Wahhabi leaders could properly explain for what political and economic reasons the British were successful in establishing their dominion in India. For this reason these movements registered "reactions not remedies, to the situation then existing."

Studying these movements it would be clear to us that in the beginning the Muslim leaders expressed their grievances against the British rule through the medium of theology. This was quite natural in the context of that time. But its consequences were far-reaching. As religion was mixed up with politics, it provoked complex reaction among the people of different religious groups which were not congenial to a country like India.

2. Deoband and Aligarh Centres of Muslim Learning

But these religious reform movements which acquired anti-British character lost their tempo by the end of the 19th century. The Faraizi-Wahhabi movements generated a hostile disposition among the British towards the Muslims. This was subsequently strengthened by the Revolt of 1857. In the meantime a section of Muslim leaders realized that the British rule was firmly established in India and it would be impossible to regenerate the Muslims by launching anti-British struggle. So these leaders made honest efforts to remove British suspicion about the Muslims. Since then new ideas began to mould the Muslim mind. The Muslim intelligentsia followed two courses—one section took the path of religious education and the other turned to Western learning. In this way both the groups tried to rouse up and defend the rights of the Indian Muslims. Serving different prescriptions to cure the same illness, two Muslim institutions were simultaneously founded in the United Provinces—one at Deoband (1867) and another at Aligarh (1875). Maulana Muhammad Qasim Nanautvi (d. 1879) and Syed Ahmed Khan (1817-1898) were respectively the leaders of these two schools of thought.

The Orthodox views were strengthened in the Muslim society by a Madrassa founded at Deoband in the Saharanpur District of Uttar Pradesh in 1867 by Maulana Muhammad Qasim, Nanautivi. This school actually replaced the Delhi School of Shah Abdul Aziz which was closed down during the revolt of 1857. The main object of the Deoband seminary was "to re-establish contact between, the *alim* and the average Muslim, and to reorientate the Muslim community to its original cultural and religious identity." The founder of Deoband school upheld certain elements of the teachings of the school of Shah Waliullah. This Seminary, of course, made efforts "to spread through its education among the religious class of Muslims the spirit of freedom".[4] But it remained aloof from practical politics. Naturally, the fervour for freedom did not take any concrete political organizational shape. Keeping intact the set-up of 'religious puritanism', the Deoband leader wanted to develop the 'love for political freedom'. As the theologians of Deoband school were staunch defenders of Islam and opponents of the trend of modernism, they had an important role in reshaping Indian Muslim society on orthodox lines which in one way or other preserved and strengthened separatist tendencies in our country.

On the other hand, Sir Syed Ahmed Khan wanted to remove the backwardness of the Muslim society through English education and Western culture. He also sincerely tried to remove misunderstanding between the British and the Muslims. With this object in view Sir Syed Ahmed founded an educational institution at Aligarh in 1875 which in course of time became the nursery of Muslim elite and politicians. In order to maintain and preserve the identity of the Muslims as a separate community and to bring them up from their present state, he urged upon the Muslims to remain aloof from the Indian National Congress, which was to him an organization of the Hindus only. Sir Syed Ahmed made determined efforts to weaken the position of the nationalists led by Badruddin Tyabji (1844-1906) and his associates. The Annual Muhammadan Education Conference (1886) founded by Sir Syed Ahmed became the main political and ideological seat of the Muslims. He also took the initiative in founding the Indian Patriotic Association (1888). Within a short time this Association became broad based and various Muslim organizations of Bengal and Bihar were affiliated with it. Moreover, in December 1893, the Muslims of upper India formed another organization at Aligarh named Muhammadan Anglo-Oriental Defence Association of Upper India. The main objects of these organizations were to oppose the Indian National Congress and to acquaint the Government officials and, the British Press with the condition and opinions of the Muslims. Thus the movement initiated by Sir Syed Ahmed got a pro-British and anti-Congress colour. The concept of 'modernism' as propounded by Sir Syed Ahmed was based on the Islamic identity mixed up with pro-British and anti-Congress ideas.[5]

All these efforts, however, could not stem the tide of the nationalist movement led by the Congress. A section of upper Indian Muslims considered the "activities of the so-called National

Congress" as subversive to "the best interests of the British rule in India." To counteract the 'discontent and unrest' generated by the Congress propaganda, they formed an Anti-Congress Committee (1899) at Lucknow. During this time the Muslims of upper India felt the necessity of forming a separate Muslim political organization and they discussed this matter at a meeting in Lucknow in 1901. Accordingly, the Muslim Political Association came into existence in 1903 at Saharanpur, U.P., under the able guidance and leadership of Mustaq Hussain Viqar-ul-Mulk (1841-1917). It was founded on pro-British and anti-Congress programme. But it survived only for three years. Yet, this Association can really be called as a precursor of the All-India Muslim League (1906). The leader of this Association Mustaq Hussain Viqar-ul-Mulk presided over that historic meeting at Dacca in 1906 where the Muslim League was founded.[6]

3. Muslim Associations in Bengal

Another important centre of Muslim awakening during the period under review was Bengal. Abdur Rauf, Nawab Amir Ali Khan Bahadur (1817-1879), Abdul Luteef (1828-1893) and Syed Ameer Ali (1849-1928), four prominent leaders of educated Muslims directed their attention to the strengthening of the position of the Muslims, mainly through educational reforms within the framework of British administration. Abdur Rauf's Anjuman-i-Islami, Calcutta (1855), Nawab Amir Ali's National Muhammadan Association (1856), Abdul Tuwef's Muhammadan Literary Society of Calcutta (1863) and Syed Ameer Ali's Central National Muhammadan Association of Calcutta (1876) played a vital role in moulding Muslim mind in Bengal and neighbouring areas. These associations enlisted the support of the Muslim theologians also. We can particularly mention the role of Maulana Karamat Ali (1800-1873) of Jaunpore, who urged upon the Muslims to give up anti-British attitude and to learn European languages for the extension of scientific knowledge. In the sphere of politics the Muslim elite and the theologians jointly blunted the edge of the anti-British aspects of the Faraizi-Wahhabi ideology. At the same time they percolated the processes of Islamization continued from the Medieval period and carried on by the Faraizi-Wahhabi movements into the body-politic of the Muslims. In fact, the entire process of modernising the Muslim society was founded on the concepts of purity of Islam as well as on the separate identity of the Muslims. For their loyalist stand, they got encouragement from the Government.[7]

On 2nd May, 1855, the Anjuman-i-Isami, Calcutta was founded by Abdur Rauf, Head of the Department of Arabic, Calcutta Madrassa and others. Abdul Luteef also was one of its founder members. The objects of this organization were to protect the fights of the Muslims and to support the English Company's administration in this country. It also advised the Muslims not to join the Revolt of 1857. The ideals of this organization were propagated by its organ, *Durbeen*, a Persian weekly, which was published in June 1855 under the editorship of Abdur Rauf. There were several branches of this organization, viz. Anjuman-i-Islami, Midnapore (1855) and Anjuman-i-Islami, Sylhet (1855). The Anjuman-i-Islami, Calcutta existed till 1876. Thus this organization had a role in creating, pro-British attitude in Bengal.

From the very beginning Abdul Luteef took an anti-Congress stand. He refused to attend the Congress Session in 1886. Ameer Ali's Association also expressed its inability to attend this Session. They thought that their association with the Congress would be harmful to the interests of the Muslims. They refused to follow "an attitude of uneasiness towards the Government". They wanted to serve the interests of the educated Muslims by mobilising them on a broad pro-British and anti-Congress platform and by making them conscious of their position as a separate and distinct community. Thus the aims and objects of the Muslim elite of Bengal were similar to the group led by Sir Syed Ahmed Khan in upper India.[8]

However, Abdul Luteef and Ameer Ali did not confine their activities to Bengal only. They even established links with the Muslims of other parts of the country. So the movement for the uplift of the Muslim community, though purely confined to the upper and middle classes, was widened to a vast area. Both of them encouraged the Muslim elite to found organizations in the mofussils.[9] The Muslim gentry of Dacca established the Dacca Muhammadan Friends

Association in 1883. The branches of Central National Association were established at Midnapore and at Hooghly. The Anjuman-i-Islamia was founded at Mymensingh as well as at Rangpur. The Anjuman-i-Mafidul Islam was established at Jingapara, Mohanganj. After the death of Abdul Luteef in 1893, Ameer Ali's Central National Muhammadan Association took the leading part in placing before the Government the difficulties of the Muslims. From that time several Muslim organizations were either connected with it or re-organised on the model of it. The Malda Muhammadan Association (1891) was re-organised on its model in 1895. The Anjuman-i-Islami established at Sirajganj in the district of Pabna in 1898 had close connection with the Central National Muhammadan Association. The Muhammadan Union (1890) and the Suburban Muhammadan Association (1901), both established in Calcutta, were also connected with Ameer Ali's Association. Even the aims and objects of the Meerut Association, the Anjuman-i-Islami of Amritsar and the Bombay Association were similar to those of the Central National Muhammadan Association. Moreover, the branches of Ameer Ali's Association were established in different parts of Bengal as well as in Lahore, Karachi and Lucknow. Several other educated Muslims, who were in legal profession, also came forward to guide the community and they established an organization in 1896 known as the Muhammadan Reform Association. All these organizations gave a concrete shape to the Muslim mind and weakened the position of those Muslim leaders who were trying to strengthen the forces of Indian nationalism by mobilising the Muslims on the Congress platform. As the Muslim elite of Bengal, who were organized in Calcutta and mofussil areas, took an anti-Congress stand, it became difficult for Rahmatullah Sayani of Bombay to go ahead with the ideals of the Congress. The speech delivered by him as a President of the Congress Session in 1896 was condemned by the Bengali Muslims.[10] As an influential section of the Bengali Muslims refused to join the Congress, the gap between the Hindus and the Muslims was greatly widened. It accelerated the process of organizing the Muslims on a separate political platform.

4. Role of the Muslim Writers

The Muslim writers also played an important part in strengthening separatist forces in the country. The literature created by the Hindu writers was considered by them as "an expression of Hindu culture and ideology". So in the spheres of literature and culture, the reaction of the Muslim writers "took the shape of an outcry for Islam and the Muslims."[11] The books, and the tracts as well as the articles published in various Muslim journals either in 'Mussalmani Bengali' or 'pure Bengali', generated pan-Islamic, pro-British, anti-Congress and anti-Hindu attitude among the Muslims. The Muslim authors made determined efforts to preserve the distinctness of the Muslims by removing their ignorance on Islam as well as the influence of un-Islamic ways of life on them. Mohammad Naimuddin served this purpose by incorporating essential tenets of Islam in his Bengali Work Zobdatal Masael—Pratham Khand (1873).[12] A group of Muslim writers appeared on the scene centering round the Madrassa Literary Budget, a monthly literary journal of Calcutta *Madrassa*, edited by the Madrassa Literary and Debating Club. The first edition of this journal was published in June 1876 and continued till 1878. This journal and club made the educated Muslims aware of their Islamic identity. Then, the Bengali Muslims were acquainted with the greatness of their religion by the Islam Tattva (1887-1888). One notable work on the life of the Prophet was Sheikh Abdur Rahim's Hajrat Muhammader Jiban Charit O Dharmaniti (1888). Sheikh Abdus Sobhan in his work entitled Hindu Mussalman (1888) clearly pointed out that the Muslims were deprived of Government posts by the educated Hindus and they utilized the Congress organization for this purpose. He called upon the Muslims to unite on a common platform to safeguard their interests. *The Upadesa Sanurahe* (1891), written by Maulavi Alauddin Ahmed, gave religious instructions to the Muslims. A similar work entitled *Massayele Islam* (1905) was written by Kazi Abdul Aziz. Two other works on the biography of the Prophet were published in Bengali—*Maulud Sharif* by Syed Nawab Ali Chowdhury and *Paritrana Kavya* (1904). Muhammad Abdul Wahab Chaudhury's *Srihatte Shah Jalal* (1905) was on that Muslim saint. Thus these authors created an Islamic literature in pure Bengali.[13]

During this time Munshi Muhammad Meherullah (1867-1912) of Jessore began to preach the tenets of Islam and wrote a number of tracts in defence of Islam. He declared crusade against Hinduism and Christianity. He bitterly criticised Christianity in his work *Radde Khristan O Dalilo Islam* (1895). The hollowness of Hinduism was exposed by him in *Hindu-Dharma Rahasya O Deba Leela* (1912). Meherullah's sole object was to prove that "Islam was the best religion in the world." His ideals were carried on by his associate Munshi Sheikh Muhammad Jamiruddin of Nadia. The followers of Meherullah did their best to turn "the Bengali Muslim mind back to the religion of Islam".[14] A group of Muslim writers also moved in the same direction. *The Sudhakar* (1889-1891), a Bengali weekly published from Calcutta, served as a mouthpiece of this group. In the Muslim literary circle they were known as the 'Sudhakar Group'. The most influential anti-Swadeshi papers were the *Islam Pracharak* (1895-1910, monthly) and the *Mihir O Sudhakar* (1895-1919, weekly) organs of the Muslim zamindars. These papers propagated the greatness of Islam in comparison with Christianity, Hinduism and Brahmoism; and upheld anti-Congress and pro-British policy. Their hold on the Muslims of Bengal was much greater than that of the *Mussalman* (1906) and the *Soltan* (1902-1910), the two pro-Swadeshi papers.[15]

The Muslim writers fostered pan-Islamic feeling among the Muslims. The situation was, however, favourable to it. After the visit of famous Muslim leader Jamal-ud-Din Afghani (1839-1897) to Calcutta in 1881-82, the Muslim leaders and writers became more inclined to Pan-Islamism. The Muslims got satisfaction in establishing a link with the Caliph and became proud of the emergence and expansion of Islamic world. Pandit Reaz-al-Din Ahmed Mashhadi (1859-1910), a noted author, wrote a book entitled *Samaj O Samskarak* (1889) on the life and activities of Jamal-ud-Din Afghani. But Pandit Mashhadi and other supporters of Pan-Islamism did not care to properly fit Pan-Islamic ideas with the main stream of Indian life. As a result Pan-Islamism nourished separatism in India.

At the end of the 19th century the Muslim authors became very much vocal against the Hindu writers for slandering the "Muslim

Nation, and its 'Glorious History'." They sharply reacted to the use of the words 'Jaban', 'Mlechha', 'Nere' etc. in Bengali literature by the Hindu writers, particularly by Iswar Gupta, Rangalal Bandyopadhyaya, Hem Chandra Bandyopadhyaya and Bankim Chandra Chattopadhyaya. In 1898 Syed Nawab Ali Chowdhury moved a resolution at a session of Muslim Education Society condemning the reflection of Muslim feeling in Bengali literature. Another disturbing feature was the controversy on cow protection or cow slaughter. It was one of the factors for which communal amity was disrupted. In 1882, Swami Dayanand Swaraswati founded an Association named Gohatya Nibarani Sabha for the protection of cows. On the other hand, most of the Muslim authors defended cow slaughter on religious grounds. Thus the Muslim mind moved on a different tract, quite distinct and separate from the Hindus.

From the above discussion we can broadly divide the leading figures of the Muslim community into three groups : first, anti-British socio-religious reformers; second, pro-British and anti-Congress leaders and writers; third, anti-British and pro-Congress nationalist Muslims. The dominant element in the first group was the Faraizis-Wahhabis. Their anti-British feeling was mixed up with Pan-Islamic and Muslim revivalist ideas. The leaders of the second group pursued pro-British and anti-Congress policies keeping alive the processes of Islamization. The leaders of these groups carried on the orthodox-revivalist spirit which grew up in medieval context. The leaders of the third group were in the Congress fold and some of them took prominent part in the Swadeshi and anti-Partition Agitation of Bengal. As many of the nationalist Muslims were emotionally attached to the ideals of revivalism and Pan-Islamism, the orthodox-revivalist trend became the principal moulding factor of the Indian Muslim society. It thwarted the growth of liberal-rational-humanistic trend in Indian life. Even the prominent thinkers like Mir Mosharraf Hossain (1848-1911), Pandit Mashhadi, Delawarr Hosaen Ahmed Meerza (1840-1913) and Syed Ismail Hossain Shirazi (1870-1931) could not rise above communal thinking. At a later period Mir Mosharraf Hossain could not preserve his non-communal outlook[16] which he had boldly expressed in the Gojiban and other articles. Delawarr Hosaen Ahmed Meerza, the first Muslim graduate of Calcutta University, advocated radical reform and change in the laws and institutions of the Muslims. But at the same time strengthened the separatist forces by launching a campaign for a separate Muslim organization in the country. Syed Shirazi was once a nationalist and a member of the Indian National Congress. But afterwards he severed his connections with the Congress and became a staunch protagonist of Muslim revivalism and Pan-Islamism. He also spoke for the "separate culture and existence for the Muslims."[17]

In fact, the Muslim intelligentsia and the theologians did not make any effort to bring the followers of different faiths closer to each other for the establishment of a new human society which was slowly getting a form due to the activities of several saints and reformers in the eighteenth-nineteenth century India. No positive efforts were made by them to study the question of Muslim backwardness in its historical context under alien domination. Moreover, the Muslim leaders and thinkers did not feel any urge to promote the Muslim politics to a higher secular stage so that a new India could be built up along with other communities. As they remained absolutely indifferent to this task and as they did not undertake the responsibility of moulding Muslim mind with liberal-rational-humanistic ideas, the separatist forces gained enormous strength in a community like the Indian Muslims.

REFERENCES

1. De Amalendu, *Roots of Separatism in the Nineteenth Century Bengal* (Calcutta: Maya Prakashan), 1974, p. 4.
2. *Ibid.*
3. De Amalendu, *Islam in Modern India* (Calcutta: Maya Prakashan), 1982. p. 12.
4. Ahmad, Aziz, *Islamic Modernism in India and Pakistan*, 1857-1964 (London: Oxford University Press), 1967, p. 104.
5. *Ibid.*, Chapter II.
6. Ahmed, Sufia, *Muslim Community in Bengal, 1884-1912* (Dacca: Oxford University Press), 1974, p. 206.
7. *Ibid.*, p. 170.

8. De Amalendu, *Islam in Modern India, op. cit.*, p. 16.
9. Graham, G.F.I., *The Life and Work of Sir Syed Ahmed Khan, op. cit.*, p. 273.
10. Ahmed, Sufia, *Muslim Community in Bengal. 1884-1912, op. cit.*, p. 187.
11. *Ibid.*, p. 309.
12. De Amalendu, *Roots of Separatism in the Nineteenth Century Bengal, op. cit.*, p. 42.
13. *Ibid.*
14. Munshi Muhammad Meherullah's Works:

(i) *Hindu-Dharma Rahasya O Deba Leela* (First and Second volume), Reprinted by Muslim Anusilan Sangstha, Dacca, 1976. The first edition of this work was published after the death of Meherullah in 1912. Some leading members of the Hindu community filed a suit at the Jessore court for forbidding the circulation of this work as they were derogatory comments on Hinduism. The publisher of this book was Meherullah's eldest son. The Judge fined him and proscribed the book in 1915. (See Introduction of the new edition published from Dacca on 13 July, 1976.) The Muslim Anusilan Sangstha was founded by Dr. Ramjan Ali Sardar of Dacca University in 1972.

(ii) *Radde Khristan O Dalilol Ba Khristan Dharmer Asharata*, Reprinted by Muslim Anusilan Sangstha, Dacca, 1976. The first edition of the book was published in 1895. This new edition was published on 22 August, 1976. It was stated in a note of this new edition that the religious leaders of the Christian and Hindu communities tried to convert Bengal into a province dominated by the non-Muslims. Munshi Meherullah was one of those prominent Muslim leaders who played a vital part in retaining Bengal as a Muslim dominated province frustrating the attempts of the Christian and Hindu leaders.

(iii) *Jauabounachara Ba Khristander Prasnattor*, Reprinted by Muslim Anusilan Sangstha, Dacca, 1976. The first edition of this work was published on 26 Bhadra, 1304 B.S. The new edition states about a Chritian Missionary named John, who was defeated by Munshi Meherullah in a religious debate, embraced Islam and became known as Munshi Sheikh Muhammad Jamiruddin (see Foreword by M.A. Zaman).

(iv) *Bidhaba Ganjana*. This was not known from the works of Munshi Meherullah published by the Muslim Anusilan Sangstha when actually this tract was written by him. But it was claimed by M.A. Zaman that many Hindu widows embraced Islam after the publication of this tract by Munshi Meherullah (see Foreword by M.A. Zaman, in *Hindu-Dharma Rahasya*).

15. De Amalendu, *Roots of Separatism in the Nineteenth Century Bengal, op. cit.*, p. 19.
16. Chaudhri, Munir, *Mir-Mansam* (Dacca: Oxford University Press), 1968.
17. De Amalendu, *Roots of Separatism in the Nineteenth Century Bengal, op. cit.*, 1974, pp. 316-317.

4

BRITISH LOYALISM AND POLITICAL SEPARATISM

The East India Company turned out to be the principal casualty of the 'Mutiny' of 1857-58. The destinies of India passed from the hands of the Board of Directors of the Company to those of the British parliament and the British electorate. In a speech from the Throne in 1859, Queen Victoria proclaimed a general amnesty and a vague promise of gradual political representation for the Indian people. On 28 July 1859, 15,000 Muslims gathered in a mosque in Delhi to thank her.[1] As he addressed them, Syed Ahmed Khan found himself the leader of a defeated and demoralized community which had waged a conservative, 'archaic' struggle against the impact of foreign rule and its alien but dynamic institutions, and failed. There was only one way of survival left open, loyalism in politics and modernism in institutions.

Causes of the Indian Revolt

In 1858, Syed Ahmed Khan wrote a book entitled *The Causes of the Indian Revolt.* Originally written in Urdu (*Asbab-i-Baghawat-i Hind*), it was translated by Colvin and Graham in English in 1873. According to Syed Ahmed the primary cause of the revolt was the non-admission of Indians into process of legislation as participation of people in the councils was essential. Due to the non-admission of Indians in the legislative bodies, there was no avenue open to them through which they could register their protests and express their opinions. There was thus a great misunderstanding of the real intentions of the government. There came a time 'when all men looked upon the English government as slow poison, a rope of sand, a treacherous flame of fire.'[2] Hence in his book *The Causes of the Indian Revolt*, he deplored the absence of an effective communication and information feedback between the rulers and the subjects. He lamented that although the British government had been in the country for nearly a century, no attempts had been made to solicit the affections and good feelings of the people. He regretted that the people had no means of expressing their grievances to the rulers. Syed Ahmed had made a plea for people's participation in councils and lamented that the people in India had no means to register their protest against an unwanted measure.

Syed Ahmed wrote: "Most men agree, I believe, that it is conducive to the welfare and prosperity of government—indeed it is essential to its stability—that the people should have a voice in its councils. It is from the voice of the people that government can learn whether its projects are likely to be well received. This security can never be acquired unless the people are allowed a share in the consultation of government. The men who have ruled India can never forget that they were here in the position of foreigners...The security of government is based on its knowledge of the governed as well as its careful observance of their rights and privileges."[3]

There were some other subsidiary causes of the Indian revolt, according to Syed Ahmed, which were rooted in the primary factor of legislative non-participation Indians. These other factors can be thus classified[4]:

(i) The passing of laws and measures which went against the cherished traditions and conventions of people. Some of these laws and measures were definitely objectionable.
(ii) The government was ignorant of the desires and aspirations of the people.
(iii) The neglect by the rulers of the basic elements were requisite for the good governance of India.
(iv) The bad management of the army leading to the spread of disaffection amongst them.

British Loyalism

From the revolt of 1857, Syed Ahmed drew some lessons for political philosophy. He inculcated the necessity of friendship and sympathetic intercourse between the rulers and the ruled. Taking a botanical analogy, he said that the government is the root and the people are the growth of that root. He quoted St. Paul's injunctions regarding brotherliness. He also quoted the saying of Jesus Christ; "Therefore all things whatsoever ye would that men should do to you, do ye even so to them: for this is the law and the prophets."

In 1860 Syed Ahmed published a pamphlet on "The Loyal Mohammedans of India," extracts from which are given below:

"It is as well that the English public be reminded of eminent services rendered by our Mussulman fellow-subjects during the memorable years 1857-58; and it is also advisable to bring, after the lapse of so many years, these services and their rewards prominently before the Indian public. During and for long after the Mutiny, the Mohammedans were under a cloud. To them were attributed all the horrors and calamities of that terrible time; and that this prejudice was to a very great extent unjust, and that it was regretted and resented by the Mohammedans at large, is undoubted."[5] No one being apparently willing to take up the cudgels in their defence, Syed Ahmed threw himself into the breach and did all in his power to rehabilitate their reputation.

Verily [he wrote] it is an incontrovertible truth, that in the revolutions of time a general calamity sometimes occurs of a nature so overwhelming that man is completely prostrated and unhinged thereby, and rendered utterly helpless in his extremity. There is then, as it were, a great weight on his soul, bearing it down into the gulf of despair, for at that season of crushing trial neither virtue nor learning, nor skill nor talent, is of any avail. Undoubtedly, if a man be guilty of a really culpable act, there can be no extenuation for it; but when he is enveloped by the sombre mantle of misfortune, even his good deeds are open to suspicion and misconstruction, and are either condemned *in toto* or said to proceed from a latent sinister motive. "Certainly, good and bad are to be found in every class and creed; but the proverb that "a fish pollutes all water" has reference especially to a season of distress—for it is a peculiarity of the time, that if even one man has done ill, the entire class to which he belongs is held up to execration; and although a large number of that class may have done right well, nobody thinks of their good deeds, and they get no credit for them. Now the season of dire extremity to which I allude is that which befell the Mohammedans in 1857-58. There was no atrocity committed then of which the blame was not imputed to the Mohammedans, although the parties really guilty may have been Ramdin and Matadin. An oriental poet has well said: "There is no misfortune sent from heaven which, ere it descended to earth, did not seek for its resting-place the dwellings of Mohammedans!" Long and anxiously have I pondered upon the events which marked the terrible crisis that has passed over this country; and I am free to confess that the facts which have come to my knowledge, and which I firmly believe to be true, have been a source of genuine comfort to my soul, inducing, as they do, the proud conviction that the rumours defamatory of the Mohammedans that have got abroad from the four quarters of the world are utterly without foundation. Some of the acts of the horrible drama have already been exposed; but as day by day all the particulars are gradually brought to light, when the naked truth stands revealed, then will this one glorious fact stand out in prominent relief, that if in Hindustan there was one class of people above another who, from the principles of their religion, from habits and associations, and from kindred disposition, were fast bound with Christians, in their dreaded hour of trial and danger, in the bonds of amity and friendship, those people were the Mohammedans ; and then will effectually silenced the tongue of slander, now so loud in their condemnation."[6]

He further wrote, "I really do not see that in those days any class besides the Mohammedans displayed so much single minded and earnest devotion to the interests of Government, or so willingly sacrificed reputation and status, life and prosperity, in its cause. It is to the Mohammedans that the credit belongs of having stood the staunch and unshaken friends of the Government amidst that fearful tornado that devastated the country, and shook the empire to its centre; and who were ever ready, heart and hand, to render their aid to the utmost extremity, or cheerfully to perish in the attempt, regardless of home and kindred, of life and its enjoyments. At that momentous crisis it was imperatively their duty—a duty enjoined by the precepts of our religion—to identify themselves heartily with the Christians and to espouse their cause, seeing that they have, like ourselves, been favoured with a revelation from heaven, and believe in the prophets, and hold sacred the word of God in His holy book, which is also an object of faith with us. But I must deprecate that wholesale denunciation against Mohammedans as a race, in which the newspapers are wont to indulge."[7]

Syed Ahmed then goes on to rejoice that the Government is favourably disposed to his countrymen, as shown by the rewards which have been liberally bestowed upon all loyal Mohammedans ; and he only regrets that their loyalty and good services are rarely alluded to in the newspapers, whilst the writers on the Mutiny have "ignored them altogether."[8]

From 1859 until his death in 1898 he came to be more and more preoccupied with the problems of Muslim education in India. In 1868 he adopted a westernized way of living, developed cordial social contacts with British officialdom, and visited England in 1869-70. In 1876 he retired to devote his time entirely to the institutions of modern education he was building up at Aligarh. In 1869 he became a Commander of the Star of India and was awarded a knighthood in the same order in 1888. In 1878 he was appointed a member of the Viceroy's Legislative Council, an appointment which was a fulfilment of a suggestion that he was the first Indian to make, as early as 1859. In 1883 he resigned from the Council to meet the opposite challenge, that of the inevitable dominance of the Hindu majority over the Muslim minority in the representative or parliamentary institutions in India which Gladstonian liberalism had begun to introduce.

Apart from the political problems that were faced by him from 1859 onwards, there was also the intellectual problem of a better evaluation of Western civilization, and the theological problems of the rationalization of the basic data of faith which was bound to be challenged by the findings of the new sciences, and of meeting the challenge of Christian missionary polemics and its heritage in the more scientific study of Islam by western orientalists. Well equipped with a consummate theological scholarship in the tradition of Shah Wali Allah, he also turned to the study of Christian apologetics in the writings of the Unitarians, to a reorientation of Islam in terms of a rationalist scholasticism in the tradition of the Mu'tazila and an appreciation of Christianity in terms of what is now generally described as religious pluralism. In one sense his entire intellectual energy was devoted to trying to resolve the conflict between religion and science and to reconcile the best of both for the younger generation of the Muslim elite whom he wished to attract.

His loyalism can be measured in three stages. From 1859 to 1870, it was essentially a politically stabilizing factor, its object was to wean his own community 'from its policy of opposition' to one of acquiescence and participation, and to wean the British government 'from its policy of suppression to one of paternalism.'[9] This objective was more or less achieved in 1870. His argument was that as long as the Muslims of India enjoyed liberty to conform to their religious rituals publicly and, to propagate and defend their faith, there could be no theological case for them to rise against the British or even to aid a Muslim invader, though their emotional reaction in such an eventuality would be difficult to calculate. On the controversial question, whether India under the British remained *dar al-Islam* or *dar al-harb,* he did not commit himself. The second phase of his loyalism from 1870 to 1884 was mainly a response to the infiltration of pan-Islamic ideology, which Syed Ahmed Khan considered dangerous political adventurism. In this phase, championing the security of the loyalist *status quo,* he went to the extreme of defining the British rule in India 'as the most wonderful phenomenon the world has ever seen', with the argument that loyalty to it 'springs not from servile submission to a foreign rule, but from genuine appreciation of the blessings of good government'.[10]

In the third phase, from 1887 to 1898, his loyalism was employed to emphasize Muslim political separatism, with the advent of elective institutions and the rise of the Indian National Congress founded in 1885. Earlier he had been one of the first to assess the implications of the Urdu-Hindi controversy as the ultimate factor of cultural division between Muslims and Hindus. As early as 1867 he had told a British civil servant that the linguistic and cultural gulf between the two communities was widening so sharply that they were unlikely to co-operate in the composite development of a single nationhood. In 1884 he proposed a political pattern based on triangular unity and loyalty between Hindus, Muslims and British: 'In India peace cannot be maintained if either Hindus or Muslims rule the country. It is therefore inevitable that another nation should rule over us. We should take full advantage of these times of peace.'

Opposition to the Indian National Congress

Syed Ahmed Khan's active opposition to the Indian National Congress did not begin until 1887 when a Muslim, Badr al-din Tayyibji, was elected its president. From Syed Ahmed's viewpoint this was the beginning of an erosion in Muslim political solidarity, disastrous for the future of the Muslim community, which was numerically much smaller than the Hindu population, educationally backward, politically immature, and in economic resources and enterprise far behind the others. A political alliance with the Hindus could therefore lead only to one inevitable result, the eventual domination and the subjugation of the weaker by the stronger.

During 1888, Tyebji and Hume constantly endeavoured to secure his conciliation with the Congress. Sir Syed gave Tyebji a stunning reply (At just about that time, another honour had been conferred by the British Queen on Sir Syed). He said: 'I do not understand what the words "National Congress" mean. Is it supposed that the different castes and creeds living in India belong to one nation, or can become a nation, and their aims and aspirations be one and the same? I think it is quite impossible, and when it is impossible there can be no such thing as a National Congress, nor can it be of equal benefit to all peoples. You regard the doings of the misnamed National Congress beneficial to India, but I am sorry to say that I regard them as not only injurious to our own community but also to India at large. I object to every Congress in any shape or form, whatever, which regards India as one nation.'[11]

In August 1888, Sir Syed, with the help of the M.A.O. College Principal, Theodore Beck formed another Organization, the United Indian Patriotic Association whose membership was open to all communities, Muslim Nawabs, Hindu Rajas, titled gentlemen and some Englishmen entered the Association. Sir Syed was happy at this success and wrote to Col. Graham, a high police officer and later his biographer: 'I have undertaken a heavy task against the so-called National Congress, and have formed an association.'[12]

The aims of the Patriotic Association, as reported in the Aligarh Institute Gazette dated August 28, 1988, were: (a) to publish and circulate pamphlets, and other papers for information of members, of parliament, English journals and the people of Great Britain, in which those mis-statements will be pointed out by which supporters of the Indian National Congress have wrongly attempted to convince the English people that all the Indian chiefs and rulers agree with the aims and objects of the National Congress; (b) to inform members of Parliament and the newspapers of Great Britain and its people, by the same means, of the opinions of Mohammedans in general, of the Islamia Anukans, and those Hindus, and their societies which are opposed to the objects of the National Congress; (c) to strive to preserve peace in India and to strengthen the British rule; and to remove those bad feelings from the hearts of the Indian people, which the supporters of the Congress are stirring up throughout the country, and by which great dissatisfaction is being raised among the people against the British Government.[13]

Therefore, Beck was the honorary editor of the *Patriotic Association*, and in that capacity prepared articles and extracts for distribution in Britain and India. In one of his articles, he gave Muslims a stern warning, holding out fear of an impending mutiny: 'The worst sufferers by the mutiny would be Mohammedans. As far as savagery goes, both sides would have a good fling. At such a period men become friends, and the innocent and guilty, the strong and defenceless, share the same fate. The English nation, on whose benevolence at home the Congress-wallas lay stress would forget all about constitutions and elective councils, and cry only for vengeance. But the English would not lose their national existence, while the Mohammedans would be irretrievably ruined. This is why the Mohammedan leaders wish to keep their people from the whirlpool of political agitation. My revered chief, Sir Syed Ahmed, whose humble disciple in matters political I boast myself, has pointed out clearly. No one has even grappled with his arguments, but in place of reason, a shower of mud and abuse has been hurled at him . . . The Bengali has made enormous progress under British rule, his political star is in ascendant; how can he put himself in the position of the Mohammedan whose greatness is in the past, and who sees rain staring at him in the face? If, in spite of this he will disseminate his poisonous literature among Mohammedans, have not Mohammedan patriots a right to be angry?...This so-called self-government of the municipalities in which Mohammedans have been bound hand and foot and handed over to their rivals to be governed by them is a case in point. An order just by the Bengal Government that all minor appointments are to be given by competitive examinations—an order which will almost destroy the Mohammedan middle class which cannot for one generation at least acquire English education sufficient to compete with others—is another."[14]

Beck seldom argued his case rationally. He would not explain how the Congress agitation would lead to a mutiny; how Muslims have been bound hand and foot; how opposition to competitive examinations would inspire Muslims to raise their educational standards; why the political association of Muslims with educated Bengalis would be ruinous to the former. He did not hesitate to indulge in palpable falsehoods. In the same article, he observed: "Another Syed Ahmed, the great Wahabi, and Maulvi Ismail, his supporter, raised a great popular agitation, but urged their followers never to attack the British. They fought the Sikhs, but after that what took place? To every thoughtful Mohammedan the idea of another mutiny is as horrible, more horrible I believe, than to an Englishman, and to every Muslim lady more dreadful even than to an English lady.... If the passions of the people be stirred up about politics there is no reason why there should not be a mutiny. The soldiery will readily imbibe the sentiments, and then all will be up."[15] Beck cleverly concealed the fact that in the sixties and seventies, the Wahabis made numerous attacks on the British authority, and made numerous Muslims enemies of the British.

According to Maulvi Tufail Ahmed Malabari, who inherited a good deal of oral and written knowledge from his ancestors about the Aligarh movement, and who is the authcr of *Musahnanon ka Roshan Mustaqbil,* it was Beck who helped Sir Syed to formulate his opinions about the Congress, about politics, and about what should be the Muslim attitude towards competitive examinations. Some, who witnessed the Aligarh drama being, enacted, held the same view. One of them is Wilayat Husain. He contributed an article to the *Conference Gazette* (Aligarh) dated November 8, 1935, in which he said that after, hearing Surendranath Banerjea's speech at Aligarh on the demand for the entry of Indians into the Civil Service, the reaction that Beck conveyed to his students was that if the competitive examination for Civil Service was allowed to be held simultaneously in India as well, the only people to benefit from it would be Bengalis, and that the timid Bengalis would rule over the sturdy people of northern India; he asked the Rajputs and Pathans whether they would tolerate this. He asked with dismay what would happen if this storm, rising from Bengal, would reach northern India. Wilayat Husain further says that had not Beck, who took over the editorship of the Aligarh Institute Gazette from Sir Syed, begun abusing Bengalis and their movement through the editorial columns, relations between Aligarh and nationalism would not have become as bitter as they did. Again, according to Wilayat Husain, it was Beck who not only sponsored Muslim opposition to Charles Bradlaugh's Bill, presented before Parliament in 1889, seeking to introduce an element of democracy in India, but fraudulently obtained the signatures of Muslims on a memorial he had drafted for submission to Parliament. Batches of Aligarh students were round to various towns on a signature campaign; Beck himself accompanied one that proceeded to Delhi. He set down at gates of the famous Jumma Mosque, with his students standing beside him to carry out his behest. It was a Friday, and Muslims returning from prayers were to be asked to sign the memorial (Written in English). What should the students tell the prospective signatories? Few were capable of understanding Bradlaugh's Bill and its implications affecting the Muslims. The anti-cow slaughter movement, which some Hindus had recently started and which Muslims generally resented, suggested itself as a plausible excuse, and while asking for signatures, students, on the advice of Beck, said that they were petitioning the Government to uphold the right of Muslims to sacrifice cows. By this device, 20,735 signatures were obtained, and the memorial was presented to the British Government.[16]

United Patriotic Association

Beck devoted the best part of his energies to the promotion of the United Patriotic Association. In the name of Sir Syed, he carried on correspondence with Muslim organizations in other provinces, persuading them to open the Association's branches. Landed aristocrats and title-holders in big cities of the country caused public meetings to be held and branches formed. Copies of resolutions denouncing the Congress and welcoming the formation of the Association were forwarded to Sir Syed. The *Aligarh Institute Gazette* scrupulously published the proceedings of these meetings and their resolutions. Here is a resolution lifted from the Gaz*ette* dated December 8, 1888; it was adopted by 'a great public meeting' organized by the Anjuman Nasar-ul-Islam, Nagpur: "This meeting is of the opinion that the objects and measures of the so-called National Congress tend towards raising a spirit of disloyalty and discontent and are likely to be most detrimental: (1) to India in general, and (2) to the welfare and prosperity of Mohammedans in particular; that the demands of the Congress are not the demands of two hundred million British subjects; that its habitual assumption that it has the right to speak in the name of the majority of the people of India is fictitious and the grievances which it alleges, imaginary; that should any Mohammedan of Nagpur join or associate himself in anyway, with any Congress, meeting to be held at Nagpur or allow himself to be appointed as a delegate to the Allahabad Congress, he will be considered representing himself alone, and as a renegade from the Muslim community."[17] The resolution also said that a copy of the resolution should be sent to Sir Syed Ahmed's honorary secretary of the United Patriotic Association.

The Association also became a rallying point for Hindu landlords and aristocrats. For example, the public meeting at Jaunpur (U.P.) was presided over by the Hindu Raja of the place, and among the prominent participants were Muslim Government pensioners and others.

Mohammedan Anglo-Oriental Defence Association

The Patriotic Association, though a docile body, met and held political discussions, and gave Beck an impression that it tended to develop into a conservative counterpart of the Congress. Therefore, in December 1893, with Sir Syed's support, he founded another organization, and named it the Mohammedan Anglo-Oriental Defence Association of Upper India, with himself as its Secretary. He himself said in his inaugural address that the Patriotic Association suffered from the blemish of growing into an agitational body. Moreover, it was a cosmopolitan body, and what Muslims needed was a wholly Muslim organization. He said the new associations should affiliate no branches, and hold no public meetings, and should not engage in any agitational activity; it should have an executive council as its plenipotentiary functionary. He told his audience that the past few years had witnessed the growth of two agitations in the country: one, the Indian National Congress; the other the movement against cow-slaughter. The former was directed against the English, and the latter against the Muslims. The object of the Congress was to secure control of the country from the British and hand it over to certain sections of the Hindus. It demanded arms to be given freely to the people, reduction in military expenditure and the consequential weakening of the frontier defence. The Mussalmans could have no sympathy with these demands. The cow-protection movement of the Hindus aimed at weakening of Englishmen and Muslims so that they might be easily subjugated. The communal riots in Bombay and Azamgarh were a manifestation of this spirit. It was therefore imperative for the Muslims and the British to unite so that they could face Hindu agitators, and prevent the introduction of democratic form of government, unsuited as it was to the needs and genius of the country.[18]

The objects of the Defence Association were: (1) to acquaint the British people in general and the Government in particular with the views of the Muslim India and to protect the political rights of the Muslims; (2) to support measures designed to strengthen British rule in India; (3) to prevent political agitation from spreading among Muslims; (4) to help the Government in maintaining peace and to foster a spirit of loyalty.

In 1895, Beck proceeded to England where he addressed the annual meeting of the London branch of the Association. A summary of his speech was published in the Aligarh College Magazine of March, April and June 1895. According to it, Beck said that (1) a friendship between the British people and the Muslims was possible, but not between Muslims and followers of other religions; for example, the followers of Shivaji and those of Guru Govind Singh would never agree with the Muslims in accepting Aurangzeb as their hero; (2) Muslims would never accept a system of government in which the Hindu majority would rule over them; the Muslims of Kashmir who were living under the yoke of Brahmin officers envied the good fortune of the Muslims who were living happily under the British rule; (3) Indians themselves did not like a democratic system. They preferred monarchy; (4) Muslim behaviour during and after the Revolt (of 1857) had warned the community against agitational politics of Hindus, and they were now wisely acting on the advice of Sir Syed—it was the advice of loyalty to the British; (5) Muslims were opposed to the holding of the competitive examinations in India, for they knew that this step would mean the replacement of many impartial British Officers by anti-Muslim Hindus.[19]

Sir Syed and Beck complemented and supplemented each other; but it would be understanding Sir Syed's intelligence to suggest, as some Muslim writers have done, that in the latter years of his life, he came very much under Theodore Beck's spell. It was Sir Syed's deep rooted loyalty to the British and his own religious belief which compelled him to take the conflicting stands. Hence, circumstances one of which was the continued backwardness of Muslims in higher education and their failure to get high posts under Government, British loyalism along with communalism, made Sir Syed change his attitudes again and again, and finally, think exclusively in terms of his own community. He became a communalist for all practical purposes, but one cannot pass this judgement without sympathising with him.

Muhammedan Civil Service Association

In 1868, it occurred to Sir Syed that Indians should get a share in the Indian Civil Service by allowing them to appear for the competitive examination held in England, was then monopolized by Europeans. What happened to this proposal and how he narrowed it down later to apply only to Muslims had better, be narrated in his own words: "As far back as 1868, we had tried to form an association which should prepare Indians to undertake a journey to Europe. The members of the association were to pay two rupees each as subscription, and after these subscriptions grew into a fund, suitable Indians—Hindus and Muslims—were to be got ready to go to Europe. But alas, the proposal did not succeed. The apparent cause of the failure was that the Hindus of our country regarded a journey to Europe as impinging upon their religion and caste, and the Muslims, too, were victims of religious bigotry. The most important cause was that Indians believed that a journey to Europe was very difficult... Later, other communities made efforts, and obtained success at the civil service examinations.... But until today, there is not one Muslim who has obtained a position in the civil service. Therefore, we propose to establish a fund to send selected Muslim candidates for the civil service examination in London. Undoubtedly, the civil service examination is very hard these days; and since the maximum age was reduced from 21 years to 19, it has become extremely, difficult to pass it. And if our memory does not fail us, since the age limit was reduced, only one Indian has found entry into the civil service. Before that, about a dozen Indians had obtained success; most of them were Bengalis."[20]

The Mohammedan Civil Service Association was formed in 1883, but it did not produce any encouraging result. The Association was formed at a time when frustration had begun to be seriously felt and expressed, and men like Ameer Ali had already lost faith in the method of selection by competition. In 1882, Ameer had drafted a comprehensive memorial on the subject of 'Mohammedans grievances and claims', and submitted it to the Viceroy, Lord Ripon, on behalf of the Central Association, urging the recognition of the Muslim claim to Government jobs. It was here that the aims of the Mohammedan Association differed from those of the Indian Association. The latter demanded holding of the competitive examination simultaneously in England and India, and also increase in the age limit of candidates. But the Mohammedan Association demanded jobs for Muslims through a system of selection, and not through competition. Ameer Ali complained that 'up to the year 1865, the Government maintained a fair balance between the Muslims and Brahminical people. A sharp digression took place then, and the Muslims found themselves gradually ousted from the public services by their more adaptive compatriots.'[21]

Ameer Ali's memorial was examined thoroughly by authorities concerned, but it was not until July 1885, that a favourable resolution was adopted by the Government of India. The Governor-General-in-Council observed in the resolution (dated July 17): 'There are a large number of appointments the gift of which lies in the hands of the local Governments, the High Courts, or local officers. The Governor-General-in-Council desires that in those provinces where Mohammedans do not receive their full share of state employment, the local Governments and High Courts endeavour to redress this inequality as opportunity offers, and will impress upon subordinate officers the importance of attending to this in their selection of candidates for appointments of the class referred to.[22] The subject of the extent to which Mohammedans are employed in offices under Government might usefully be noticed in the annual reports of the provincial administration.

It was the strikingly disproportionate number of Muslims in the Government services of Bengal that had mainly given Ameer Ali cause of grievance, and. it will be appropriate to examine the actual condition and the reasons for it in that province. With a view to give effect to the wishes of the Government of India, the Bengal Government asked heads of departments to ascertain and report to what extent the services of Muslims were being utilized. The reports said that of the 215 ministerial officers in the 24-Parganas, only six were Muslims. The proportion was more or less the same in other districts of Bengal. In several offices at Calcutta, there were no Muslims at all.

The cause of the disparity, according to the Bengal Government's findings as contained in its resolution dated October 8, 1886, is to be sought primarily in the predilections of the Mohammedans themselves, who prefer Persian and Arabic learning, now of little use in the conduct of business, to the English education given to their children by Hindus. Even the Mohammedans who go through classical languages in addition have less time to devote to studies more immediately remunerative.[23]

A few years earlier, W.W. Hunter in his capacity as the President of the Education Commission for India, observed in his reply to an address presented to him by the managing committee of the Anglo-Oriental College Fund Committee (August 8, 1882): 'In each province of India, the Commission has heard much of the special difficulties which beset the higher education of the Muslims. In almost every province, we see, bright and eager in our primary schools, while in the upper schools, they dwindle in numbers, until in some parts of India, they are scarcely represented in the colleges at all. Many explanations of this state of things have been urged in memorials and by witnesses. But among such explanations, we almost everywhere find the pleas of the poverty of the Mohammedan population, and the necessities of their religion... Before a Mohammedan child begins his secular education in our schools, he has to obtain the rudiments of his religious training in a mosque or some Mohammedan institution. He starts heavily weighted in our primary schools; and in our higher schools, the best of the Mohammedan youths are tempted from the broad road which leads to secular honours into the bypaths of sacred learning... while the young Hindu is devoting his whole energies to obtaining a single education on a purely secular basis, the young Mohammedan is struggling to acquire a double education on both a secular and religious basis.'[24]

However, the branches of the Central Mohammedan Association in their periodical reports submitted to the Association's head office at Calcutta, often complained of Muslims being deliberately ignored by appointing authorities. In its report for the period 1885-88, the Central Association also said: 'Instances have come to the knowledge of this Association in which claims of qualified Mohammedan candidates have been completely ignored and overridden by shuffling of cards in the departmental offices.'[25] The instances are not quoted in the report, and it is difficult to accept or reject the complaint.

But from the memorial the Association submitted to the Lieutenant-Governor of Bengal (which included Bihar and Orissa) in March 1888, it appears that in other provinces there was no cause for grievances. The memorial said: 'In the presidencies of Bombay and Madras, the proportion of Mohammedans and Hindu in the Statutory Civil Services is extremely fair, and in the North-West Province, the number is exactly equal. In Bengal alone, disparity between the number of Mohammedans and Hindus in the statutory civil service is too marked to escape your notice, for whilst there are nine Hindus, there are only two Mohammedans. The explanation of this difference between the number of Mohammedan statutory civilians in the Madras and the Bombay Presidencies and the North-West Province and of those in Bengal is to be found in the fact that the Governments of these provinces have followed a consistent rule of selecting probationers, according to their merit and ability, instead of submitting them to the uncertain test of competitive examinations. We will not presume to call your Honour's attention to the fact that competitive examinations are, at the best, most fallacious tests of merits and ability. And so far as the Mohammedans are concerned, an unfortunate and uncertain test.'[26]

The Lieutenant-Governor dismissed the memorial by saying that 'Government of India's resolution was meant to meet a temporary occasion and was not intended to prescribe the method by which nominations to the statutory civil service will be made.' This reply made Ameer Ali and his Association more earnest in their purpose, and they sounded their branches to consolidate themselves for a common cause.

From the developments, recorded above, it is clear that the grievances of the Muslims of Bengal were different from those of Northern India where Sir Syed's writ prevailed. In the latter territory, the Muslims were over-represented in services below the rank of Indian Civil Service, and this provides us with the reason why Sir Syed and his Aligarh school later adopted, so far as the Indian Civil Service was concerned, Ameer Ali's tactics of opposition to competition. But in effect the two kinds of grievances were similar: Hindus were devouring the Muslim share. It was not any animosity between Hinduism and Islam which caused this feeling; Muslim lack of preparedness for higher services was due to the emphasis at early stages on religious education.

Muslims themselves realized this and openly admitted it again and again in the addresses they presented to official dignitaries. The establishment of the Mohammedan Anglo-Oriental College at Aligarh and several Muslim high schools at other places in the country and the subsequent development of the Aligarh College into a University does not offer proof that for secular education also Muslims wanted separate institutions. The establishment of the few separate institutions was not dictated by any religious urge, but by the anxiety to extend the facilities of education to Muslims. At these institutions, religious education did not occupy a dominating position. The establishment of Allahabad University was jubilantly welcomed by the Mohammedan Education Congress of 1887, which resolved to send a memorial to the Lieutenant-Governor of the North-West Provinces and another to the Vice-Chancellor of the University to the effect that greater attention should be paid to imparting 'high English education'. Sir Syed joined in the jubilation by saying in his speech that the country, 'and particularly the Muslims' badly needed instruction in 'high English education'. The ambition of the Aligarh College to grow into a university was natural, as it was of any school to grow into a college, and, of the Central Hindu College of Benares to grow into a Hindu university, actually obtained its fulfilment before the Aligarh Muslim University came into being.

There is no truth in the belief, commonly held, that the Aligarh College attracted many Muslims for degree courses. According to figures collected for 1898-1902, the total number of Muslim graduates in India was 1,184. Out of this, Aligarh's contribution was 220, Allahabad's 410, Calcutta's 398, and the Punjab's 255. In 1890-91, for the first time, Aligarh sent one Muslim candidate up for the M.A. examination; in 1891-92, two; none in the next two years; in 1894-95, two. The number declined to one by 1901-02, and to zero in 1902-03. Between 1882 and 1887, a period of intense propaganda for employment of Muslims in Government departments, the Aligath College produced only ten graduates.[27] Thus, Aligarh's contribution to the education of Muslims during the life time of Sir

Syed was insignificant, and there is no warrant for the assumption that but for the Aligarh movement, Muslims would not have received higher education.

The most prominent and conspicuous among those who wanted this assumption to prevail, were the English principals of the Aligarh College. The second principal, Theodore Morrison advocated denominational institutions: 'The general principle which I believe is capable of very wide application is that a university should be the university of a community, not of an area; there should, for instance, be a university for the Mohammedans, for the Paris, for the Hindus of Eastern India, etc., but no university for the Punjab or Madras or Bombay."[28] He cited the Central Hindu College at Benares and the Mohammedan College at Aligarh as worthy examples to be emulated and observed: 'I cannot help recognizing that a large number of English-educated Mohammedans, incontestable as are their merits in other directions, are indifferent to religion, and many of them have no faith at all. This is an acknowledged evil which is growing with the spread of English education.'[29]

Aligarh was in a whirlpool of confusion. While the cause of the lack of higher English education among Muslims was the disproportionate emphasis on religious instruction, the English principals of the M.A.O. College preached religious exclusiveness with a view to withholding Muslim students from the rising current of political consciousness. While the object of the College was to concentrate on English education, the emphasis was shifted to creating an anti-political and anti-patriotic atmosphere; the *Aligarh Institute Gazette,* instead of devoting itself to educational matters, specialised in abusing and deriding political activities; published and reproduced articles condemnatory of these articles. In the whole series of the *Gazette* and contemporary speeches delivered in the College premises, one hardly comes across an endeavour to prepare Muslims for life in the competitive world. On the contrary, they were told that unqualified co-operation with the Government and loyalty to the British would get them Government jobs as a matter of course. Under the inspiration of the College authorities, campaigns were carried on against competitive examinations and political India's demand for the holding of the Civil Service examination simultaneously in England and India. Here is a sample of one such campaign as reported in the *Aligarh Institute Gazette* dated September 1, 1893: 'A very large public meeting of the local Mohammedan community was held last evening to memorialise Parliament against simultaneous examinations. Syed Nizam-ud-din, a graduate in arts and law, presided. Several telegrams and letters expressing sympathy were read. Mr. Mohammed Yassin moved a resolution: "That this meeting, considering that simultaneous examination would be unwarranted in the present condition of the country, prays that the House of Commons be pleased not to give effect to the resolution affirming its desirability."[30] In a long and vigorous speech, he said that 'educated India was divided into two camps—one of Muslim moderates who would leave the country's progress in the hands of its rulers, the other of red-hot radicals who claimed the most comprehensive surrender, the latter consisting of Babus and Brahmans, who arrogated to themselves the power of controlling the destinies of the country.'

The two Muslim leaders were now transformed almost unrecognizably. Sir Syed, the sponsor of a fund to prepare Indian students, and later Muslim students, for the Civil Service competitive examination, had now reversed his position.

Occidentalism

Real politik loyalism was only a fraction of the far more significant approach towards a closer understanding of western civilization. Syed Ahmed Khan's journey to England in 1869-70 'to study the culture and institutions of Europe for the progress and betterment of India' is the outstanding landmark of his 'occidentalism'.[31] Compared with the travels of Abu Talib Khan seven decades earlier, Syed Ahmed's impressions of the West present interesting parallels and contrasts. On the steamship during his voyage through the Mediterranean he met de Lesseps who was profoundly impressed by his idealism and patriotism. He admired the elegance of the architecture of Versailles, and in the art galleries of Paris and Versailles, he enjoyed the work of the French Romanticists. He was distressed by a painting depicting the capture of 'Abd al-Qadir's *da'ira* in Algeria and the rape of his harem by French soldiers. He regarded 'Abd al-Qadir as a great soldier who resisted the French without guile and with honesty and chivalry until he was overwhelmed, and the theme and the exhibition of the painting of the dishonour of his *da'ira* as a disgrace to the French traditions of honour and chivalry. He admired another painting in which Napoleon III is shown releasing 'Abd al-Qadir from an unjust and treacherous imprisonment and shaking hands with his mother. Napoleon III, whom he never met, is for Syed Ahmed Khan an image of humanity and honour, enlivened by the glitter of his smart army and the 'glamour and array' of Paris where the Indian traveller admired the Arc de Triomphe, the Bois de Boulogne, the great boulevards, and the exterior of Notre-Dame.[32]

He was favourably impressed by London, by the tasteful decor of the London hotels, by the impeccable dignity of English butlers, and by the good manners of British housemaids. He was impressed by the extent of equality of opportunity for both sexes during his visit to the observatory of Mt. St. Vincent at Clifton which worked under the direction of a woman, and he wrote back to the annoyance of orthodox theologians in India, that 'European women were as shocked to hear that Indian women were generally illiterate as Indians would be if they saw a woman walking naked in the bazaars'. He recorded his satisfaction that at least in Turkey and Egypt there had been some progress in female education and no absolute complacency in 'compound ignorance'.

In England his contacts included Lord Lawrence, Lord Stanley of Alderley, and Sir J.W. Kay, the Under-Secretary of State for India; and he was presented at the levees of the Prince of Wales (later Edward VII) and Queen Victoria. He was elected a fellow of the Royal Asiatic Society and a member of the Athenaeum club. He attended the last reading given by Charles Dickens, and met Thomas Carlyle, whose 'Hero as a Prophet' he admired and with whom he discussed the project on the life of Muhammad. He visited the University of Cambridge and carefully studied its structure, government, and syllabus as the model of the educational institution he was planning to set up in India.

His contacts with the British ruling bureaucracy in India were even more extensive and influential. To the growing racial snobbery of the British in India and to the first signs of a growing racial prejudice in Britain his attitude was ambivalent, critical when it was openly discriminatory, tolerant in the perspective of the western cultural advancement. With the adoption of the western style of living since 1868 he and some of his friends had chosen a bicultural social life, which gave rise to some biting satire from friend and foe, such as a novel by his protege Nazir Ahmed, *Ibn al-waqt* (The Time-Server), and some facetious verses by the brilliant conservative poet Akbar Allahabadi. The theologians frowned and the majority looked askance at his eating with the English masters meat killed contrary to the prescribed Muslim ritual, a position for which he offered a scholarly apologetic defence in his treatise on eating with the 'People of the Book'.[33]

REFERENCES

1. Ahmad, Aziz, *Islamic Modernism in India and Pakistan 1857-1964, op. cit.*, p. 31.
2. Khan, Sir Syed Ahmed, *Asbab-i-baghawat-i Hind* (Agra: Mufid-i am Press), 1892, p. 12.
3. *Ibid.*
4. *Ibid.*
5. Graham, G.F.I., *The Life and Work of Sir Syed Ahmed Khan, op. cit.*, p. 40.
6. *Ibid.*, p. 41.
7. *Ibid.*, p. 42.
8. *Ibid.*
9. Smith, W.C., *Modern Islam in India* (London: V. Golancz), 1946, p. 16.
10. Address presented to Viceroy, Lord Lyffon in Speeches and Addresses Relating to Muhammadan Anglo-Oriental College (Aligarh: Institute Press, 1888), pp. 24-31.
11. Quoted in Source Material for a History of the Freedom Movement in India, Collected from Bombay Government Records, Vol. II, 1885-1920, (1958), p. 71.
12. Graham, G.F.I., *The Life and Work of Sir Syed Ahmed Khan, op. cit.*, p. 273.
13. Ram Gopal, *Indian Muslims, op. cit.*, p. 68.
14. *Ibid.*, pp. 68-69.
15. *Ibid.*
16. *Ibid.*, p. 70.
17. *The Aligarh Institute Gazette*, 9-10-1988
18. Ram Gopal, *Indian Muslim, op. cit.*, p. 71.

19. *Ibid.*
20. The Annual Report of the Mohammedan Education Conference, 1887.
21. The Indian Central Committee Report, 1928-29
22. Ram Gopal, *Indian Muslim, op. cit.*, p. 54.
23. *The Aligarh Institute Gazette*, 19-10-1886.
24. *Ibid.*, 8-8-1882.
25. The Report of the Committee of the Central Mohammedan Association for 1885-1888, p. 15.
26. *Ibid.*
27. Morrison, Theodore, *The History of the Mohammedan Oriental College, Aligarh, from its Foundation to the Year 1903* (Aligarh: Institute Press), 1904.
28. *Ibid.*
29. *Ibid.*
30. *Aligarh Institute Gazette* 1-9-1893.
31. Ahmed Aziz, *Islamic Modernism in India and Pakistan 1857-1964, op. cit.*, p. 34.
32. *Ibid.*, p. 35.
33. *Ibid.*, p. 36.

5

ON EDUCATION AND CULTURE

Linguistic Differences

While the jealousy between the upper and middle classes of Muslims and Hindus over Government jobs was still persisting, a controversy whether the court language should be Urdu or Hindi leading to another difference, appeared in Northern India in the seventies of the 19th century. In Bengal, the controversy took different form: Muslim leaders demanded that the Bengali language to be fit for Muslim students should have an admixture of Persian rather than Sanskrit words. In order to understand these controversies, we must acquaint ourselves with the prevailing indigenous system of education in India, and see how it was being replaced by the British system.

In many parts of the country, Hindu indigenous schools were different from their Muslim counterparts. The former were attached to Hindu temples and the latter to Muslim mosques. There were no regular classes, each boy taking his lessons independently from the teacher. The pupils came to the private house of the teacher or to those houses which suited the teacher's convenience. Quite often the compounds of temples and mosques were used for teaching boys of the neighbourhood. The Hindu schools included a course on religious books such as the Ramayana and the Bhagavad Gita. At Muslim schools, the Koran was a compulsory subject. The medium of instruction at the former was Sanskrit or Hindi, whereas at the latter, Persian, Arabic or Urdu. There were secular schools too for both the communities, but in a Muslim secular school exclusion of the Koran was unthinkable. It differed from the religious one only in its emphasis as it paid greater attention to the teaching of other subjects.

In the Arabic schools which existed in large towns only, the masters were generally the maulvis renowned for their knowledge of the Arabic language. The Koran schools were generally taught by *hafizs* (those who learnt the Koran by heart) and who could read and recite the Koran correctly. The Sanskrit schools were conducted by men highly reputed for their Sanskrit learning. However, the Hindi schools were ill-equipped: they had to content themselves with teachers who knew a little of Hindi and arithmetic.

The most conspicuous feature of these schools was that while there was to be found a good number of Hindu students at the Arabic, Persian and Urdu schools, there were practically no Muslims at the Sanskrit and Hindi schools. The reason was apparent. Persian had been the official language for several centuries, and Urdu had replaced it in the whole of Northern India as the court language. Arabic enriched these two languages as a stone did a ring. While Hindus took to enjoying and writing Persian and Urdu poetry, it was seldom that Muslims were attracted to Sanskrit and Hindi literature. A few Muslims did compose elegant verses in Sanskrit and Hindi, but while they can be counted on the fingers of the hand, the number of Hindu poets who wrote in Urdu runs into hundreds.[1]

Indigenous System vs. New System of Education

The indigenous system of education continued throughout the first half of the 19th century, in spite of the appearance of modern schools imparting English education. These schools were few and far between, and most children continued to receive the old system of education. Scrupulously cautious about the religious susceptibilities of the people, the British rulers did not disturb the indigenous schools but opened their own in addition to these. The Government village schools which made their appearance at the tehsil headquarters in pursuance of a Government resolution of February 9, 1850, were intended to enable the land-holders and cultivators to protect themselves from fraud on the part of the *patwaris* by teaching them to read and write, and to comprehend the system under which their rights are recorded, their payments entered, and arrears specified in the patwaris' books. Incidentally, these schools gave an opportunity of bringing Hindu and Muslim students under one roof. The schools provided a course of instruction in Hindi, Urdu, accounts, mensuration of land according to the Indian system, geography, history, geometry, and other subjects. But they did not teach English. Only schools in the towns taught English.

Muslim boys freely entered the Government-managed schools, and, in proportion to their population, did not lag behind Hindus. Sometimes their number proportionately exceeded that of Hindu students. According to the educational returns for 1880-81 of the North-West Provinces (now Uttar Pradesh), there were 769 Hindus and 112 Muslims in colleges; for 'anglo-vernacular' middle schools the figures were respectively 1,70,478 and 32,619.[2]

Yet, the assumption persisted among leading Muslims even in Northern India that Muslims generally were not taking advantage of English education, the reason being that Muslim landlords and aristocrats considered it derogatory to their position to allow their children to associate with commoners at educational institutions. The Hindu landlords exhibited the same mentality, and preferred to deprive their children of modern education. But rich Hindus of the towns did not join the boycott of the aristocrats.

That Muslim commoners went in for English education as a result of the persuasive efforts of Sir Syed Ahmed Khan, which had started in the early seventies, is not a fact. There were three colleges and nine 'anglo-vernacular' schools in the North-West Provinces in 1843, educating about 2,000 boys. Of these pupils 1,598 were Hindus, 385 Muslims and the rest Europeans or Eurasians. Nor were Muslim commoners averse to receiving secular education with Hindus.[3] They mixed freely in Government schools and also joined those that were started by Hindu charitable institutions. As far back as 1818, a Hindu philanthropist, named Jai Narain Ghosal, started at Benares a charitable school which taught English, Persian, Hindi and Bengali. Muslim students freely entered in it.[4] In the course of time, the religious schools were relegated to the background as secular schools became more popular among the Muslims as well as Hindus.

Curiously, the Muslim aristocracy remained ignorant of this development. Several Muslim witnesses grievously asserted in their evidence before the Education Commission of 1882 that compared to their Hindu brethren, Muslims were backward in education and fewer in numbers at schools and colleges. They were surprised when they were told by a member of the Commission that according to the census returns of 1881 the percentage of children under instruction to total population is larger for the Mohammedan than for the Hindu community. The evidence of one Rev. B.H. Badley brought home this fact more precisely. He said that while the Muslims formed about 10 per cent of the population in the North-West Provinces, Muslim students at schools and colleges numbered about one-fourth of the total.[5]

For several decades, the aversion of the Muslim aristocracy to the new system of education was interpreted as an aversion of the entire Muslim community. There was no design in it. Muslim leaders had close association only with aristocratic classes, and the sight of young boys moving about aimlessly set them thinking. The causes of the indifference were investigated. Sir Syed believed that the 'aversion of the Muslim community' was 'due to the fact that when in the reigns of the Caliphs of Baghdad the Greek sciences of logic, philosophy, astronomy and geography were translated into Arabic, they were accepted by the whole Mohammedan world without hesitation, and with slight modifications and alterations, they gradually found their way into the religious books of the Mohammedans, so that in course of time these sciences were identified with their very religion, and acquired a position by no means inferior to that of the sacred tradition of faith.' Again, according to Sir Syed, European learning 'founded on the results of modern investigations, differed widely in principle from these Greek dogmas, and the Mohammedans certainly believed that the philosophy and logic taught in the English language was at variance with the tenets of Islam, while the modern sciences of geography and astronomy were universally regarded, and are still regarded by many, as altogether incompatible with the Mohammedan religion. As regards literature, it must be admitted that it is a subject which is always more or less connected with the religion of the nation to which it belongs; and, such being the case, the Mohammedans, as a matter of course, viewed this branch of knowledge too, in anything but a favourable light. Their antipathy was carried so far, indeed, that they began to look upon the study of English by a Mussalman as a little less than the embracing of Christianity, and the result was that Mohammedans generally kept aloof from the advantages offered by Government institutions.[7]

'Practical steps' for the spread of education in the Muslim community began in 1871, and in this year the Government of India adopted a resolution through which the attention of the local governments was invited to the subject. Calcutta was the headquarters of the Government, and the Muslims of Bengal were really educationally backward. The Muslims of Bengal had for years been under the Wahabi influence, and the Government of India's resolution was in pursuance of a policy of appeasement of the Muslim sentiment. The frustrated Muslim community of Bengal badly needed to be helped to catch up with Hindus, and the realization embodied in the resolution came none too. In 1880-81, as against 36,686 Hindu pupils at the English High Schools, there were only 363 Mohammedans at English middle schools, the figures respectively were 29,469 and 4,346. These figures naturally shocked Muslims, for they were more numerous in Bengal than Hindus.

But the Government resolution received a warmer welcome in Uttar Pradesh, and leaders like Sir Syed applied themselves the heart and soul to the task of Muslim education. For several years, Sir Syed had been persuading his co-religionists to take to English education, and in 1871 he took a positive step by appointing a committee to investigate the causes of the aversion of Muslims to English education, and to suggest means by which their attitude could be changed. The committee's findings nearly tallied with the picture he had formed in his own mind.

He gathered around him a body of influential Muslim gentlemen, and opened a high school for Muslim boys at Aligarh in 1875. Within three years, the school was raised to a second-grade college. The original object of some of the supporters, according to Sir Syed himself, was to confine the college to the Muslims, but 'so much goodwill, sympathy, and generosity were displayed by the Hindu nobility and gentry' that the college was declared open to Hindu students also. The Aligarh College, though similar in courses of instruction to other colleges, differed from them in one respect: it gave instruction in Islam and encouraged Muslim boys to visit the mosque regularly for prayers, Sunnis and Shias praying separately. Sir Syed's efforts succeeded admirably, and boys of Muslim aristocracy from distant parts of the provinces began to seek admission in the Aligarh College. Besides the educational institutions conducted by Christian missionaries, there was no College which combined secular education with compulsory religious instruction. This combination greatly assuaged Muslim antagonism towards English education.

But if Muslim commoners were ahead of Hindus in education, though the Muslim aristocracy held aloof, why was the number of Muslim graduates in arts and sciences strikingly low compared to that of Hindus? In 1878, Sir Syed had a comparative statement prepared for the preceding twenty years. There were 3,155 Hindus as against 57 Muslims holding graduate and post-graduate degrees, civil engineering, arts, medicine, etc. Muslims were absolutely unrepresented among doctors of law, law honours graduates, civil engineers, doctors of medicine and honours-graduates in medicine. Out of 1,373 bachelors of arts, there were only thirty Muslims; the proportion of masters in arts was 326 to 5. For an explanation of this paradox, one has again to turn to that phase of history which professionally distinguished the upper and middle classes of Muslims from their Hindu counterparts. Most Muslim classes were landlords; most Hindus were businessmen, traders, contractors, etc. While the former imbibed the aristocracy of the Muslim rulers, the latter had no prejudices, social or religious, to send their boys for higher education. The poorer classes of Muslims, who educated their children up to the high school and intermediate level, could not pay for higher education. In paying capacity, only the landed aristocracy of Muslims matched Hindus of the towns. The sense of preservation of the respectability of their order kept Hindu landlords away from English education longer than it did the Muslim aristocracy. In Uttar Pradesh, both Hindus and Muslims were far behind the Hindus of Bengal in higher education; therefore, while the comparative statement gave a cause of grievance to the rich Muslim houses of Bengal, the Muslims of Uttar Pradesh had little to complain of.

Persian and Urdu-knowing Muslim gentlemen were subordinate judges even in the last quarter of the 19th century; this was not so in Bengal. When a Muslim of U.P. ridiculed English education, he was conscious of the fact that he was missing little by ignoring it. Early in the 'eighties, a Hindu inspector of schools suggested to two Muslim subordinate judges (of U.P.), both ignorant of English, that they should put their boys in an English school. 'They will be spoilt', the judges argued; and their argument was that from the little they had heard of English. They concluded that the English language lacked the delicacy of Persian and/or Urdu. How jarring, they said, it was to the ears to hear 'tor, tor' every now and then, as in 'collector, administrator, debtor, waiter.'[8]

Therefore, it was clear to Muslim reformers that the removal of bigotry, conservatism and prejudice was a prerequisite to the spread of higher education among Muslims. English was gradually becoming the official language all over the country, and the sooner this realization dawned upon the Muslims the better. Propaganda was disseminated by Sir Syed and his colleagues through journals and public speeches. Sir Syed even exhorted Muslims to enter missionary institutions, telling them that the study of the Bible did not offend Islam; on the contrary, 'it affords a valuable help in acquiring a knowledge of English literature'.[9]

While Northern India had in Sir Syed an ardent reformer, Bengal whose need was greater, never possessed one. A change of attitude was, no doubt, brought about by the Muslim leadership of Bengal, but it was a change from anti-British to anti-Hindu. Hunter's finding in his *Indian Mussalmans* became their text. Hunter had observed: 'The truth is that our system of public instruction ignores the three most powerful instincts of the Mussalman heart. In the first place, it conducts education in the vernacular of Bengal, a language which the educated Mohammedans despise, and by means of Hindu teachers, whom the whole Mohammedan community hates. The Bengal schoolteacher talks his own dialect and a vile Urdu, the latter of which is to him an acquired language, almost as much as it is to ourselves. Moreover his gentle and timid character unfits him to maintain order among Mussalman boys.'[10]

Hunter had in mind those Muslims of Bengal whose mother-tongue was Persian or Urdu, and who belonged to Persia or

Northern India, and not to Bengal. These Muslims assumed the leadership of the Muslim masses, who, being converts, were the children of the soil and whose mother-tongue was the same as that of Bengali Hindus. It was this fact which the Government of Bengal had in mind when it observed in its resolution dated November 19, 1881: 'The ordinary primary schools of the country are believed to be in general as fully suited to the requirements of Mohammedan as of Hindu pupils, the vernacular of the former being in nearly all the cases that of the people among whom they live; but the, Lieutenant-Governor is glad to observe that the practice of subsidizing Mohammedan Maktabs on condition of their teaching the vernacular and a little arithmetic in addition to the Koran, has been extended with successful results.'[11] Bengal, at that time, had Bengali as the court language, and that was the justification for emphasis on Bengali; and since Muslims, under the Wahabis, had developed too much attachment to religion, complete indifference to religious education was considered inexpedient.

Ameer Ali, one of the foremost Muslim leaders of Bengal whose forefathers belonged to Persia, demanded in his evidence before the Education Commission that 'Urdu should be to the Mohammedans what Bengali is to the Hindus of Bengal, and Arabic and Persian should take the place of Sanskrit'.[12] Another Muslim leader Nawab Abdul Luteef Khan Bahadur, taking his inspiration from the above quoted paragraph from Hunter, said that the ordinary Bengali school was unsuited to the requirements of the Mohammedan peasantry. 'There is too much of Hindu influence. The guru, in almost all cases, is a Hindu; so are many of the pupils, and there is not much of sympathy between them on the one hand and the Mohammedan pupils on the other.'[13] He suggested that the language of the school in which Muslim boys might be able to study, must be a mean between the highly Sanskritised Bengali of the Hindu school on the one hand, and the Muslim Bengali patois on the other, which was thickly intermingled with Persian and Arabic terms. Bengali, laden with Persian and Arabic terms, was in fact, the local dialect of the Bengali Muslim aristocrats of foreign origin. But since they were the religious preceptors of the Muslim masses of Bengal they had acquired a right to speak for them. Abdul Luteef, however, wanted a different system of education for the upper and middle classes of Muslims. In order that they might be 'respected in their own society as educated men', they 'should possess a thorough knowledge of Urdu, a fair knowledge of Persian, and, if possible, some acquaintance with Arabic'. He desired Urdu to be recognized as their medium of instruction. He made no secret of his reason: 'The middle and upper classes of Mohammedans are descended from the original conquerors of Bengal, or the pious, the learned and the brave men who were from Arabia, Persia, and Central Asia to the services of the Mohammedan rulers of Bengal, or from the principal officers of Government, who, after the absorption of the province into the empire of Delhi, were appointed and sent from the Imperial court, and many of whom permanently settled in these parts.

Whether the Hindu teachers of the Bengali schools were too saturated with Hinduism or whether the Muslim leadership was without cause prejudiced against them, it is difficult to say at this distance of time: there is no evidence clearly supporting one assertion or the other. On behalf of the Hindus, it might be said that the natural language of the converts should be the language of their forebears; Muslims might argue that for a Muslim to be true to his faith, a background of Arabic, Persian and Urdu is necessary. Whatever be the reasons, the separatist tendencies, which arose from the jealousy over jobs, received strength from a public discussion as to the system of education that would suit the Muslims. Separate teachers were demanded for Muslim boys. Ameer Ali's argument was that the Muslim English teacher won obviate the difficulty under which the Muslim students laboured 'owing to the Hindu teachers in Bengal not knowing Urdu'. Mohammendan maulvis were wanted for district schools to teach Persian and Arabic. These tendencies, whether communalist or religious, brought forth separate schools. They became an accomplished feature of the social and political life, and a contemporary eminent Hindu politician and reformer, Rai Rajendralala Mitra made an implicit admission of this fact while expressing himself on the scheme of self-government. He said: 'Each village or a group of villages, having a school should have a panchayat; and it may be necessary at times (but not often) to have both a Hindu and a Mohammedan panchayat in the same village where there are separate schools for the two classes of persons.'[14]

Hindi-Urdu Controversy

At about the same time, that is in the seventies and eighties, there was a conflict between protagonists of Hindi and Urdu, dividing the learned men and social institutions of the two communities. The Persianised form of Hindi or Hindustani is known as Urdu, a name derived from the Urdu-e-Mu'alla, or royal military bazaar outside Delhi Palace, where it took its rise, during the Khilji period. Muslim foreign troops, settled in and around Delhi, had to learn the local dialect for intercourse with the local people. Ailahuddin Khilji had a book prepared in which Persian and Arabic equivalents of common Hindi words were collected. The book was named *Khalikbari* and numerous copies of it were distributed among Muslim troops and others. It was impossible to expect these foreigners to speak a one hundred per cent chaste Hindi, and often the dialect they spoke, which later came to be known as Urdu, contained many Persian or Arabic words. For some five hundred years, Urdu remained just a spoken language. With Persian words scattered through it, Urdu later became a literary language and produced a galaxy of poets. Even when Urdu had developed a beautiful style of expression, there were some Muslim litterateurs who employed Hindi laden with Sanskrit words for their works. Persian words were freely thrown into the spoken dialect, because current coin, and as if by right, found their way into Sanskritized Hindi works of Hindu poets, now occupying the topmost position in the world of Hindi literature. Urdu employed Persian characters, and this is what pre-eminently distinguished it from Hindi whose script was Devanagari. Urdu developed its own elegant style of poetry.

But, until after the collapse of the Mughal Empire, Urdu had no access to the public offices and courts. It was only in the 19th century that Urdu began to replace Persian, and reached the highest pitch when Bahadur Shah read out his own Urdu verses before his court poets. With Government patronage, Urdu rose in importance over Hindi, and many Hindus, descendants of officials, preferred to acquire a proficiency in the former only because it helped to get Government jobs. Urdu was the court language throughout Northern India when the British seized power. And the British deliberately retained it as such in the interests of continuity.

The official position of Urdu was a damper to Hindi; but the Hindus never abandoned it. In fact, the assumed superiority of Urdu provoked Hindi protagonists to work harder for the progress of their own language. They murmured that Hindi, in an Indian character, and not Urdu written in Persian, should be the court language in the seventies, and these murmurs developed into noisy protests. In Bihar, which then formed part of Bengal, the Government of Bengal issued orders in 1873 for the use of Hindi and the Nagari character in the courts and offices of the Patna, Bhagalpur, and Chhota Nagpur divisions, and directed that all processes, notifications and proclamations should be made in Hindi; the official records should be kept in Hindi; petitions should be received at the option of the presenters in the *Hindi* or Urdu character; a knowledge of the Hindi character should be insisted on in the case of police and ministerial officers. These orders having practically proved a dead letter, reminders were issued in April 1874 and July 1875. Again, there was no co-operation forthcoming; petitions, police orders, diaries, reports and registers, as well as collectorate and other official papers continued generally to be written in Persian character, and even forms of notices, etc., printed in Hindi were filled up in Persian. Therefore, in April 1880, Sir Ashley, the Lieutenant-Governor of Bengal, finding that no real advance had been made in giving effect to the wishes of Government, came to the conclusion that the changes enjoined by Government would never be thoroughly introduced until Nagari was made the character for exclusive use in official documents in Bihar. He accordingly directed that this character should be exclusively used from January 1881, and that the issue from the courts or the reception by the courts of any document in Persian character, except as exhibits, should be absolutely forbidden. Police officers were also warned that if they could not read and write the Nagri character by January 1881, they would be replaced by those who could. An inquiry showed that those who insisted on ignoring the Government orders were ministerial officers, pleaders, mukhtars and touters, both Hindu and Muslim, who monopolized all power and had virtually made these offices hereditary.[15]

These orders, and the doggedness with which they were pursued, antagonised Muslims against the Hindus at whose instance Urdu had been displaced. Angry representations were made to the Government, and the grievance was ventilated whenever an opportunity offered itself.

In Uttar Pradesh also, the battle for Hindi did not succeed, and this gave many Hindus a cause of grievance which they nurtured for several decades. But the differences between the two communities grew quite as acutely as they did in Bihar. The Hindi-Urdu controversy arose in 1883, with an innocent-looking suggestion that the character of the court language should be changed from Persian to Devanagari; the replacement of Urdu by Hindi was not specifically mentioned. But the intention was obvious, and the entire Muslim official world arrayed itself against the proposal. The public platform and newspapers were invoked by the protagonists of the two languages, and the agitation seemed to draw a demarcation line between educated Hindus and Muslims. Arguments and figures were collected in support of the case for Hindi: that 71 per cent of the boys at schools, as stated in the North-West Provinces Education Report for 1873-74, 'spontaneously chose to be taught in Hindi in preference to Urdu'; that Urdu, being the spoken and written language of a minority in the towns, was unintelligible even to Hindi-knowing educated Hindus; the Hindi-knowing persons had to pay a few annas to learn the contents of court summons, and a rupee or a half for writing out a small petition; that in all countries of the world, the language and the character of the country were the language and character of the offices and courts; that Hindi and the Devanagari script were easier to learn and that a change-over would cause little difficulty to Muslims; that with Urdu as the official language, Muslims monopolised Government employment that even the Director of Public Instruction in the North-Western Provinces (he was an Englishman named Griffith) observed in his report for 1877-78 that 'as a rule Hindi is the true vernacular of the province and is used by the rural population with greater or less purity according to the greater or less influence of Mohammedan rule and colonisation.'

Two orders of the local Government issued in 1878 sharpened the edge of the agitation for Hindi. One said that the possession of the middle-class certificate was a *sine qua non* in getting an appointment; another laid down that a certificate would not be given even if the candidate had passed the examination creditably, second language was not Urdu. This was construed as a conspiracy against Hindi designed to discourage its study. Surprise was expressed as to why Urdu was taught in villages wholly peopled by Hindus, and a demand was put forward that instruction must be given in Hindi where the number of Hindu boys was 60 per cent of the total.

Muslims of several towns—Aligarh, Bulandshahr, Roorkee, Meerut—conjointly represented that the Persian character had been commonly used by every class of people in India for hundreds of years. Urdu has been for two centuries and a half the native tongue in these provinces. 'Nagari character will take longer time to write.' The Hindu leadership of the Hindi movement countered the argument on the basis of their helplessness during the time of the Muslim rulers.

Muslims learnt their Persian alphabet and Koran at their own schools; when they came to the secular schools, they chose Urdu as medium of instruction, and with them a fair sprinkling of Hindus did so also. But nothing alienated the two communities towards each other as did the Hindi-Urdu controversy. (Again the word 'communities' is used in its limited sense to mean the Muslim aristocracy and middle classes, and the upper Middle classes of Hindus.)

In the Punjab, Hindus were far behind Muslims in the teaching profession, as Muslims were in Bengal, and when Hindus grew conscious of this fact and swarmed the profession, Muslims became apprehensive of losing what they had enjoyed for a long-time. The Hindu consciousness grew in volume when pointed attention was drawn by Captain Fuller, Director of Public Instruction, in the Education Report for the Punjab for 1860-61. The Report said: 'The preponderance of Muslims among teachers, who are trained in these institutions, is very apparent; there being to 111 of Hindus and six of other castes. There seems no way of equalising the proportion very readily. Except in the Ambala circle, vernacular education is in the hands of the Muslims, and we cannot supersede them so long as they retain their popularity.

'District officers, however, might prepare the way for a gradual change by encouraging more Hindus to qualify as teachers, and appointing them to schools where the residents are not too strongly prejudiced in favour of Muslim instructors.'[16]

Fuller's observation coincided with the spread of the Wahabi influence in the Punjab; during the sixties, most educated Muslims in the Punjab, as elsewhere, were suspected of alliance with Wahabis. But, in the absence of direct evidence, one can only conjecture that Hindus were thought of at that particular time as safer persons for the teaching profession. If a generous interpretation is put on the observation in the annual report, it may as well be believed that there was a genuine desire to extend opportunities of employment to Hindus. In any case, the increasing number of Hindus in the teaching profession and the corresponding decrease in the employment of Muslims, inevitably caused bitterness among educated persons. In the Punjab, the cause of difference between the two communities was economic, and not cultural or sentimental, because in spite of the ascendancy of Hindus in the sphere of education. Urdu continued to be the medium of instruction, and Hindi remained practically unknown in educational institutions until the appearance of the Arya Samaj influence.

In the ultimate analysis, jobs were the cause of differences over language and script also.

Thus we can conclude that Syed Ahmed Khan's educational programme which was to change the intellectual, political, and economic destiny of Muslim India had its humble beginnings in the critical year of 1859. From that date onwards the inescapable emphasis on the use of English as the medium of instruction was one of the main planks of his programme. In 1864 he founded a Scientific Society for the introduction of western sciences primarily among Muslims in India. The Society translated works on physical sciences into Urdu and published a bilingual journal. In 1864 he founded a modern school at Ghazipur, and in 1868 promoted the formation of educational committees in several districts of northern India. He prepared his blueprint for the higher education of Muslims during his visit to England in 1869-70. In 1874 the scheme of his Anglo-Muhammadan Oriental College at Aligarh assumed a concrete shape, the school classes were opened in 1875 and college classes in 1878. The institution, intentionally modelled on Cambridge University, soon assumed a form and personality of its own. Meant primarily for Muslims, it was interdenominational, providing for Sunni as well as Shia theological education, and included a fair percentage of Hindu students. It aimed at the liberalization of ideas, broad humanism, a scientific world view, and a pragmatic approach to politics. It strove for a steady increase of educated Muslims in the government services. It smoothed the transition of the younger generation of Muslim elite from almost medieval conservatism to at least superficial modernism. And, finally, it was to produce the leadership for Muslim political separatism in India as a counter-balance to the growing influence of the Indian National Congress.

In 1886 he founded the Muhammadan Anglo-Oriental Educational Conference for the general promotion of western education in Muslim India, for the enrichment of Urdu through translations of indispensable scientific works, to exercise political pressure for the acceptance of Urdu as the secondary language in all government and private schools, to emphasize the necessity for educating women as essential for the balanced intellectual development of future generations, and to formulate a policy for the higher education of Muslim students in Europe, who were discouraged from marrying abroad in order that they should remain involved with the problems of their own land of origin. The question of religious education at the Muhammadan Anglo-Oriental College (MAO College) at Aligarh was complex. Personally opposed to denominational education, and disapproving of the existence of denominational colleges even in the great universities of England as anachronistic and a heritage of medieval obscurantism in the West, Sayyid Ahmad Khan left the direction of the compulsory theological studies to a committee which included some of his fiercest orthodox critics. He thus succeeded in his objective that however unpopular his own religious radicalism was, it should not interfere with the popularity of the College among all sections of the Muslim upper classes. But the chasm between the pragmatic premiss of modern physical sciences and the data of revealed religion alarmed him as tending to a vacuum threatening to engulf the younger generation of Muslims whom he was leading from the past to the present. The motive and the entire methodology of his speculative modernist theology was intended to bridge this chasm.

REFERENCES

1. Ram Gopal, *Indian Muslim, op. cit.*, p. 31.
2. *Ibid.*, p. 32.
3. Report of Education Commission, 1882, *North West Province*, p. 8.
4. *Ibid.*, p. 7.
5. *Ibid.*, p. 151.
6. *Ibid.*, p. 292. (Evidence by Sir Syed Ahmed Khan).
7. Letter of Sir Syed Ahmed Khan to the Director, Public Instructions, North West Province, dated June 1881, quoted in the report of Education Commission, p. 151.
8. Ram Gopal, *Indian Muslim, op. cit.*, p. 36.
9. Report of Education Commission, *op. cit.*, p. 295.
10. Hunter, W.W., *Indian Mussalman, op. cit.*, p. 178.
11. *Ibid.*
12. Report of Education Commission, *op. cit.*, p. 222.
13. *Ibid.*, p. 213.
14. *Ibid.*, p. 329.
15. Ram Gopal, *Indian Muslim, op. cit.*, p. 40.
16. *Ibid.*, p. 42.

6

ON RELIGION AND NATURE

Wahabi Movement

Early in the 19th century, a Muslim adventurer, hailing from the district of Rae Bareli in U.P. and fired by Islamic zeal, took it into his head to plant the Crescent throughout every district of India. His name was Syed Ahmed. He was a visionary and believed that he could by reviving the true spirit of Islam re-establish a lasting empire in India. He had begun life as a horse soldier in the service of one Amir Khan Pindari, afterwards Nawab of Tonk, and according to W.W. Hunter, 'for many a year harried the rich opium-growing villages of Malwa'. But his ambition took him to a Muslim *maulvi* of high repute at Delhi to study the sacred law of Islam. He attributed the downfall of Islam in India to the abuses which had crept into the faith. He became a preacher and zealously attacked the abuses, obtaining a turbulent following. This was in the second decade of the 19th century. He styled himself, and was verily regarded as a prophet. His piety and the steadfastness of his purpose travelled ahead of him, and wherever he went multitudes came forward to join his standard. Men of rank and learning ran like common servants, with their shoes off by the side of his palanquin. It was now apparent that he could raise an army for the mere asking. 'In Calcutta the masses flocked to him in such numbers that he was unable even to go through the ceremony of initiation by the separate laying on of hand. Unrolling his turban, therefore, he declared that all who could touch any part of its ample length became his disciples.'[1] Money was necessary for his future campaigns, and he appointed agents to go forth and collect during his long itineraries, a tax from the profits of trade in all the large towns which fell on his route. He assumed the authority of spiritual and temporal command over his co-religionists and, like the Mohammedan Emperors, issued *farmans* (orders). In 1822, he made a religious journey to Mecca, and came under the influence of the Wahabi cult, whose success in Muslim countries gave him greater confidence and vigour. Within a short period of six or seven years, his influences spread over two thousand miles of thickly populated area, from the Peshawar Frontier to the delta of Bengal.

The Wahabis involved the British rulers of India in several costly wars on the Frontier. There was a network of conspiracies in the provinces, and each war on the Frontier produced its corresponding State trial of non-belligerents. Each case gave clues which led to a whole crop of others. Between 1864 and 1871, there were five great State trials, as a result of which dozens of Muslims were awarded capital punishment, transportation for life, and heavy sentences of imprisonment. As a matter of policy, in every case, a capital punishment was commuted to transportation for life. At the time of the 1871 trial, the Muslim bitterness against the British reached its climax, and the Chief Justice of Bengal, John Paxton Norman was stabbed to death by a Muslim on the steps of his own Tribunal. He had imposed heavy sentences on some Wahabi Muslims. The same year, Viceroy Mayo was murdered in the Andaman Islands by a Wahabi convict, Sher Ali.

Mayo had fallen to the blow of a Wahabi, but he had already laid out a clever tactic to break up the movement. For half a century, Muslim rebels had tried without success to convert the *Darul-Harb* (land ruled by the Infidel), that was India under British rule, into *Darul-Islam* (a country ruled by the Faithful), but their spirit remained unsubdued and their followers were not disheartened. It was apparent that the victory of British arms on the Frontier did not secure to the Government the obedience of most of the Muslims and could not quell the unrest. If doctors of the Muslim law continued to declare India *Darul-Harb,* Muslims would consider it their religious duty to help the rebellion against the Infidel. Quite naturally, therefore, it had occurred to Mayo that if one set of doctors declared British territories as *Darul-Harb,* another could be secured to interpret it as *Darul-Islam* in which *jihad* was a sin. Accordingly, a discussion was started throughout the country as to whether India was *Darul-Harb* or *Darul-Islam.* Obviously, nobody would come forward openly to suggest that she was *Darul-Harb;* such a suggestion would have landed the maker of it in gaol or made him a suspect in the eyes of the authorities. The discussion was, therefore, one-sided. Orthodox and semi-orthodox doctors came out with new interpretations, and forcefully suggested that the Wahabi interpretation was wrong and misleading. Opinions were obtained from certain Muffis of Mecca who, in effect, said that 'as long as some of the peculiar observances of Islam prevail in a country, *it is Darul-Islam'*. Doctors of Muslim law in Northern India, who were approached by the Personal Assistant of the Commissioner of the Bhagalpur Division said: 'The Muslims here are protected by Christians, and there is no *Jihad* in a country where protection is afforded.'[2] The Mohammedan Literary Society, founded in Calcutta at about the time of the Wahabi trial of 1863 by Nawab Abdul Latif, had been opposing the Wahabi agitation. It was a pro-British organization, and lent support to the favourable interpretation. Sir Syed Ahmed Khan also participated in the discussion, and in a letter in the *Pioneer* dated, April 14, 1871, he wrote: 'Mohammedans, be they dwellers in *Darul-Harb* or *Darul-Islam*, are prohibited from rebellion against a government which interferes in no way with the free worship of their religion.'[3]

Already, before Mayo had propounded his new policy, men like Sir Syed who had been loyal to the British had been trying persistently to wean Muslims away from the Wahabi influence. Sir Syed was one of those Muslims who had a great personal risk, and in spite of their having been condemned by learned doctors of Islam, rendered invaluable help to the British during the Great Revolt of 1857, and he continued to support the Government throughout the Wahabi agitation. Many Muslims had enlisted willingly in the British armies during the long northern wars and even marched with those armies to Kabul and Kandahar. The Muslims fought for the British against the wild tribes on the debatable frontier lands between India and Afghanistan. During the 1857 Revolt also, there were many Muslims, as there were Hindus among the Company's troops and informers. But the British authorities and chroniclers turned fiercely on Muslims, and held them mainly responsible for the Revolt, believing that its success would re-establish Muslim rule, rather than that of the Marathas or the Sikhs. The conciliatory policy of the British Government, after the failure of the Revolt and Queen Victoria's announcement that Indians 'will be freely and impartially admitted to the offices' in Government services, may have brought about a change in the attitude, but the resumption of Wahabi activities hardened the Government's attitude towards the Muslims. This conclusion is supported by the fact that the discrimination against Muslims was applied vigorously in Bengal, for example, where the Wahabis had firmly entrenched themselves. In the territories now called Uttar Pradesh, which had main battleground of the Revolt, the Wahabis could not flourish, and Muslims were trusted with Government jobs, while in the eastern provinces, almost every Muslim was a suspect or a rebel.

The Muslim aversion to the European system of education kept Muslims out of other-new professions. They despised the English sciences of medicine, and did not offer themselves for training at medical colleges. In 1869, the year in which attention began to be drawn prominently to the 'pitiable plight' of the Muslims, out of 104 Licentiates of Medicine, there were 98 Hindus, five Englishmen and only one Muslim. Among the graduates of Medicine in Calcutta University, there were four doctors, three Hindus and one Englishman. For many years, the Muslims continued to lag behind the Hindus in all branches of learning and, consequently, in the State services, despite Mayo's policy of lifting the discrimination against them. Even after the Wahabi movement had died out, and the Muslim leaders of the pro-British school had constantly advised their co-religionists to take to European arts and sciences and English education, the orthodox maulvis continued to exercise a dominating influence over the Muslim mind; British jurisprudence as against Islamic law and the Kazi system; the European system of medicine as against the time-honoured *Tabib, Hakim* and *Jarrah*; exclusion of the Koran from the textbooks, and emphasis on secularism as against theocracy; substitution of Persian by English; the teaching of European arts and sciences, which were considered inferior by learned Muslims—all offended against the tradition of centuries. Hindus, in this respect, were distinctly different from Muslims. During the six hundred years of Muslim rule, they had made themselves remarkably adaptable. During Muslim rule, they not only learnt Persian and Urdu with equanimity but produced eminent scholars and poets. The subordinate revenue services and clerical jobs were being open to them under the Muslim rulers, and they learnt the official language without allowing any thought to enter their minds that they were doing something offensive to their religion. The Hindu priesthood did not withhold Hindus from Persian schools and service under the Muslim rulers. With the Muslims, the case was different. Whether in Persia or as invaders, rulers and administrators in India, they were never faced with an occasion to make a departure from the traditional way of life. When it came, the powerful influence of the *maulvis* applied a brake.

History so shaped itself in the half a century just surveyed that Muslims grew jealous of Hindus, and Hindus became unfriendly to Muslims. Again, let it not be forgotten that the jealousy and unfriendliness did not extend to the Muslim and Hindu masses, but were restricted to the aristocracy and the middle classes of the two communities whose living depended on the Government jobs and Government favours. Yet naturally, this minority shaped and influenced the entire politics of the country. Muslim politics began, as did Indian politics (in practical result, Hindu politics) with the pertinent question: What was to be the representation of Muslims in the services ? Would a time ever arrive when Muslims would have their share? Muslim leaders, in these circumstances, put a sensible question to their co-religionists: What should be their immediate interest in public life, education or politics ?

Theological Speculation

Syed Ahmed Khan's Islamic reformism has some fundamentalist data as its starting point, originating in the school of Shah Wali-Allah, in which he received his early theological training.[4] Wali-Allahi fundamentalism had already mitigated the influence of the watertight compartmentalization of Muslim jurisprudence by permitting a believer to choose on any point the ruling of any of the four great

Sunni juristic schools; it had rejected *bida'* (innovations) and accretions borrowed from extraneous and alien cultural contacts by Islamic traditionalism. It had reiterated Ibn Taymiyya's significant anti-traditionalist thesis that the *bab al-ijtihad* (the gate of individual reasoning) was still open and should not be considered closed. Of the three disciplines of Islamic theology, the Qur'anic *tafsir* (exegesis), the science of *hadis,* and *fiqh* (jurisprudence as worked out by the four great juristic schools), the last had already been subjected to some anti-traditionalist dialectics by Shah Wali-Allah. This break-through had been absolutely unconnected with any western influences, and was inspired by internal spiritual and historical forces that had led to a stock-taking of theological data in the early eighteenth century during the period of the decline of the Mughal and the Ottoman empires.

Syed Ahmed Khan's first theological work *Rah-i sunnat wa radd-i bid'at* (1850), is directly in this tradition. Since then, and specially after 1870, he turned to Wali-Allahi fundamentalism again and again, but only to transfer and reinterpret it in terms of his own revolutionary modernism. The key phrase of Shah Wali-Allah, 'The time has come for Islamic theology to be brought in the field fully armed with dialectics'[5], actually referred to the need of a reorientation of the classical methodology of disputation. But Syed Ahmed Khan used it as the starting point for limitless rationalist speculation.

Though no other writer has been quoted and discussed more frequently in Syed Ahmed Khan's writings than Wali-Allah, and though he often returns to anti-traditionalist sources within Islam, such as the views of the Mu'tazila and of the Ikhwan al-Safa (Brethren of Purity), some features of his speculative system show the unmistakable influence of Unitarianism. He regards religion as a discipline essential for the establishment of ethical criteria. Its essence is truth rather than faith, which distinguishes a true creed from a false one. Faith is one of the ingredients of this essence. Truth, in so far as it is cognizable by human reason, is identical with nature and its laws, which determine the organizational causality of all material and non-material phenomena. These natural laws also posit moral criteria which constitute the basis of human social ethics.

And the logic of the natural laws points necessarily to a Final Cause, a Prime Mover, God.[6]

He interprets Islam, freed from the traditionalist accretions it has accumulated in its long history, according to his own criteria and on the basis of a rationalist reinterpretation of the Qur'an. As he analysed the corpus of traditional exegetical literature, he found it almost solely preoccupied with such secondary problems as the relation of the Qur'an to the theological sciences of *fiqh* and *kalam* (scholasticism), or with the 'miraculous' nature of its i'jaz (style), or with minutiae of differences of interpretations among the classical exegetes. There was hardly any material available on the chronological order or classification of the verses of the Qur'an, on its underlying principles of guidance for future ages in widely different climes, or on its position as the ultimate source for the resolution of any problems that the Muslim community might face in circumstances very different from those of the Arabs of the early seventh century. This led him to formulate his own principles of exegesis. He accepted in principle the thesis advanced by his associate and critic, Muhsin al-Mulk, that the Qur'an can only be interpreted given an accurate understanding of the Arabic idiom in the Prophet's time, but reserved for himself or any individual Muslim the right not only of a literal but also of a symbolic or analytical interpretation. The bases of interpretation were to be the underlying principles (*usul*) and not the minutiae or details (*furu*) derived therefrom or the verses in the Qur'an referring to specific historical situations.[7]

Fifteen Principles

He outlined fifteen basic principles for his own exegesis: (i) God is omnipotent, omnipresent, and the Creator of the universe; (ii) He has sent prophets, including Muhammad, for the guidance of mankind from time to time; (iii) the Qur'an is the authentic *wahy* (revelation), the Word of God; (iv) it was conveyed to Muhammad's mind by a process of *wahy*, and it is immaterial whether it was conveyed to him by the Archangel Gabriel, or whether its sense as well as its words were received directly by Muhammad's prophetic intuition;

(v) the Qur'an contains nothing which could be wrong or incorrect or anti-historical; (vi) the attributes of God mentioned in it exist only in their essence; (vii) they are identical with His Self and are eternal; (viii) these attributes can have no limitations, but in His wisdom and freedom God has created the laws of nature and maintains them as the disciplines of creation and existence; (ix) therefore there can be nothing in the Qur'an contrary to the laws of nature; (x) the present text of the Qur'an is complete and final without any interpolations or additions; (xi) the verses of every *sura* in their present sequence follow a chronological order; (xii) *naskh,* accepted as a textual and exegetical reality in classical Islam, is a doctrine which must be rejected in the study of the Qur'an; (xiii) the *wahy* of the Qur'an has developed in gradual stages; (xiv) Qur'anic eschatology, angelology, demonology and cosmology cannot be contrary to scientific actuality and must be interpreted in its terms; and finally (xv) linguistic research is necessary to study the sociological *mores* and possibilities of development of human society contained in the direct and indirect expressions of the Qur'an.[8]

It follows from these fifteen principles that wahy and natural law are identical. Wahy operates as natural instinct in lower forms of life. Man's problem in relation to wahy is much more complex. Unlike most animals he is compelled to live in society; through social organization alone he survives and overcomes the hostile forces around him. The natural necessity of social organization imposes upon him another necessity, that of an ethical code, without which society cannot hold together as an entity. For the human individual and society revelational law is necessarily in consonance with human rationality. In human society wahy and reason are, therefore, identical. Reason as a natural revelational instinct operates in man's scientific investigations as much as in his concept of the deity, his distinction between good and evil, his views on divine judgment and retribution, and his belief in life after death. With the passage of history these revelational instincts are imprinted as clear and fixed images upon the human mind.[9]

The capacity of revelational cognition of rational reality is not possessed by all men in equal degree. Certain individuals, for whom Shah Wali-Allah has used the term *mufahhimun* (the understanding ones), are endowed with this faculty to a much higher degree than certain others. These former leaders of men include philosophers, statesmen, founders of classical juristic schools, and outstanding mystics, and culminated in the prophets. The natural revelational instinct of a prophet is the highest form of its development in man. It comes as a sudden flash, often unconnected with any immediate causation. The impact of this flash has received many names in theology including that of Gabriel. The more highly developed the instinctive flashes of a prophet, the more consistent they would be with divinely ordained laws of nature. Reason revealed through prophetic intuition is the most developed form of true faith in God. Prophets can be true or false. False ones are those in whose intuitional cognition the message of divine reality has gone astray and is, therefore, contrary to human rationality and the norms of human ethics. But they may also attract followers and create societies which are, however, inclined towards evil.[10]

The term 'nature' is used by Syed Ahmed Khan in the sense in which the nineteenth-century scientists interpreted it 'as a closed system of the universe which obeys certain laws of mechanics and physics and which is invariably characterized by a uniformity of behaviour in which there cannot be any exception'. Analysing this point further, B.A. Dar aptly comments that the purely theistic view of Nature in its totally anti-theistic interpretation, current during his days.. was a totally illegitimate transition from a mechanical to a teleological view of nature.'[11] But, partly at least, his 'naturalism' was an orthogenetic heritage of the Mu'tazila, especially Nazgam, and other Muslim speculative thinkers, including al-Jahiz and Ibn Tufayl.

A 'naturalistic' commentary on the Qur'an raised certain problems. One of these was to explain the 'folklore' which is encrusted in it, as in the scriptures of other religions. To meet this difficulty, Syed Ahmed Khan redefines the familiar classical distinction between two kinds of Qur'anic verses, the 'clear' and the 'ambiguous', as 'essential' and 'symbolic', the former constituting the irreducible minimum of Islamic faith and creed, the latter being open to two or more interpretations, permitting deductions appropriate to other ages and circumstances, different from those of Arabia in the early seventh century.

Another problem, basically of considerable textual, legal and historical significance, was that of *naskh,* or the supersession of one Qur'anic injunction by another, a principle affirmed in the Qur'an itself. On this question Syed Ahmed Khan takes the view that a single scripture like the Qur'an is a monolithic eternal reality. The principle of *naskh* can only be valid in terms of comparative religion, where a later prophetic religion abrogates an earlier one. Thus Christianity abrogates Judaism, and Islam Christianity. But the principle is quite irrelevant to the Qur'an. The Qur'an abrogates the Old and the New Testament with chronological finality.

The first in modern Islam to experience the impact of Darwinian evolutionism, Syed Ahmed Khan was also the first to search for a formula to reconcile it with the Islamic tenets of Creation and the Fall of Adam. The Qur'an affirms that the law of evolution is observable in relating one species of created beings to another. The 'symbolic imagery' of 'semen' or 'seed' as the nucleus of life refers to the primeval movement of life emerging out of inert matter. The literal reference in the Qur'an, as in the Old Testament, to the genesis of the universe is the use by God of a popular belief for the sake of argument. For the scripture must necessarily approach and address the people among whom it is revealed in terms of their folklore, store of knowledge, and understanding, and within the conceptual framework comprehensible to them. The legend of the Fall of Adam is likewise metaphorical. Adam connotes human nature.[12]

Syed Ahmed Khan views the soul as a pragmatic reality which is 'proved' in animal as in man, though human reason cannot grasp its exact nature. The animal soul is primarily circumscribed by instinct. The human soul is capable of unlimited action. It can evolve or suffer decline and can range from scientific research to gross inhumanities. It is incapable of absorbing or rejecting good or evil at its choice. It exists in essence and is, therefore, immortal. In its immortality it is accountable for the good or evil it has chosen to absorb. This account it will have to render on the Day of Judgement which begins for each individual at the moment of his death. There is also a final and collective Day of Judgement, on which all humanity will be resurrected, but in a different physical sense, with a physical personality which would be different from the human body in this life.

Prophets are the promulgators of the divine law of nature. The concept of a miracle contradicts this law wrongfully and anarchically. Miracles mentioned in the scriptures have, therefore, to be interpreted as either symbolical or metaphorical or legendary. The laws of nature are immutable. They are 'pledges' of God to his creation and cannot be broken. To believe in a miraculous suspension or reversal of these laws amounts therefore to repudiation of faith in the divine 'pledges' and to accuse God of falsehood. True, we do not know all the laws of nature. Everyday new laws are revealed to us. But known or unknown to us, these laws do exist independent of our knowledge, and by analogy we may perceive that they exist in regularity and harmony, and are not contradicted by miracles.

The only miracle attributable to the Prophet of Islam is his great prophetic role, which is revelational in nature but thoroughly consonant with reason. The great miracle traditionally attributed to Muhammad, the isra' (his ascension to heaven and vision of God on a night of beatitude), was neither a physical nor a spiritual experience but a dream. On the question of man's capacity to perceive the vision of God, Syed Ahmed Khan accepts the orthodox Sufistic view of Shaikh Ahmed Sirhindi that it can only be a mystical and spiritual and not a physical experience.

A similar process of rationalization is applied to Islamic angelology and demonology. Angels are the 'properties' of created things like hardness in stone, fluidity in water, and intuitive cognition of reality in man. In Qur'anic terminology, a secondary sense of the 'concept' angel is the divine moral support which encourages man in his struggle against overwhelming odds. Satan, the fallen angel, is metaphorically mentioned in the Qur'an as created of fire. This signifies the dark passions of man.

In Muslim demonology, commenting on the identity of *jinn* whom the Qur'an has mentioned on several occasions, Syed Ahmed Khan tries to determine their position in the comparative data of animistic folklore: 'Not only the pagan Arabs but medieval Jews and Zoroastrians believed in supra-human invisible creatures, created from fire, with attitudes benevolent or malevolent towards men.'

Then he argues that on five occasions the word 'Jinn' used in the Qur'an is synonymous with 'jann' and refers to the pagan belief in these creatures without actually recognizing their existence. In the Qur'an they are projections of evil, diseases, and other calamities. On certain other occasions the Qur'an uses the term for 'wilder men living in forests, hills and deserts'. This later theory of the historicity of the jinn is based upon the biblical researches and apologetics of Syed Ahmed Khan's more radical associate, Chiragh 'Ali. The devils referred to in the Qur'an are evil human beings who misinterpret divine decrees 'and inhibit free will by astrological calculations'.

References in the Qur'an, as in the Bible, to natural calamities as visitations of divine punishment on sinful peoples have roots in popular superstition, and have been restated in the scriptures not as historical verities but with an ethical motive borrowing the popular legendary framework. This bold exegetical approach should have been enough for Syed Ahmed Khan, but he vitiates it in detail when he indulges in apologetics explaining away the 'folklore' of the Old and the New Testament and of the Qur'an in terms of untenable historical hypotheses. Thus the Seven Sleepers of Ephesus are interpreted as members of a "Unitarian" Christian sect persecuted by Diocletian. They did not remain literally asleep for several years but were dead and mummified by the temperature and soil of the caves they lived in.153 Rejecting al-Razi's identification of the Qur'anic Zu'l *qarnayn* (the two-horned one) with Alexander the Great, Syed Ahmed Khan advances a theory identifying him with the Chinese emperor Chi Wang Ti (C. 247 BC), and Gog and Magog with the races of Chinese Turkestan (Mongolia?); and he makes the interesting but rather anachronistic observation that a number of legends are common to Chi Wang Ti and the *Alexander Romance* of the Muslim poets, showing that the two had become confused and telescoped together in the medieval Muslim mind.[13]

However startling his speculative rationalization of Muslim faith and dogma, on the question of prescribed ritual he was conformist and a conservative. The prescribed form of the Muslim ritual prayer *(salat)* he considered logically perfect and structurally immutable.

Of the four sources of Islamic law, the question of a modernist interpretation of the first, the Qur'an, was by far the most difficult.

It is not surprising therefore that by far the greater part of Syed Ahmed Khan's theological work concerns itself with exegetics. The next most important source of law, the *hadis,* was easier to deal with. To begin with, by all traditional accounts it was well recognized that during the first three centuries of Islam a vast corpus of apocryphal traditions was fabricated and attributed to the Prophet; and that two sciences, that of the study of *hadis ('ilm al-hadis)* and of biographical verification *(asma' al-rijal),* had to be developed by the classical discipline of the ninth and tenth centuries to sift truth from falsehood. Syed Ahmed Khan's views on the doubtfulness of even the six great classical collections of *hadis* are not very different from the conclusions arrived at by western orientalists like Goldziher and Schacht. Among motives for the fabrication of *hadis* attributed to the Prophet, he advances the loss of the focus of reality with the passage of time, popular credulity for the unusual and the extraordinary, uncritical faith in the narrated word, confusion between the incident and the injunction, political manipulations in the context of dynastic rivalries, mischief-making by the dissemblers *(munafiqun),* and fabrication as a purely psychological phenomenon. Supernatural incidents were woven in, in consonance with the credulity, common to all ancient and medieval cultures. He objects to the methodology of classical *hadis* criticism, including that of Bukhari and Muslim, on the same ground as did the western Islamists later, that it is based entirely on the personal reliability of the individuals in the *isnad* (chain of narrators) and not on a logical or rational criticism of the text (*matn*) of a hadis itself. The hadis in the great classical hadis collections, therefore, constitutes, generally speaking, not so much an infallible source of law as a historical reflection of the ideas and attitudes of the first few generations of Muslims.[14]

Syed Ahmed Khan's own theory of hadis criticism, later more elaborately developed by Chiragh Ali, postulates that the greater part of the classical hadis which is repugnant to human reason should be rejected forthwith. One should also reject a hadis which is repugnant to the dignity of prophethood. Authentic ahadis can only be of three varieties; those which are in consonance with the Qur'an and repeat its injunctions; those which explain or elucidate these injunctions; and those which deal with basic legal formulations not touched upon in the Qur'an. Any hadis which contradicts the Qur'an is necessarily a fabrication. Even in the hadis which are accepted at their face value as genuine statements of Muhammad, a distinction has to be established between those which he made as the Prophet of God and those which reflect his personal views or his likes and dislikes as a human being.[15]

Much of the modern methods of re-explanation and reinterpretation of such points of sensitivity to western criticism among traditional Islamic institutions as jihad or the permissibility of polygamy and slavery begins with Syed Ahmed Khan, his associates, and his critics, including Jamal al-din al-Afghani and Shaykh Muhammad 'Abduh, partly as genuine historical research and partly as apologetics. Even T.W. Arnold's view of jihad as purely defensive is inspired by Syed Ahmed Khan, whose basic theory regarding the Prophet's *maghazi* (militant expeditions) is in the historical context of pagan Arabia, as indeed in the international code of war in all times, reconnaissance forays and raids against the enemy have been a recognized institution of defensive warfare. Hebrew prophets occupied themselves in similar warfare without any apologies.

On the question of slavery, his argument is based on the principle that freedom and slavery are mutually exclusive; they cannot co-exist or evolve together. Therefore, both of them cannot be in accordance with divine approval. Man has been created free, endowed with reason, consciousness, and organs, mental and physical, over which he has been given full control. If he is his own master, he cannot be anybody else's slave. His soul is free and cannot be enslaved under any circumstances. Most societies based on religion or philosophy, Jewish, Christian, and Graeco-Roman, however, sanctioned slavery. Islam alone limited and rejected slavery, condemning it on moral grounds. Historical Islam has indeed, like Graeco-Roman, Hindu, the Byzantine, and American societies, patronized the institution of slavery in disobedience to divine injunctions. Some contemporary Muslim states failed to abolish it when the West decided to do so. In such cases the institution has its roots in history and not in Islamic religion. Ideal Islam has no place for slavery, judging from the famous hadis that there is nothing more pleasing to God than the manumission of slaves, and the Qur'anic injunction in verse 47:5 laying down that all prisoners of war should be set free gratuitously or for a ransom.

Historical Islam came in the wake of two cultures, pagan Arab and Judaeo-Christian, both of which sanctioned and maintained slavery as an institution. Islam's solution of this problem was a gradual mitigation of the lot of the slave, and to recommend his manumission as one of the greatest acts of piety. A loan was made available to a slave from the state treasury to purchase his freedom. The injunctions in the Qur'an refer only to the slaves then existing; there is no evidence in its text that fresh enslavement was encouraged or even permitted. The entire corpus of reference to slavery in the Qur'an refers to the slave-owning social order inherited from pagan Arabia, which could only be gradually abolished 'within a generation'. The verse 47:5 of the Qur'an states:

Then set them free, either by grace or ransom marks therefore the watershed and the point of prohibition of fresh enslavement for the future. This verse is termed by Syed Ahmed Khan and Chiragh 'Ali as the 'verse of liberation' (*aya hurriyya*), and its revelation dated to 629, the year of the occupation of Mecca. This view stands in opposition to the general opinion of classical jurists, who date the verse to the occasion of the Battle of Badr (622), and therefore regard it as abrogate by other verses in the Qur'an referring to slavery as an institution.[16]

In the later decades of the nineteenth century the question of slavery in Islam was a burning political issue and one of the principal points of British propaganda against the Mahdi of the Sudan. The stand taken by the Indian modernists was to argue that the theory of Islam was innocent of the guilt, which should be laid at the door of the historical inheritance of the Muslim states.

The institution of polygamy had been one of the main bastions of Sir William Muir's polemics against Islam. Syed Ahmed Khan examines it from three points of view: in terms of natural law; in the context of its social use and abuse; and as a religious dogma. He sees no biological objection to the permissibility or practicability of polygamy in terms of natural law, as a male is naturally equipped to fertilize several females. As a social problem he argues that in certain societies remarriage is a necessary evil, to safeguard the woman's economic, though not her psychological or emotional interests. Coming to the third point, he and Chiragh 'Ali advanced the famous theory based on a liberal and modernist interpretation of the Qur'anic verse 4:2-3:

> *If you fear that you will not act justly*
> *towards the orphans, marry such women*
> *as seem good to you, two, three, four;*
> *but if you fear you will not be equitable,*
> *then only one, or what your right hands own;*
> *so it is likelier you will not be partial.*

This argument, which has formed the basis of family law reforms in several Muslim states, contends that justice in a man-woman relationship can only be synonymous with love; and since a man is emotionally incapable of loving more than one woman equally at any given time, polygamy has been prohibited and criticized by demonstrating its underlying shortcomings. In these arguments, he ignores the problem of concubinage. Syed Ahmed Khan then takes the counter-offensive by arguing, unlike the Qur'an, that polygamy as an unjust institution is forbidden neither in the Old nor clearly in the New Testament. Christ's celibacy, he argues, was not based on any moral or theological principle but was due to the fact that the Jews regarded him as illegitimate and therefore not an eligible husband for a Jewish girl; and in any case he died young.[17]

Interest on loans (*riba*) is categorically forbidden in the Qu'ran. On this question, which has been one of the greatest significance in relation to the development of an Islamic state in modern times, involving the future of banking and finance, Syed Ahmed Khan's interpretation is that compound interest might be considered forbidden, but simple interest, specially bank interest or interest on government bonds, should be considered permissible.

In the final analysis, Syed Ahmed Khan's modernism can be discerned as grappling with two broadly distinct problems: the rationalization of the minutiae of non-essential dogma, and the liberalization of Islamic law. In regard to the first of these he shows signs of psychological pressures which occasionally result in some easily avoidable apologetics as well as certain extreme rationalist positions which were repugnant to the traditionalists. In regard to the second, in spite of some slight apologetic residue, his work is dynamic and constructive, and as such it has made a tremendous impression on modern Islam in general, and on Indian Islam in particular. It contains an undercurrent of juristic change, facing the question of the adjustment of law to the contemporary as against the historical context. He tried to resolve the difficulties inherent in the four traditional sources of Muslim law by a dialectical rationalist exegesis of the Qur'an; by historical scepticism in scrutinizing the classical data of the *hadis;* by an almost unlimited emphasis on *ijtihad* as the inalienable right of every individual Muslim; and finally, by rejecting the principle of *ijma* in the classical sense which confined it to the '*ulama*'.[18]

Comparative Religion

Chronologically Syed Ahmed Khan's Commentary on the Bible (1862) precedes his exegesis of the Qur'an (1880-95). He seems to have turned to comparative religion within five years of the Uprising of 1857, primarily to understand the religious *mores* of the rulers of his country, and secondly, to pursue the counter-offensive against the Christian missionaries into their own territory. In this he chose the path of understanding and eclecticism. He made some effort to learn Hebrew and to study the Old Testament in the original, though he relied largely on the Persian translation.[19]

His exegetic thesis of the Bible turns on the crucial argument that revelation is a secret disclosure to man of the will and purpose of God. It can be either prophetic or non-prophetic. In the latter sense the Apostles could also be considered as inspired, though their inspiration is neither perfect nor accurate. The difference between the revelational character of the Qur'an and the New Testament is that whereas the latter includes a number of non-revelatory traditions narrated by the Apostles, the former contains nothing except the authorized word of God. The corpus of the Old and the New Testaments has, therefore, to be tested for veracity by comparison with the indisputably divine message in the Qur'an.

On the question of *tahrif* (corruption and interpolation) in the Bible, Syed Ahmed Khan's views are at this stage closer to Muslim orthodox theory. He divides the totality of the Old Testament into three broad categories: genuine revelation, the sections that have been lost, and the sections which have been deleted by later Christian or Jewish compilers. The New Testament could likewise be divided into an authentic canonical part and an apostolic apocrypha. In the Commentary on the Bible he applies the classical Muslim technique of *isnad* criticism (examination of the reliability of persons involved in a chain-link narrating a *hadis* of the Prophet) to distinguish what he considers genuine revelatory passages from the apocrypha. He interprets the classical Muslim theory of *tahrif* as referring essentially to exegetical interpretations rather than actual verbal corruption of the text. On textual criticism of the Bible he draws attention to the historical fact of the multiplicity of earlier manuscripts, to the accumulated errors that might have crept in through centuries of copying, and to the complicated problems of translation.

The Commentary itself is guided by the basic principle, which he later followed in his Commentary on the Qur'an, that between the work of God (nature) and the word of God (revelation) there can be no contradiction. His biblical apologetics has therefore to rely equally on his exegetical subtlety.

In his identification of biblical and Qur'anic concepts of monotheism, he asserts that he could find no trace of the Trinitarian dogma in the New Testament itself, and that by emphasizing the humanity of Christ, the Qur'an simplifies Christian dogma, reducing it to a consonance with the laws of nature. Revelational reference to Christ in Matthew iii, 17 as 'My beloved Son' leads to his equating the biblical term 'Father' with the Qur'anic term *rabb* (the provider), a paternalistic concept of the deity, which is interesting in view of the later development of the theory of *rububiyyat* (divine providence) in its relation to man's economic and social life in the subsequent exegetical speculations of Azad and Parwiz.

More methodically than some medieval Muslim scholars, but in their tradition, Syed Ahmed Khan interprets certain passages in the Old Testament as referring specifically to the advent of

Muhammad, and in the case of the New Testament he follows Godfrey Higgins in interpreting John xiv, 25-26 and xvi, 7 as also referring to the Prophet's advent.[20]

The study of Christianity in the Commentary is essentially sympathetic. It is groping its way towards a religious pluralism in an age in which the western theologians had taken no significant step in that direction. It is all the more regrettable that Syed Ahmed Khan's *experience inter-religionale* should have died out not only in Indian Islamic speculation but also in his own later writings.

REFERENCES

1. Ram Gopal, *Indian Muslim, op. cit.*, p. 22.
2. *Ibid.*, p. 25.
3. *Ibid.*
4. Hali, Altaf Hussain, *Hayat-i-Jawed, op. cit.*, p. 16.
5. Ahmad, Aziz, *Islamic Modernism in India and Pakistan, 1857-1964, op. cit.*, p. 41.
6. Khan, Sir Syed Ahmed, *Khutbat-i-Ahmadiya* (Aligarh: Institute Press), 1983, pp. 1-5.
7. Khan, Sir Syed Ahmed, *al-Tahrir fi usul al-tafsir* (Agra: Mufid-i-am Press), 1892, pp. 8-9.
8. *Ibid.*, pp. 32-56.
9. Khan, Sir Syed Ahmed, *Tasfir al-Quran* (Aligarh: Institute Press), 1880, Vol., VIII, pp. 9-12.
10. *Ibid.*, pp. 14-18.
11. Dar, B.A., *The Religious Thought of Syed Ahmed Khan* (Lahore: Ashraf), 1957, pp. 150-52.
12. Ahmad, Aziz, *Islamic Modernism in India and Pakistan, 1857-1964, op. cit.*, p. 46.
13. *Ibid.*, p. 48.
14. Khan, Sir Syed Ahmed, *Tasfir al-Quran, op. cit.*, Vol., IV, pp. 118-23.
15. Khan, Sir Syed Ahmed, *Khuttrut-I a, op. cit.*, pp. 334-35.
16. Ahmad, Aziz, *Islamic Modernism in India and Pakistan, 1857-1964, op. cit.*, pp. 51-52.
17. *Ibid.*, pp. 52-53.
18. Hali, Altaf Hussain, *Hayat-i-Jawed, op. cit.*, p. 256.
19. *Ibid.*, p. 97.
20. Ahmad, Aziz, *Islamic Modernism in India and Pakistan, 1857-1964, op. cit.* p. 56.

BIBLIOGRAPHY

Abdullah, S.M., *Spirit and Substance of Urdu Prose* (Lahore: Ashraf), 1940.

Ahmad, Aziz, *Islamic Modernism in India and Pakistan, 1857-1964* (London: Oxford University Press), 1967.

Ahmed, Sufia, *Muslim Community in Bengal, 1884-1912* (Dacca: Oxford University Press), 1974.

Ahmad, Nazir, *Ibn ul Waqt* (Lahore: Sheikh Mubarak Ali), 1949.

Ahmad, Jamil-ud-Din (ed.), *Speeches and Writings of Mr. Jinnah*, Vol. I (Lahore: Ashraf), 1960.

Ahmed, Akbar S., *Jinnah, Pakistan and Islamic Identity* (Karachi: Oxford University Press).

Ahmad, Aziz, *Islamic Modernism in India and Pakistan 1857-1964* (London: Oxford University Press), 1967.

Ahmad, Rizwan (ed.) *The Quaid-e-Azam Papers* (Karachi: East & West Publishing Co.), 1976.

Ahmad, Rizwan (ed.) *Iqbal's Letters to Quaid-e-Azam* (Lahore: Friends Educational Service), 1966.

Akbar, Ahmad, *Jinnah Pakistan and Islamic Identity* (London: Routledge), 1997.

Albiruni, A.H., *Makers of Pakistan and Modern Muslim India* (Lahore: Ashraf), 1950.

Almeida, Prakash, Jinnah Man of Destiny (Delhi: Kalpaz Publications), 2001.

Ambedkar, B.R. *Pakistan or the Partition of India* (Bombay: Thacker), 1946.

Ambedkar, B.R., *Pakistan or the Partition of India* (Bombay: Thacker), 1946.

Ambedkar, B.R., *What Congress and Gandhi Have Done to the Untouchables* (Bombay: Thacker & Co.), 1946.

Azad, Maulana Abul Kalam, *India Wins Freedom* (Calcutta: Longmans), 1959

Aziz, Beg, *Jinnah and His Time* (Islamabad: Babur and Amer Publications), 1986.

Aziz, K.K., Rahmat Ali—A Biography (Lahore: Vanguard), 1987.

Aziz, K.K. *The Making of Pakistan* (London: Chatto & Windus), 1967.

Bakshi, Illahi, *With Quiad-e-Azam During His Last Days* (Karachi: Quaid-e-Azam Academy), 1978.

Baig, M.R.A., *In Different Saddles* (New York: Asia Publications), 1967.

Bamford, P.C., *Histories of Non-Cooperation and Khilafat Movements* (New Delhi: Deep and Deep), 1974.

Bannerjea, D.N., *India's Nation Builder* (London: Headley), 1919.

Beck, Theodore, *Essays on Indian Topics* (Allahabad: Pioneer Press), 1888.

Bhardwaj, K.K., *Pakistan's March to Democracy and Liberalism* (New Delhi: Anmol Publications), 1996.

Bhutto, Zulfikar Ali, *The Myth of Independence* (London: Oxford University Press), 1969.

Blunt, W.S. *India Under Ripon: A Private Diary* (London: T. Fisher Unwin), 1909.

Bolitho, Hector, *Jinnah: Creator of Pakistan* (London: John Murray), 1954.

Bose, Subhas Chandra, *The Indian Struggle Part II* (Calcutta: Published for Netaji Publishing Society), 1945.

Buski, Shahid Javed, *Pakistan, The Continuing Struggle for Nationhood* (Boulder Colo. West View Press), 1991.

Chagla, M.C., *Roses in December: An Autobiography* (Bombay: Bharatiya Vidya Bhawan), 1978.

Chandra, Bipin, *Communalism in India* (New Delhi: Vani Educational Books), 1984.

Chandra, Bipin, *India's Struggle For Independence 1857-1947* (New Delhi: Viking), 1988.

Chandra, Bipin, *Modern India* (New Delhi: NCERT), 1976.

Chandra, Bipin, *Nationalism and Colonialism in Modern India* (New Delhi: Orient Longman's Ltd.), 1979.

Chaudhry, Binayandra Mohan, *Muslim Politics in India* (Calcutta: Orient Longman), 1946.

Chaudhry, Kailash, *Tragedy of Jinnah* (Lahore: Varma Publishing Co.), 1943.

Chaudhri, Munir, *Mir-Mansam* (Dacca: Oxford University Press), 1968.

Chaudhary Rahmat Ali, *Pakistan: The Farther Land of Pak Nation* (London: The Pak National Liberal Movement), 1947.

Chaudhry, Sandhaya, *Gandhi and Partition of India* (New Delhi: Sterling), 1984.

Chiral, Valentine, *India, Old and New* (New Delhi: Light and Life Publishers), 1975.

Chiral, Valentine, *The Indian Unrest* (New Delhi: Light and Life Publishers), 1979.

Cohen, Stephen Philip, *The Idea of Pakistan* (New Delhi: Oxford University Press), 2005.

Collins Larry and Dominique Lapierre, *Freedom at Midnight* (New Delhi: Vikas Publications), 1973.

Constituent Assembly of Pakistan Debates, 11 August 1947, Vol. I, No. 2, pp. 18-20.

Countess Mary of Minto, *India Minto and Morely 1905-1910* (London: Macmillan), 1934.

Coupland, R., *The Indian Problem Part II* (New York: Oxford University Press), 1944.

Cunning John (ed.), *Political India 1832-1932* (London: Oxford University Press), 1932.

Damodar P. Singhal, *Pakistan* (New Jersey: Prentice Hall), 1972.

Dar, B.A., *Religious Thoughts of Syed Ahmed Khan* (Lahore: Institute of Islamic Culture), 1961.

Das, Durga, *India from Curzon to Nehru and After* (New York: John Doby), 1970.

Datta, S. K. and Rajiv Sharma, *Pakistan from Jinnah to Jehad* (New Delhi: UBSPD), 2002.

De Amalendu, *Roots of Separatism in the Nineteenth Century Bengal* (Calcutta: Maya Prakashan), 1974.

De Amalendu, *Islam in Modern India* (Calcutta: Maya Prakashan), 1982.

Dodwell, H.H. (ed.), *The Cambridge History of the British Empire*, Vol. 5 (London: Cambridge University Press), 1932.

Dutt, R. Palme, *India Today and Tomorrow* (London: Lawrence and Wishart), 1955.

Dwarkadas, Kanji, *India's Fight for Freedom: An Eye Witness Story, 1913-37* (Bombay: Popular Prakashan), 1960.

Embree, Ainslie T., *Imaging India: Essays on Indian History* (London: Oxford University Press), 1989.

Escott, T.H.S. (ed.), *The Pillars of the Empire* (London: Chapman & Hall), 1879.

Faruqi, Zakir Hussain, *Muslim League Kiyyum?* (Bombay: Maktaha-Sultani), 1947.

Gaba, K. L., *Inside Pakistan* (Delhi: Raj Kamal Publications), 1948.

Gandhi, M.K., *An Autobiography or The Story of My Experiments With Truth* (Ahmedabad: Navajivan Publishing House), 1983.

Gandhi, M.K., *Hind Swaraj* (Ahmedabad: Navajivan Publishing House), 1982.

Gopal, S., *Selected Works of Jawaharlal Nehru*, Vol. I (New Delhi: Orient Longman), 1972.

Graham, G.F.I., *The Life and Work of Sir Syed Ahmed Khan* (London: Oxford University Press), 1974.

Gunther, John, *Inside Asia* (New York: Hamilton), 1938.

Hali, Altaf Hussain, *Hayat-i-Jawed* (Delhi; Idarah-i-Adabiyat-i-Delhi), 1979.

Hamid, Abdul, *Muslim Separatism in India* (Lahore: OUP), 1967.

Hamid, Shahid, *Disastrous Twilight* (Leo-Cooper: Oxford University Press), 1986.

Hassan, Javed, *India: A Study in Profile* (Rawalpindi: Army Book Service), 1990.

Hasan, S.S., *Plain Mr. Jinnah: Selections from Quaid-e-Azam correspondence relating mainly to personal matters* (Karachi: Royal Book Company), 1976.

Hedayatullah, Mohammad, *Sayyid Ahmad Khan: A Study of the Religious Reform of Movement of Sayyid Ahmad Khan of Rae Bareli* (Lahore: Ashraf), 1970.

Hudson, H.V., *The Great Divide* (Karachi: Oxford University Press), 1969.

Hussain, Azim, *Fazl-i-Husain* (Bombay: Longmans), 1946.

Iqbal Afzal (ed.), *Select Writings and Speeches of Maulana Mohamed Ali* (Lahore: Ashsaf), 1944.

Ikram, S.M., *Modern Muslim India and the Birth of Pakistan* (Lahore: S. M. Ikram), 1965.

Jain, M.S,. *The Aligarh Movement: Its Origin and Development 1858-1906* (Agra: Sri Ram Mehra), 1965.

Jayakar, M.R., *The Story of My Life*, Vol. II (Bombay: Asia Publishing House), 1959.

Jawed, Ajeet, *Secular and Nationalist Jinnah* (New Delhi: Kitab Publishing House), 1998.

Jinnah, Fatima, *My Brother* (Karachi: Qaid-e-Azam Academy), 1987.

Jinnah, M. A., *History of the Origin of Fourteen Points* (Bombay: n.d), (Australia: Flinders University).

Joachim, Alva, *Leaders of India* (Bombay: Thacker and Company), 1943.

Kanji, Dwarkadas, *Ten Years to Freedom* (Bombay: Popular Prakashan), 1968.

Karunakaran, *Indian Political Thought 1832-1921* (New Delhi: Peacock), 1976.

Khaliquzzaman, Chaudhri, *Pathway to Pakistan* (Lahore: Pakistan Longman), 1961.

Khan, Sir Syed Ahmed, *Asbab-i-Baghavat-i-Hind* (Agra: Matba-i-Mufidi), 1859.

Khan, Sir Syed Ahmed, *Khutbat-i-Ahmadiya* (Aligarh: Institute Press), 1983.

Khan, Sir Syed Ahmed, *Sirat-i-Faridiyah* (Agra: Matba-i-Mufidi), 1886 (Translation by Chr. Schackle).

Khan, Sir Syed Ahmed, *al-Tahrir fi usul al-tafsir* (Agra: Mufid-i-am Press), 1892.

Khan, Sir Syed Ahmed, *Tusanif-i-Ahmadiyah* (Aligarh: Institute Press), 1883.

Khan, Wali, *Facts are Facts – The Untold Story of Partition* (New Delhi: Vikas Publications), 1987.

Khurshid, K.H., *Memories of Jinnah* (Karachi: Oxford University Press), 1990.

Lal Bahadur, *The Muslim League, Its History, Activities and Achievements* (Agra: Agra Book Stores), 1954, p. 23.

Lentizion, Nehemia (ed.), *Conversion to Islam* (New York: Holmes and Meir), 1979.

Letters of Iqbal to Jinnah, published by Muhammad Ashraf quoted in Rafiq Zakaria, The Man Who Divided Pakistan (Mumbai: Popular Prakashan), 2002.

Malik, Hafeez, *Muslim Nationalism in India and Pakistan* (Washington D.C: Public Affairs Press), 1963.

Malik, Hafeez (ed.), *Pakistan Founders' Aspirations and To-days Realities* (New York: Oxford University Press), 2001.

Mansrgh, Nicholas, E.W.R. Lumby and Penderel Moon, *The Transfer of Power 1942-47* (London; Her Majesty Stationery Office), 1970-83.

Masani, R.P., *Dadabhai Naoroji* (New Delhi: Publications Division, Ministry of Information and Broadcasting, Government of India), 1960.

Mazumdar, A.K., *Advent of Independence* (Bombay: Bharatiya Vidya Bhawan), 1963.

Majumdar, B.B. *Indian Political Association and Reforms of Legislatures (1818-1917)* (Calcutta: Minerva), 1945.

Mazumdar, R. C.; Rayachaudhary, H.C. & Dutta, Kali Kumar, *An Advanced History of India* (Madras: Macmillan), 1963.

McGrath, Allen, *The Destruction of Democracy in Pakistan* (Karachi: Oxford University Press), 1972.

Menon, V.P., *Transfer of Power*, Vol. VIII (New Delhi: Orient & Longman), 1968.

Merriam, Allen Hayes, *Gandhi Vs Jinnah—The Debate Over the Pakistan of India* (Calcutta: Minerva), 1980.

Mirza, Humanyun, *From Plassey to Pakistan* (New York: University Press of America), 1999.

Mody, Hormi, *Pherozeshah Mehta* (New Delhi: Publications Division, Ministry of Information and Broadcasting, Government of India), 1963.

Mohan, Sulakshana, *Pakistan Under Musharraf* (New Delhi: Indian Publishers), 1999.

Moon, Penderel, *Divide and Quit* (London: Chatto & Windus), 1964.

Morley, John Viscount, *Recollections*, Vol. II (London: Macmillan), 1918.

Morrison, Theodore, *The History of the Mohammedan Oriental College, Aligarh, from its Foundation to the Year 1903* (Aligarh: Institute Press), 1904.

Mustafa, Zubeida (ed.), *The South Asian Century: 1900-1999* (London: Oxford University Press), 2000.

Naidu, Sarojini (ed.), *Mohammad Ali Jinnah, An Ambassador of Unity; His Speeches and Writings* (Madras: Ganesh), 1918.

Nanda, B. R., *Gandhi, Pan-Islamism, Imperialism and Nationalism in India* (Bombay: Oxford University Press), 1989.

Nehru, Jawaharlal, *An Autobiography* (London: The Bodley Head), 1937.

Page, D., *Prelude to Pakistan* (Delhi: Oxford University Press), 1982.

Panipati, M. Ismail, *Maqalat-i-Sir Sayyid* (Lahore: Majlis-i-taraqqi-i-adab), 1972.

Prashad, Rajendra, *India Divided* (Bombay: Kitabs), 1947.

Pirzada, Syed Sharifuddin, *Quaid-e-Azam Jinnah's Correspondence* (New Delhi: Metropolitan Book Company), 1981.

Pirzada, S. S. (ed.), *Foundations of Pakistan, All India Muslim League Documents 1906-1947* (New Delhi: Metropolitan Book Company), 1982.

Pirzada, Syed Sharifuddin, *Some Aspects of Qaid-e-Azam's Life* (Islamabad: National Commission on Historical and Cultural Research), 1978.

Pirzada, S.S. (ed.), *The Collected Works of Quaid-e-Azam Mohammad Ali Jinnah*, Vol. I (Karachi: East West Publishing), 1969.

Radhakrishnan, S. (ed.), *Mahatma Gandhi* (London: George Allen), 1949.

Rajendra Prasad, *India Divided* (Bombay: Hind Kitabs), 1946.

Ralhan, O. P. (ed.), *Hindu Mahasabha*, Vol. II (New Delhi: Anmol), 1997.

Ramani, Hashoo Kewal, *Pakistan X-Rayed* (Delhi: New Age Publication), 1955.

Ram Gopal, *Indian Muslim* (Bombay: Asia Publishing House), 1959.

Rawlinson, H.G., *The British Achievements in India* (London: William Hodge), 1948.

Resolutions of the All India Muslim League from March 1941 to April 1942 (Delhi: All India Muslim League).

Robinson, F., *Separation Among Muslims* (Cambridge: Cambridge University Press), 1974.

Roy, M.N., *Men I Met* (New Delhi: Lalvani Publications), 1968.

Sahni, J.N., *The Lid Off* (Bombay: Allied Publishers), 1971.

Sarojini, *Speeches and Writings* (Madras: G.A. Natesan), 1945.

Sayeed, K.B., *Pakistan: The Formative Phase 1857-1948* (London: Oxford University Press), 1968.

Sayed, Khalid B., *Pakistan The Formation Phase* (London: Oxford University Press), 1968.

Sayed, Zaifullah and Samuel Baid, *Pakistan: An End Without a Beginning* (Delhi: Lancer International).

Sayed, K.B., *Pakistan: The Formative Phase 1857-1948* (London: Oxford University Press), 1968.

Sayid, M.H., *The Sound of Fury: A Political Study of Mohammad Ali Jinnah* (New Delhi: Akbar Publishing House), 1983.

Spear, Percival, *India Pakistan and the West* (London: Oxford University Press), 1958.

Sitaramayya, B. Pattabhi *The History of Indian National Congress, Vol. I, 1885-1935* (Bombay: Padma Publications), 1946.

Seervai, H.M., *Partition of India – Legend and Reality* (Bombay: Emmenem Publishers), 1989.

Sharma, Jai Narain, "Irreligious Jinnah Wanted A Religious Pak", *The Tribune*, Chandigarh, 6 July 1997.

Sharma, Jai Narain, *Power, Politics and Corruption: A Gandhian Solution* (New Delhi: Deep and Deep), 2004.

Sharma, M.S.M., *Peeps Into Pakistan* (Patna: Pustak Bhandar), 1954.

Sharma, Rashmi (ed.), *Sonia Versus Vajpayee* (New Delhi: Deep and Deep), 2004.

Sharma, T.L., *Hindu Muslim Relations, 1913-1925* (Delhi: B. R. Publishing Corporation), 1987.

Sharif, Al-Mujahid, *Qaide-e-Azam* (Delhi: Low Price Publications), 1993.

Sherwani, Latif Ahmad, *Pakistan Resolution to Pakistan* (Delhi: Daya Publishing House), 1985.

Sikander Hayat, *Pakistan Resolution Revisited* (Islamabad: National Institute of Historical and Cultural Research), 1999.

Singh, Anita Inder, *The Origin of the Partition of India 1936-47* (Bombay: Oxford University Press), 1987.

Sri Prakash, *Pakistan: Birth and Early Years* (Delhi: Meenakshi Prakashan), 1965.

Sitaramayya, Pattabhi, *History of Indian National Congress* (Delhi: S. Chand & Co.), 1969.

Smith, W.C., *Modern Islam in India* (London: V. Golanez), 1946.

Sri Prakash, Pakistan: Birth and Early Days (New Delhi: Meenakshi Publications), 1956.

Suda, J.P., Main Currents of Social and Political Thought in India, Vol. III (Meerut: K. Nath & Co.), 1973.

Symonds, Richard, *Making of Pakistan* (London: Faber and Faber), 1950.

Tara Chand, *History of Freedom Movement in India* (New Delhi: Publications Division, Ministry of Information and Broadcasting, Government of India), 1962.

Tendulkar, D.G., *Mahatma, 8 Vols.* (New Delhi: Publications Division, Ministry of Information and Broadcasting, Government of India), 1958.

Troll, Christian W., *Sayyid Ahmad Khan: A Reinterpretation of Muslim Theology* (New Delhi: Vikas), 1978.

Varma, V.P., *Modern Indian Political Thought* (Agra: Luxmi Narain Agarwal), 1961.

Wells, Ian Bryant, *Jinnah's Early Politics: Ambassador of Hindu Muslim Unity* (Delhi: Permanent Black), 2005.

Wolpert, Stanley, *Jinnah of Pakistan* (New York: Oxford University Press), 1984.

Wolpert, S., *Tilak and Gokhale: Revolution and Reform in the Making of Modern India* (Barkeley: University of California Press), 1961.

Zaidi A.M. and Shaheda Zaidi (eds.), *The Encyclopedia of Indian National Congress, Vol. IV, 1901-1905* (New Delhi: S. Chand & Co.), 1978.

Zakaria, Rafiq, *The Man Who Divided India* (Mumbai: Popular Prakashan), 2002.

Zakaria, Rafiq, *Price of Partition* (Mumbai: Bharatiya Vidya Bhawan), 1998.

Zulfikar, G.H., *Pakistan: As Visualised by Iqbal and Jinnah* (Lahore: Bajm-e-Iqbal), 1989.

Index

ENCYCLOPAEDIA OF EMINENT THINKERS

VOLUME-XXIV: **LOKMANYA BAL GANGADHAR TILAK**

Volumes by the same author

The Political Thought of ***Veer Savarkar***
The Political Thought of ***M.A. Jinnah***
The Political Thought of ***Mohammad Iqbal***
The Political Thought of ***K.B. Hedgewar***
The Political Thought of ***M.S. Golwalkar***
The Political Thought of ***Lokmanya Bal Gangadhar Tilak***
The Political Thought of ***Pandit Deendayal Upadhyaya***
The Political Thought of ***Gopal Krishna Gokhale***
The Political Thought of ***Maulana Abul Kalam Azad***
The Political Thought of ***Sir Syed Ahmed Khan***

About the Author

Dr. Jai Narain Sharma (*b.* 1951) is Professor and Chairman of the Department of Gandhian Studies, Panjab University, Chandigarh. He is also Hon. Director of Gandhi Bhawan; member of Board of Studies, Nagpur University, Nagpur and Mahatma Gandhi Kashi Vidyapith, Varanasi; member of Research Degree Committee of the Department of Political Science, H.P. University, Shimla: General Secretary of Indian Soviety of Gandhian Studies; and member on the Presidium of the Alliance for Sarvodaya. He regularly writes for leading newspapers, and has published more than hundred research papers in professional journals of repute. Dr. Sharma has many books to his credit including *"Gandhi's View of Political Power", "Economics of Defence: A Study of SAARC Countries", "Economic Thought of Mahatma Gandhi", "Human Resource Management", "Alternative Economics: Economics of Mahatma Gandhi and Globalisation", "Power, Politics and Corruption: A Gandhian Solution"* and *"Research Methodology: The Discipline and its Dimensions.*

ENCYCLOPAEDIA OF EMINENT THINKERS

VOLUME-TWENTY FOUR

THE POLITICAL THOUGHT OF LOKMANYA BAL GANGADHAR TILAK

Dr. Jai Narain Sharma
Professor and Chairman
Department of Gandhian Studies
Panjab University
Chandigarh

CONCEPT PUBLISHING COMPANY, NEW DELHI-110 059

Cataloging in Publication Data—DK
Courtesy: D.K. Agencies (P) Ltd. docinfo@dkagencies.com

Encyclopaedia of eminent thinkers.
p. cm. — (Gandhian studies and peace research series ; 11)
Vols. 11- lack series statement.
In Indian context.
Includes bibliographical references.
Includes indexes.
Contents: v. 24. The political thought of Lokmanya Bal Gangadhar Tilak / Jai Narain Sharma.
ISBN 13: 9788180695841
ISBN 10: 8180695840

1. Statesmen—India. 2. Political science—India. 3. India—Politics and government. I. Sharma, Jai Narain, 1951- II. Pasricha, ashu, 1967- III. Series: Gandhian studies and peace research series ; 11.

DDC 954.035 22

ISBN -13: 978-81-7022-684-0 (Series)
ISBN -10: 81-7022-684-8 (Series)
ISBN -13: 978-81-8069-584-1 (Vol. XXIV)
ISBN -10: 81-8069-584-0 (Vol. XXIV)

First Published 2009

Published and Printed by
Ashok Kumar Mittal
Concept Publishing Company
A/15-16, Commercial Block, Mohan Garden
New Delhi-110059 (India)

Phones: 25351460, 25351794
Fax: 091-11-25357103
E-mail: publishing@conceptpub.com

DEDICATED
TO
THE SACRED MEMORY
OF MY
MENTOR
(Late) SHRI INDERJEET SHARMA
(AMBALA CITY)

PREFACE

The standard of greatness which our country has set to its leaders is high indeed, but Bal Gangadhar Tilak has surpassed it, and stands first amongst his peers. There have been not a few personages whose memory our people cherish with respect, but there is hardly any other personality than that of Tilak who has touched the deep-seated and most responsive chord of the hearts of the people. There are always to be found persons who, despaired of winning the esteem of the people seek to disparage the benefactors of the public. They call them "popularity hunters"; but it is a language of spleen, malice, despair and ingratitude. Popularity, and especially abiding popularity, is neither cheap nor a chance. It comes only after the crucial test of honest, sustained and benevolent efforts. Therein lies the secret of Tilak's hold over the people. He loved his people, trusted his people, helped his people and actually suffered for his people. There is no sacrifice which he would not have made for them, and no assistance which he would not have rendered to further their cause. By espousing the popular cause he had nothing to gain, but everything to lose. For the sake of the people, however, he risked everything—his prospects, wealth, health, liberty and life. Yet none of Tilak's acts was done without the exercise of prudence and foresight; for providence had blessed him with every manly virtue of which we all may be proud of. He had a subtle intelligence, spotless private character, splendid public spirit and above all superb courage without which no merit can stand or endure. People have long known that during the protracted, arduous struggle which Tilak waged, every danger that he braved and every hardship that he suffered was for their sake. To him it was a matter of duty which expected no reward.

What was the reason for his hold upon his countrymen? I think the answer is simple. His patriotism was a passion with him. He knew no religion but love of his country. He was a born democrat. He had an iron will which he used for his country. His life was an open book. His tastes were simple. His private life was spotlessly clean. He had dedicated his wonderful talents to his country. No man preached the gospel of the *Swaraj* with the consistency and the insistence of Lokmanya. His countrymen, therefore, implicitly believed in him. His courage never failed him. His optimism was irrepressible. He had hoped to see *Swaraj* fully established during his life time. If he failed, it was not his fault. He certainly brought it nearer by many years.

Lokmanya Tilak, one of India's greatest nationalist leaders, is also one of the India's most misunderstood prophets. His life and work constitute a great heritage, yet the meaning of his message has often been obscured. He has been called a disciple of expedience, meaning he was a political realist, while at the same time his philosophy was based on the highest idealism. He has been called a communalist, while actually he was the one who first taught the need for overcoming communal disagreements in the name of national unity. He has been called a provincialist, while actually he first retaught the meaning of love of country. He has been called a revolutionary, which is true, provided it is remembered he was a constructive revolutionary, far more interested in building than tearing down. He has been called an extremist, yet he was a moderating force. He has been censured for sacrificing everything for the cause, but he was always the first to sacrifice himself. And he was the first, and only, Lokmanya of India. His message, his political philosophy, must not only be remembered but also clearly understood in India, and also, because it has a world significance, in the world, else we shall be the poorer for not using the legacy he has left behind.

My work has benefited from the advice and suggestions of Professor R.N. Pal, former Pro-Vice Chancellor, Panjab University; Patiala; Dr. K.S. Bharti, Head, Department of Gandhian Thought, Nagpur University, Nagpur; Dr. A.D. Mishra, Deputy Director, National Gandhi Museum, New Delhi; Dr. R.P Diwedi, Head,

Department of Gandhian Thought, Mahatma Gandhi Kashi Vidyapith, Varanasi; Professor B.R. Duggar and Dr. Anil Dhar, Jain Vishwabharati Institute, Deemed University, Ladnun; Professor Raj Singh, Department of Sociology, H.A.U., Hissar; Professor Rakesh Dutta and Dr. (Ms) Meena Dutta, Department of Defence and Strategic Analysis, Panjab University, Chandigarh.

I am deeply indebted to my colleagues in the department—Dr. M.L. Sharma and Dr. Ashu Pasricha—who were good enough to read through a draft of the book and from whose many penetrating criticisms and constructive suggestions I have benefited more than I can say.

There are many other teacher colleagues and students who have contributed in so many ways and I express my thanks to them.

To my wife Rashmi, I owe the deepest debt for her emotional support, her unfailing encouragement and her indispensable contribution towards providing the environment in which I could complete this work.

Thanks are also due to my publisher Shri Ashok Kumar Mittal for the keen interest he has shown in this project.

Chandigarh **JAI NARAIN SHARMA**

Encyclopaedia of Eminent Thinkers Series

Vol. I. The Political Thought of Mahatma Gandhi/ *K.S. Bharti*
Vol. II. The Political Thought of Nehru/ *K.S. Bharti*
Vol. III. The Political Thought of Rabindra Nath Tagore/ *K.S. Bharti*
Vol. IV. The Political Thought of Radhakrishnan/ *K.S. Bharti*
Vol. V. The Political Thought of Vinoba/ *K.S. Bharti*
Vol. VI. The Political Thought of Aurobindo/ *K.S. Bharti*
Vol. VII. The Political Thought of Jayaprakash Narayan/ *K.S. Bharti*
Vol. VIII. The Political Thought of Vivekananda/ *K.S. Bharti*
Vol. IX. The Political Thought of Ambedkar/ *K.S. Bharti*
Vol. X. The Political Thought of M.N. Roy/ *K.S. Bharti*
Vol. XI. The Political Thought of Dadabhai Naoroji/ *Ashu Pasricha*
Vol. XII. The Political Thought of Veer Savarkar/ *Jai Narain Sharma*
Vol. XIII. The Political Thought of M.A. Jinnah/ *Jai Narain Sharma*
Vol. XIV. The Political Thought of Tej Bahadur Sapru/ *Ashu Pasricha*
Vol. XV. The Political Thought of C. Rajagopalachari/ *Ashu Pasricha*
Vol. XVI. The Political Thought of Subhas Chandra Bose/ *Ashu Pasricha*
Vol. XVII. The Political Thought of Mohammad Iqbal/ *Jai Narain Sharma*
Vol. XVIII. The Political Thought of K.B. Hedgewar/ *Jai Narain Sharma*
Vol. XIX. The Political Thought of Bhagat Singh/ *Ashu Pasricha*
Vol. XX. The Political Thought of M.S. Golwalkar/ *Jai Narain Sharma*
Vol. XXI. The Political Thought of Sir Syed Ahmed Khan/ *Jai Narain Sharma*
Vol. XXII. The Political Thought of Mahadev Govind Ranade/ *Ashu Pasricha*
Vol. XXIII. The Political Thought of Pandit Deendayal Upadhyaya/ *Jai Narain Sharma*
Vol. XXIV. The Political Thought of Lokmanya Bal Gangadhar Tilak/ *Jai Narain Sharma*
Vol. XXV. The Political Thought of Annie Besant/ *Ashu Pasricha*

Forthcoming

The Political Thought of C.R. Das/ *Ashu Pasricha*
The Political Thought of Gopal Krishna Gokhale/ *Jai Narain Sharma*
The Political Thought of Lala Lajpat Rai/ *Ashu Pasricha*
The Political Thought of Maulana Abul Kalam Azad/ *Jai Narain Sharma*
The Political Thought of Sir Pherozeshah Mehta/ *Ashu Pasricha*

CONTENTS

1

LIFE AND ACTIVITIES

Ratnagiri literally means a "mountain of jewels", on the west coast of India, where Bal Gangadhar Tilak was born on July 23, 1856. Like many other such place names, this one also belies itself because Ratnagiri, and the Konkan to which it belongs form one of the poorest and most backward regions in the whole country. The appellation, however, is redeemed by a number of eminent sons to whom Ratnagiri has given birth in the last 300 years. And among them none else in modern times was greater—a more precious jewel—than Tilak.

Nothing in the circumstances of his birth pointed to his future eminence. The modest house where he was born is preserved as a national monument. His family held the hereditary office of Khot of the village of Chikhalgaon, which gave it some prestige but a bare pittance. Tilak's father was a school-master who rose to become an inspector of primary schools. Tilak imbibed the love of Sanskrit and mathematics from his father who passed away when he was sixteen, his mother having died six years earlier. In keeping with the practice of those days, Tilak was married at 16, a few months before his father's death, to Tapi of the Bal family in a neighbouring village.

It was an orthodox family in which the young Tilak was brought up with its rigid adherence to ritual, observance of the time-honoured proprieties and devotion to learning. His father's transfer to Poona when Tilak was 10 was a lucky accident, as it facilitated his schooling under the best of teachers. Tilak matriculated in his sixteenth year and joined the Deccan College as a resident student where he spent the five happiest and most carefree years of his life. The Deccan

College then boasted of renowned professors like Wordsworth, Shoot and Chhatre, but Tilak relied for his education more on his independent and extensive reading than on their lectures and notes. Among his fellow-students were many who rose to eminence, such as M.B. Chaubal, N.G. Chandavarkar, G.S. Khaparde, R.N. Mudholkar and D.A. Khare. The closest friendship was formed between Tilak and G.G. Agarkar, a friendship which was to develop later into bitter antagonism in public life.

Tilak could hardly be called a model student. He was eclectic in his scholastic pursuits and was never bound by the academic curriculum. In fact, he devoted the first year of college life entirely to physical culture. This led to his failure in the annual examination but, in the meantime, it had transformed the weakling that he was when he entered college into a well-built and robust youth. Like all high spirited young men, he loved pranks and there are many tales of practical jokes played by him upon his friends. He also cultivated a love for controversy and a dialectical skill which were to earn him the nickname "Mr. Blunt" and to serve him well in later life. Even in those carefree days, the thoughts of political subjection and the economic plight of their country assailed these young men. A contemporary record mentions Tilak asking his friends "to look back to the year 1632 and forward to 1930". Many were the nights that Tilak and Agarkar spent together arguing what they would do after graduation, arguments which yielded early and rich harvest.[1]

Tilak took his B.A. degree in 1877 with first class in mathematics and two years later he became a Bachelor of Laws. He did not succeed, however, in qualifying as an M.A. despite two attempts. Even before he left the portals of his *Alma Mater,* he had charted the course of his life:

"It was in July or August 1879, when I was living at the Deccan College studying for the LL.B. examination, that Mr. Agarkar and myself first discussed the importance and practicability of establishing private schools on the model of the missionary institutions. There was no difference of opinion as to the need for native enterprise in education, but the question was how to make it successful. Self-sacrifice was evidently the only means for men like us. After many prolonged discussions the conclusion at which

we arrived was that, if we applied ourselves to the task with the determination of carrying out our idea at any sacrifice, it was not an impossibility."[2]

For a young man with a first-class degree to take a vow of self-sacrifice and dedication to public service was unheard of in 1879. Many must have been the old heads which shook in disapproval of Tilak's decision and even his fellow graduates, who lost no time in securing well-paid jobs, must have pitied Tilak for his impractical outlook. Government service was then the be-all and end-all of educated men and even those who were inspired with the zeal of public service like Mahadev Govind Ranade made it a secondary occupation. The bar awaited those who desired to remain independent and it was then considered the royal road to fortune. Legal luminaries like Pherozeshah Mehta and Vishwanath Narayan Mandlik served as beacons to many young men of the 'eighties'.

What were the influences which prevailed on Tilak to strike a new path of selfless and patriotic endeavour? In 1879 the country had recovered from the stunning impact of the 1857 revolt. Indeed, in 1878 Wasudev Balvant Phadke had raised the standard of another armed uprising in Maharashtra. An unprecedented famine held the country in its grip and exacted a heavy toll of life. The early glamour of British rule had begun to vanish. In 1876 Dadabhai Naoroji read a paper under the auspices of the Bombay branch of the East India Association on "The Growing Impoverishment of India", which was later to develop into that statistical masterpiece *Poverty and Un-British Rule in India.*[3]

Under the direction of Ranade the Sarvajanik Sabha, which was established in Poona in 1870, was ventilating public grievances in a methodical and constructive manner and infusing a new spirit in public life. It did pioneering work in many fields such as investigating agrarian conditions and encouraging the use of *swadeshi* goods. In 1874, it sent a memorial to the British Parliament asking for representation for India on that body. And the next year it was vigorous in defending Mulharrao Gaekwar, the ruler of Baroda, who was accused of poisoning the British Resident and deposed. This incident created great concern in Maharashtra.

All these developments must have produced a deep impression on the minds of the young men who were on the threshold of their career. They must have also come under the spell of Vishnushastri Chiplunkar's *Nibandh-Mala,* which was preaching a revivalist philosophy in a trenchant literary style and with great polemical vigour.[4] Vishnushastri was an ardent admirer of English education which he called "the milk of a tigress". But this did not prevent him from defending Indian culture and traditions, from the onslaught of the Christian missionaries or from deriding the British claim that they had come here only for our good.

There is a belief that Vishnushastri Chiplunkar was mainly responsible for influencing Tilak and Agarkar to join hands with him in starting the New English School, but it is not borne out by contemporary evidence. The idea seems to have germinated in their own minds, though, of course, the help of an elder and well-established person like Vishnushastri Chiplunkar was to prove valuable in translating it into action. Recalling those days of his youth, Tilak said: "We were men with our brains in a fever heat with the thoughts of the degraded condition of our country and after long cogitation we had formed the opinion that the salvation of our motherland was to be found in education alone."[5]

The pioneering trio inaugurated the New English School on January 1, 1880, a red-letter day in the history of national education, although work actually started the next day. Agarkar, however, took leave of absence for a year to complete his M.A. Chiplunkar and Tilak were soon joined by Mahadev Ballal Namjoshi and later by Vaman Shivaram Apte, whose high academic attainments and reputation as a disciplinarian lent distinction to the school. Within three months the number of students on its rolls rose to 500, justifying the proud assertion of Chiplunkar at the end of the term :

"The New English School is a fully accomplished fact, accomplished in the midst of a thousand difficulties, amidst popular apathy, in utter disregard of despondent opinion, in contemptuous indifference to showers of epithets like mad, hopeless, chimerical and utopian—which are the inevitable lot of everyone who would be so bold as to disturb the dull routine of things."[6]

The school proved such a success that within four years the number of its students crossed the four-figure mark, and it proved a formidable competitor even to the Poona High School conducted by the Government. It established an impressive record at the matriculation examination both in the percentage of passes and the number of scholarships won. The initial unwillingness of its organisers to ask for Government grants imposed a severe strain on them neither; Tilak nor Chiplunkar being able to draw a rupee as salary in the first year. Chiplunkar's premature death on March 17, 1882, robbed the school of his guidance. How successfully the institution had established itself by then may be seen from the testimony given to it by Dr. W. W. Hunter, Chairman of the Education Commission, when he visited the school in September 1882:

"This institution, the work of some zealous, able and intelligent educated youths actuated by ideas of self-support and self-dependence, though not receiving any aid from the Government, can rival and compete with success not only with the Government High Schools of this country, but may compare favourably with the schools of other countries too."[7]

The school did not fully absorb the ebullient energies of its founders and within a few months of its opening they were searching for fresh fields and pastures new of public service. They were not long in realising that there could be no more powerful instrument of national regeneration than newspapers. The country's press was then dominated by Anglo-Indian journals which could be best described as jackals of British imperialism. The national newspapers were struggling for existence and chafed under the Vernacular Press Act of 1878. Poona had half a dozen journals, including an English weekly, but none of them was distinguished either for character or for contents.

It did not take the young crusaders long to decide to start simultaneously two weeklies, the *Mahratta* in English and the *Kesari* in Marathi, from the beginning of the next year (1881), thus marking a break with the current fashion of publishing bilingual journals. While the *Mahrana* kept in view "the more advanced portion of the community", the *Kesari* was intended to be an organ of the masses. The prospectus of the *Kesari* stated: "We are determined

to discuss every subject in an impartial manner and in the light of what we think to be true. There is undoubtedly a growing tendency towards flattery under the British-rule, and all honest people would admit that this tendency is undesirable and detrimental to the interests of the people. The articles in the proposed newspaper will be in keeping with the name given to it *(Kesari* meaning lion)."[8]

Although the title *Kesari* was suggested by Tilak and the two words have since become synonymous in the Marathi language, it was Agarkar who took charge of that paper, while Tilak was responsible for the *Mahratta.* There was no legal compulsion then for the imprint of the editor's name, and the two journals remained the joint responsibility of their founders and, after the formation in 1885 of the Deccan Education Society, of its members in their individual capacity. Tilak did not concern himself with the running of the Kesari except for topics like law and religion assigned to him.

Like the New English School, the two journals proved an instantaneous success, the *Kesari* becoming the largest circulated Indian language newspaper within two years and *the Mahratta* gaining a reputation as the mouthpiece of educated opinion in Western India. Both were produced in a vigorous and pungent style, and every public issue was grist to their mill. In the words of Prof. P. M. Limaye: "They were always ready to strike at any abuse however well-established and any injustice however strongly entrenched. It was because they took to championing their cause with more enthusiasm than caution that Agarkar and Tilak had to pass through their first ordeal by fire."[9]

Opinion in Maharashtra was agitated by the plight of the minor Maharaja of Kolhapur. The Maharaja's adoptive mother was alleged to be intriguing to deny him the *gaddi* on the ground of his insanity and the State's Diwan, M.V. Barve, was said to have aided and abetted her and the British guardians of the Maharaja. Apart from writing leading articles to expose the alleged plot, both the *Kesari* and the *Mahratta* published letters purporting to be written by Barve which implicated him in a foul conspiracy. Other journals like the *Dnyanprakash* also published these letters and the scandal was freely ventilated on the platform by influential persons.

Moral certainly, however, does not amount to legal validity, and in an omnibus suit for criminal defamation filed by Barve against several papers and persons, the letters were declared to be forgeries. Some of the defendants got off with an apology, but it could not save Agarkar and Tilak who were sentenced to four months' imprisonment on July 17, 1882. The young and courageous editors had their initiation of "Her Majesty's guest-house", to which Tilak was to return more than once for longer stays. He lost 24 lbs. in weight during his imprisonment but gained a measure of popular respect for his spirited and selfless championship of the helpless Maharaja, who subsequently died in suspicious circumstances. Hundreds of people gathered at the portals of the jail to welcome Tilak and Agarkar on their release. The latter has left a vivid account of their life in prison which, though it did not prove a hermitage, steeled their resolve to serve their country on the lines they had already chalked out.

The death of Vishnushastri Chiplunkar and the imprisonment of Tilak and Agarkar did not affect the New English School. When they resumed work on October 12, 1882, they found to their great relief that, far from diminishing the popularity of the institution, their suffering, in a public cause had actually helped to increase it. The Kesari and the *Mahratta* were also doing well and the young men set to work with renewed vigour. Their horizons had widened and their differences over social reform occasionally erupted in the columns of the journals, but the bonds of their friendship remained firm.

Their immediate concern was to put the school on a sound basis and to establish an arts college as its logical extension. The idea of founding an educational society on missionary lines for that purpose was in their mind from the very beginning, but it received the first public expression in the school's annual report for 1883. It notes: "We have undertaken this work of popular education with the firmest conviction and belief that, of all agents of human civilisation, education is the only one that brings about material, moral and religious regeneration of fallen countries and raises them up to the level of the most advanced nations by slow and peaceful revolution."[10]

A positive step was taken towards that end on October 24, 1884, with a meeting of sympathisers for forming a society and electing a council of trustees. Among those who attended were Mahadev Govind Iftanade, Sir William Wedderburn, a founder of the Indian National Congress, Dr. R.G. Bhandarkar, Prof. Wordsworth and K.T. Telang. The ability and zeal of the young men had earned not only warm public approbation but also the active sympathy of the Government.

The Deccan Education Society was thus born under the happiest auspices. Among its patrons were the Viceroy, the Marquis of Ripon, and the Governor of Bombay, Sir James Fergusson. Their example was followed by a number of Princes, and before the end of the year donations worth Rs. 75,000 were promised for the building fund of the college. It was named after Sir James Fergusson and opened on January 2, 1885, in the Gadre Wada, Poona.

Like a giant banyan tree, the Deccan Education Society has thrown its branches all over Maharashtra during the last 75 years. It remains the premier institution of its type conducting a number of schools, and colleges, and its pioneering example has been widely copied. Even the Arya Samaj drew inspiration from the Deccan Education Society, according to the testimony of Lala Lajpat Rai.

The success of the Fergusson College was assured although its initial recognition by the University of Bombay covered only the first academic year. Its original life-members made a brilliant team of professors. V.S. Apte, the first principal, taught Sanskrit, Tilak mathematics, G.G. Agarkar history and logic, V.B. Kelkar English and M.S. Gole physics. Fired by the same spirit of patriotic self-sacrifice other young men were not slow in joining them, the most notable being Gopal Krishna Gokhale.

Although the average student found it difficult to follow Tilak's lectures, G.S. Sardesai, the famous historian, who belonged to the first batch of Fergussonians, talks highly of him as a teacher :

"While teaching permutations and combinations, Tilak gave illustrations from everyday life and made the subject very interesting. We were very much impressed with his minute observations. He was never reluctant to solve the difficulties of students. After the college was over, on his way home, be walked in the company of

students and had discussions with them on many subjects. He could easily identify himself with the audience while speaking on any subject. We never saw him lose his temper. There was never any light-heartedness in his class."[11]

So well did the Fergusson College progress and such favourable impression did the D.E. Society make on the public and the Government that the latter proposed in 1887 that the Society take over the management of the Deccan College run by the Government and amalgamate it with the Fergusson College. This must have no doubt flattered the life-members of the Society, who would have been favourably inclined towards the offer, had it not been for the fantastic conditions attached to it, one among them being that two European professors should be retained on the staff on their existing salaries. Its rejection resulted in the petulant discontinuation of the annual grant-in-aid of Rs. 3,000 by the Government of Bombay. This was sought to be justified on the ground that "money in Poona is being wasted which is urgently required for primary, secondary and technical schools throughout the country".[12]

While the College and the Society were thus making commendable progress, ominous clouds began to appear on the horizon in the shape of differences among the life-members. Mention had already been made of the divergence between Tilak and Agarkar on the issue of social reform. What really began to irk Tilak more and more was the increasing tendency of his colleagues to supplement their income from other sources. This, in his view, transgressed their Jesuitical pledge and harmed the interests of the institution. As his protests against the alleged departure of his colleagues from the vow of self-denial became strident, the gulf among the life-members began to widen perceptibly.

There was not the least doubt that not a few life-members were devoting themselves to extra-mural work. The writing of textbooks was a weakness shared by many professors then as it is now. There was also a clamour for an increment in their emoluments which were originally fixed at Rs. 75 per month and an insurance policy of Rs. 3,000.Tilak derided and attacked this tendency:

"Once in easy circumstances the patriotic position of 1881-83 came to be talked of with scorn.... We longed for more, excusing

ourselves on the grounds of distrust in the life policy or growing, wants of the family. The cry was catching as it must necessarily do and more so in the case of life-members who were admitted later. These new members had but a dim perception of why and how the sacrifice principle was adopted by us. I only wonder how in the face of these facts we still liked to be called Jesuits. I have tried to gauge the strength of the Jesuitical principle, and I am sorry to say that I have found it in the minority."[13]

It was a minority of only one–no other member sharing Tilak's fanatical insistence on rectitude. It may be, as his enemies said then, that Tilak sought to put himself on a pedestal of probity, only to put his colleagues in the wrong. Agarkar especially who had a bitter argument with Tilak over the sharing of the Holkar grant in 1888, was fed up wilh Tilak's constant references to Jesuitical principles and practices and openly disparaged them:

"It is more than doubtful whether the Jesuitical organisation has done more good than harm to civilisation and the world and, therefore, nobody can imitate its discipline without making important modifications in it. For no Jesuit is a married man; no Jesuit has private property nor is he allowed to make any; the Jesuits have a common aim, and they lodge in a common house. Above all, they are a religious body in which free thought is strictly forbidden."[14] It is thus no surprise that the Society's records for the years 1886 to 1889 are "full of skirmishes, running fights and pitched battles between these two comrades-in-arms". Whatever might be the justification of Tilak's scruples over his colleagues earning money elsewhere, he undoubtedly carried them too far in objecting even to their undertaking honorary public service. The issue came to a head with Gokhale's desire to accept the secretaryship of the Sarvajanik Sabha, which entailed two or three hours' daily work. Tilak sternly objected "to such diversion of energy", and pointed out that he himself had refused the secretaryship earlier. He drew the analogy of Government's ban on its servants taking up other work.[15]

Not content with this argument in which logic was on his side, though his own practice sometimes departed from profession in so far as honorary public service was concerned, Tilak gave gratuitous offence to Gokhale:

"There was still ample scope for Mr. Gokhale's energies in the duties of the professor of English literature in the Fergusson College. If we wished to compete with other colleges, we must at least show that we were not behind in reading and work, as we admittedly were."[16]

A crisis was reached when Gokhale did accept the secretaryship of the Sarvajanik Sabha. Tilak's efforts to reopen the question only brought him a vote of censure from the Society's council. He sent in his resignation on October 14, 1890, which became effective five months later. It was sorrow rather than anger which overwhelmed Tilak when the actual moment of parting arrived. The concluding words of his 15,000-word letter of resignation end on a note of pathos :

"By constantly insisting on the settlement of outside work and salary I have alienated the sympathies of almost everyone and rendered myself extremely unpleasant—so much so that I am regarded almost as an obstacle in the way of others, and every fault of mine, however trifling, is at once caught hold of and magnified to an incredible extent.

"I am giving up my life's ideal, but the thought that by separating myself from it I shall serve it best is my consolation. While I have been with you, I have not spared myself in serving the interests of the institution and I shall not imperil its existence by continuing longer with you... I bid you, my dear colleagues, good-bye with my heart burdened with a load of sorrow, but in the hope that by severing myself from you, I may perhaps help you in preserving harmony, so very essential to the welfare of our institution. It is for the sake of that harmony that I am making this sacrifice of myself."[17]

Uncharitable critics have suggested that Tilak was constitutionally incapable of working on equal terms with others but such criticism appears churlish, considering that Tilak had spent the ten best years of his youth in the service of the New English School and the Deccan Education Society. This could not have been possible without an accommodating spirit and capacity to pull on with others.

On the other hand, it cannot be denied that he had made himself thoroughly unpopular with his colleagues and had offended not a few of them by his sneezing references to their shortcomings. His

departure was considered a good riddance, and it helped restore the smooth working of the Society.

Tilak found it impossible—or made it impossible for himself—to continue in the Deccan Education Society in 1890. Twenty-five years later, Mahatma Gandhi found it impossible even to enter the Servants of India Society. Gokhale, its founder and first member, had the highest opinion of Gandhi and presumably considered him, as a possible successor. But after his death in 1915, the other members felt distinctly uneasy at the prospect of associating with so unorthodox a person. They were scared by the greatness of Gandhi as the life-members of the Deccan Education Society were repelled by that of Tilak. Mountain peaks may appear inviting and impressive at a distance, but it is no easy task to live in close proximity to them. So it is with great men. While the members of the D.E. Society took five long years to realise this and force the resignation of Tilak, the members of the Servants of India Society were more shrewd and fought shy of admitting Gandhi, who chivalrously put them at ease by withdrawing his application for admission.

In retrospect, both events resulted in the immeasurable good of the nation enabling the two men to strike out their independent paths. The immediate problem before Tilak, however, was to find another source of livelihood which would allow sufficient time to devote himself to public service. For, not even in that hour of disillusionment did the thought of joining Government service or starting legal practice cross his mind. The law class, started in 1889, brought him a modest but regular income. But the ginning factory at Latur in Hyderabad State, which he had purchased in partnership with two friends, hardly proved the profitable investment it was expected to become.

Tilak's resignation from the D.E. Society enabled him to devote more time and attention to the *Kesari* and the *Mahratta.* These newspapers had established a reputation for vigorous journalism, but they continued to be losing concerns for several years.

The years 1890 and 1891 were of vital importance in the career of Tilak. They marked the great divide of his life. He stood midway assessing the past and trying to visualise the future. Ten years as an educationist had only culminated in estrangement with his

colleagues and, perhaps, disillusionment with his early ideals. On the other hand, he had won his spurs as a journalist and had experienced both the hazards and the rewards of public life.

REFERENCES

1. Jog, N.G., *Lokmanya Bal Gangadhar Tilak* (New Delhi: Publications Division, Ministry of Information and Broadcasting, Government of India), 1962, p. 11.
2. *Ibid.*
3. Naoroji, Dadabhai, *Poverty and Un-British Rule in India* (New Delhi: Publications Division, Ministry of Information and Broadcasting, Government of India), 1950.
4. Chiplunkar, Vishnushastri, *Nibandh Mula* (Poona: S.V. Bapat), 1926.
5. Jog, N.G., *Lokmanya Bal Gangadhar Tilak, op. cit.*, p. 13.
6. *Ibid.*, p. 14.
7. Parvate, T.V., *Bal Gangadhar Tilak* (Ahmedabad: Navajivan Publishing House), 1958, pp. 22-23.
8. *Ibid.*
9. Jog, N.G., *Lokmanya Bal Gangadhar Tilak, op. cit.*, p. 16.
10. *Ibid.*, p. 18.
11. *Ibid.*, pp. 19-20.
12. *Ibid.*
13. Keer, Dhananjay, *Lokmanya Tilak* (Bombay: Popular Prakashan), 1969, p. 26.
14. Athalye, D.V., *The Life of Lokmanya Tilak* (Poona: Annasahib Chiploonkar), 1921, p. 17.
15. *Ibid.*, p. 19.
16. Jog, N.G., *Lokmanya Bal Gangadhar Tilak, op. cit.*, p. 22.
17. Parvate, T.V. *Bal Gangadhar Tilak, op. cit.*, p. 48.

2

IDEOLOGY AND PERCEPTION

Tilak started life with a basic comprehension of the classical values of the Indian civilization. He believed in the Aryadharma. As a child he learned the history of free Maharashtra. He studied India's great classics in Sanskrit. He rediscovered for himself the traditions of India's philosophy and absorbed the scientific and realistic approach to problems that was the methodology of that philosophy. From these beginnings he developed a frame of reference by which to judge the great issues of his day. His was obviously different from the frame of reference of the deracinated Westernizing social reformers, primarily because Tilak had not been uprooted from his heritage but rather had become devoted to it. When he began his career as an editor, the three great issues of the day were social reform, the awakening of India, and the beginning of agitation. To understand his position on these vital questions, we must continually keep in mind the frame of reference that afforded him his perspective.

Criticism of Westernized Social Reformism

Tilak believed in the Aryadharma, but he was never a blind follower of orthodoxy. He refused to overlook or to excuse the obvious evil of the atrophied social system which were repellent to the social reformers and instigated them to take action. However, he became the foremost of those in India who opposed the extremist measures of these social reformers. But the very fact that he was educated and that he refrained from joining the reformers indicated him as a

defender of orthodoxy in the eyes of the extremists. Abuse was heaped upon him, he was accused of opposing all progress; he was condemned as a reactionary, as the spokesman for backwardness. Nothing could be farther from the truth. He earnestly hoped to see the evils of the Indian social system removed, the entire system reformed, and to this end he brought forward his own concrete proposals for improving social conditions. He was a staunch advocate of progress. At the same time, he relentlessly fought against the grandiose schemes of the Westernizing reformers. Instead of schemes he wanted concrete programmes for the alleviation of real and pressing needs of the people. His reform work was direct, as in the case of famine relief programme, the textile workers' assistance, the plague prevention work. Tilak was not an armchair reformer, he was a worker with and for the people.

His objection to the social reformism of men like Justice Ranade and his disciple Gopal Krishna Gokhale, Professor Bhandarkar, Byramji Molbari, Agarkar and the others, was twofold. First, without a full appreciation of the values that had been preserved and transmitted by the social system these men were willing to discard virtually everything, to make India almost totally in the image of the West, and to base Indian social forms on the values they had learned from their Western education. To Tilak, it was folly, it was criminal, to banish everything created by India's civilization because Indian values and Indian religion did not coincide with the nineteenth-century European notions of materialism, rationalism and utilitarianism. He knew their obsession was contrary to common sense and good practice. He once wrote:

> "... a number of our educated men began to accept uncritically the materialistic doctrines of the Westerners. Thus we have the pathetic situation of the new generation making on their minds a carbon copy of the gross materialism of the West."[1]

And he went on to remind the social reformers that 'our present downfall is due not to Hindu religion but to the fact that we have absolutely forsaken religion'.[2] Second, since the reformers could not inspire mass popular support for their imitative social reform

programme, they sought to enforce reform through administrative fiat, a rely upon the coercive power of the state of the British Raj, to effect social change. From Tilak's point of view, to remake India in image of the West would mean to destroy her greatness; and to use the force of an alien *raj* to impose any kind of reform would be to make that reform itself immoral.

His first battle was directly with the leaders of the social reformers. He realized that they conceived their schemes for reform from the frame of reference of the Western value system. This frame of reference made them anti-traditionalist and iconoclastic. They were prepared to believe that virtually everything Indian was, by definition, degraded, unprogressive and evil. The cause of this, Tilak believed, was that the Westernized reformers did not understand either the classical ethic or the classical methods of meeting problems, that they operated from a frame of reference which, in effect, produced a blind spot as far as India's way of life was concerned. He wrote:

> "As the works of purely materialistic philosophers on Ethics are principally taught in our colleges, the fundamental principles of the Karma-Yoga, mentioned in the Gita, are not well understood even by learned persons among us, who have had an English education."[3]

He objected that those who did not know the old were preparing to construct the radically new. No civilization could withstand such an all-encompassing attack on all its beliefs and way of life. If they were successful in bringing about such reform, Tilak feared that all the classical values would be lost, that the moral stamina of the people would be undermined, and that the national will would be broken. When national awakening was what was needed, he could not tolerate the possibility of (well-meaning) national suicide. Tilak knew that reforms were necessary, but not in such a way as to destroy the civilization which would be reformed. As Aurobindo Ghose warned:

"Westernized India, a brown ape of Europe, might emerge from the chaos [of conflicting civilizations] keeping some elements only

of her ancient thought to modify, but no longer to shape and govern her total existence. Like other countries she would have passed into the mould of occidental modernism; ancient India would have perished."[4]

Believing as he did, Tilak was inevitably drawn into the controversy over social reform. In 1891, at the time of the Age of Consent Bill, the reformers were insisting that the British Government pass a law raising the age of consent for girls in Hindu marriages. Tilak certainly did not disagree with the objective of this measure, but he took violent exception to the reformers' pleading for the employment of coercion by an autocratic and alien state to enforce the reform measure. Tilak denied that a foreign bureaucracy had a right to sit in legislative judgement on the Indian society, and more particularly, he held that the social reformers were totally misguided in endeavouring to use such measures to bring about morally-defensible reform. If there were political freedom, self-rule, in India, and the people themselves could enact legislation and thereby use the power of the state to promote social reform, then this procedure would be democratic and morally justifiable. He further argued that since the people do not have self-rule, then it is only by education and not coercion that you can hope to have the people accept necessary reform, that this was the only way in the present circumstances to make the reform democratic and moral. Reform no matter how necessary, must not, in Tilak's eyes, be inspired by a small group of reformers and enforced upon the community by the power of an alien state. Such a procedure was indefensible if the reformers were to make any claims to having morally elevated or reformed the Indian social system. Let there be social reform, he would say, but educate the people to its necessity and have the people initiate it. A minority's desire to imitate an alien social order is not a justification for social action. Tilak's position has been summed up by his colleague, Aurobindo Ghose, when he wrote:

"The nineteenth century in India was imitative, self forgetful, artificial. It aimed at a successful reproduction of Europe in India, forgetting the deep saying of the *Gita*, 'Better the law of one's own being though it be badly done than an alien *dharma* well-followed;

death in one's own *dharma* is better, it is a dangerous thing to follow the law of another's nature.' For death in one's own *dharma* brings new birth, success in an alien path means only successful suicide." Let India, following her own path, set her own house in order, build upon her own values.[5]

Programme for Social Reform

To have been satisfied with criticism of the Westernized version of social reform without offering a constructive programme of his own would certainly have made Tilak liable to the charge of being negative and disruptive. Tilak was, however, an ardent advocate of social reform. He said, 'I am a liberal Hindu' and in the *Mahratta* he wrote, 'We have always been advocates of reform, reform we say, but not of rebellion or licence.'[6] For Tilak's reformism was the product of his moral frame of reference based on the philosophy of life of the Indian civilization, and planned in accord with his own thoroughgoing realism. He would not content himself with analyzing the evils of the existing social order, and then dreaming up ideal reforms that were so impractical that they could not be accepted by the people, or that were so alien that they had no relation to the culture of India. The first basis of his programme for reform was that those who were educated and posed as leaders of the community, should be the first to practice the reforms they advocated. In this way he believed the reform leaders could set an example for all of society, and, to the extent that society followed their example acceptance of the reforms would be democratic and moral. But before he preached he practised. The Age of Consent Bill had been designed to raise the age of marriage of Hindu girls from ten to twelve years. Tilak fought this Bill with all his editorial might. Yet in his own family he postponed the marriage of his daughters until the limit, sixteen years, sanctioned by the classical books of law. He was loyal both to his convictions about the need for reform and to the classical heritage which was his guide.

He further urged that if legislation was going to be employed to bring about social reform, then it should not be used to enforce reformed practices on the masses who neither understood the

reforms nor appreciated their potential benefit. If anything, he advocated that social legislation be passed to bind the educated members of society, especially those who advocated reforms and the use of state power to enforce them to live up to the reforms they preached, he was himself willing to be bound by such laws, and urged that if other social reformers would join him in this procedure, then the example which they would set would inspire confidence and imitation in the people. He proposed that laws be passed, applying to all educated reformers, to the effect that (1) their daughters, should not be married until they reached the age of sixteen (instead of twelve as the reformers had advocated) and that boys should not marry until they were twenty; (2) unless they were prepared to marry widows, men should not marry after they were forty years old; (3) the educated reformers be absolutely prohibited from taking alcohol; (4) the reformers and their families be prohibited from accepting dowries in marriages; (5) there be no disfigurement of widows; (6) one-tenth of the monthly income of every reformer should be devoted to public purposes. With the exception of the third and sixth suggestions, all of these measures, usually in a less liberal form, had been advocated by the Westernized social reformers, and, moreover, the British Government had been urged to enforce these measures on the public at large.

If the educated want to take up the social education factor, they must mix with the common people. Those who want to be the leaders of the people must be in touch with the people to understand what are their needs, how much religious ardour they have got and to what channel their energy should be turned in order to gain national good. Tilak believed it was much more important for the social reformers to practise what they preached than to lobby, for general legislation.

The next thing the reformers could do, Tilak urged, would be to mix with the people and to educate them to the necessity of reforming the decadent aspects of the caste-ridden social order. He argued that the social reformers must not remain aloof from the people in their dignified, intellectual societies but rather mix with the people, speak their language, and through education encourage them to desire social reform. He believed that this procedure would be

beneficial not only to society but to the social reformers themselves, for by mixing with the people they might begin to appreciate the values that they seemingly had been educated away from. He wrote,

"If the educated want to take up the social education factor, they must mix with the common people. Those who want to be the leaders of the people must be in touch with the people to understand what are their needs, how much religious ardour they have got and to what channel their energy should be turned in order to gain national good."[7]

Reform, to Tilak's mind, must grow from within the people. Since he accepted this proposition as true, it logically followed that attempts to coerce the community to accept reform were absurd. Reform would have to be based on the value system of the people and not on the values taught to the Westernized few in an alien system of education. The answer lay, he believed, in popular education which must be initiated with an understanding of the classical values and must proceed to recreate the vitality of those values in the forms of social order. Since the classical values were thoroughly intermixed with popular religion, he believed that '*religious education will first and foremost engage our attention*.[8] In this way a new spirit will be born in India. India need not copy from some other civilization when she can rely on the spirit of her past greatness. As D.V. Athalye has written, 'The difference was this, that while Ranade was prepared, if convenient, to coquette with religious sanction to social order, Tilak insisted that there should be no divorce between the two."[9] Tilak proceeded to take action in accordance with his conviction.

Because he wanted genuine reform and not simple imitation of Western life and manners and because he believed such reform must come from the people and not from a foreign government, Tilak was led to advocate two causes which were to become his life's work. First, he struggled to awaken India to her past and to base her future greatness on her past glories, Second, knowing fully well that real progress can only be made by a self-governing people, knowing that moral progress can only be made through moral and democratic decisions, knowing, therefore, that *Swaraj* or self-rule was the prerequisite of real social, political, economic,

cultural and spiritual progress, Tilak began to think in terms of the restoration of *Swaraj*. The social reformers were prepared to criticize almost everything Indian, to imitat the West in the name of improvement, and to rely upon the power of a foreign government to bring about this improvement. They were convinced that only by social reform could they earn political reform; that, therefore, social reform must precede political reform. Tilak argued just the contrary, that political reform must precede social reform, for it is only popular self-government that is moral government, that it is only moral government that can create moral social change; and, therefore, self-rule is necessary, and the first object which must be pursued is the awakening of the people to their heritage of self-rule.

His Battle against the Spirit of Orthodoxy

Tilak was a realist. He perceived more surely the root causes of social abuses of the Indian society than did his social reform opponents. He recognized that it was not simply the forms and practices of society which had to be changed if meaningful social reforms were to be brought about. He perceived that abusive 'social practices were the direct outgrowth of the spirit of orthodoxy', which filled the forms of social order and inertly resisted change. This spirit had resulted from a thousand years of instability, defeat, foreign overlordship, defensiveness and inflexibility. Effective reform, Tilak believed, must ultimately depend upon a reawakening of the true, vital, life-affirming spirit of the Indian people and civilization. Instead of criticizing, social form as the great evil, he began his battle with the atrophied spirit of orthodoxy while still engaged in his battle with the Westernized reformers. He wrote, "... just as old and orthodox opinions (and their holders the Pandits, etc.) are onesided, so the new English educated "reformers" are also one-sided and dogmatic. The old *Sastries* and *Pandits* do not know the new circumstances whereas the newly educated class of reformers are ignorant of the traditions and traditional Philosophy of Hinduism. Therefore, a proper knowledge of the old traditions and philosophies must be imparted to the newly educated classes, and the *Pandits* and *Sastries* must be given information about the newly changed and changing circumstances."[10]

His battle was not characterized by abhorrence for this old spirit because he understood it and the role it had played. The spirit was locked up in forms, rituals, customs that had survived their usefulness. Now the forms had become virtually dead things. The orthodox spirit had served its purpose because it had transmitted classical values to a new generation who could understand them and bring about the necessary rebirth and reapplication of those values.

The degraded aspects of the spirit of orthodoxy were lethargy, indolence, exclusiveness and inaction. They had fed on disunity and divisiveness born of defensiveness and rigidity, and from this had arisen casteism in all its worst manifestations, defeatism and fatalism, the loss of the ideal of harmonious social cooperation, of courage and of self-respect—in a word, the dynamics of the classical philosophy of life had been perverted into negation and passivity. This spirit, Tilak believed, was the opponent of India's progress, and it was with this spirit that he did battle. Atrophied orthodoxy had no spirit was in part the perversion and negation of the world and of the classical concept of the fulfilment of the purpose of life, the union of man with his creator. Because he was a Sanskrit scholar, learned in the Vedas, Tilak was able to teach. If man seeks unity with the Deity, he must necessarily seek unity with the interests of the world also, and work for it. If he does not, then the unity is not perfect, because there is union between two elements out of the three (man and Deity) and the third (the world) is left out. I have thus solved the question for myself and I hold that serving the world, and thus serving His Will, is the surest way of Salvation and this way can be followed by remaining in the world and not going away from it.'[11]

But learned philosophical disputations were not enough. A nation had to be awakened.

His first task was to reach the people, for he knew that lasting change, that a rebirth of values required change in the hearts of people and not, as the reformers believed change in the forms of institutions. As an editor who had always dedicated himself to popular education, he first reached the people. As his chief colleague, N.C. Kelkar, wrote; 'Through his paper, the *Kesari*, he exercised an

immense influence over the masses, and it is this influence that is mainly responsible for the infusion of a new spirit among the people."[12] He was a sincere, forceful speaker, and he taught from both the classroom and the public platform his new message of awakening India. Perhaps the most effective way in which he reached the people was through the employment of national festivals. He was instrumental in popularizing two great festivals, one to Ganapati, the Hindu deity of learning and propitiousness, and a festival to revive the memory and glory of Shivaji, the liberator of Maharashtra, and the restorer of *Swaraj* through his battle with the Mogul Empire. He especially emphasized the dynamic spirit of Shivaji. He wrote, the spirit which actuated Shivaji in his doings that is held forth as the proper ideal to be kept constantly in view of the rising generation.[13] To keep this spirit in constant view, Tilak worked ceaselessly to reach the people, and to educate them through the festivals. Throughout Maharashtra, he carried his doctrine, he waged his battle. Education through religion and history, through the association in the popular mind with gods and heroes, through recreating an appreciation of the heritage of the past as a guide to the future—this was the way he conducted his battle. He soon became the first articulate spokesman for the no-longer-silent, tradition-directed masses of India. He became the defender and the awakener of India's philosophy of life.

He taught first the *Dharma* of action. He reminded the people that India had not become a great nation through negativism and indolence, but rather through a dynamic willingness to meet the problems of the day and to solve them morally. This was the greatest need of the present day. He often said such things as,

'No one can expect the Providence to protect one who sits with folded arms and throws his burden on others. God does not help the indolent. You must be doing all that you can to lift yourself up, and then only you may rely on the Almighty to help you.'[14]

He taught that no society can survive, let alone prosper if its people refuse to assert themselves actively on their own behalf. 'Action alone' he said, 'must be our guiding principle'. He taught the necessity of a vital, energetic, self-reliant approach to life, one that would instil self-respect, for self-respect was the necessary

foundation for effective action and for eventual self-rule. To inspire this spirit of activism, Tilak was constantly appealing to the greatness of the religious faith of the people and to the lessons of the history of India. And he taught that whether one went to the Vedas for his guide to conduct or whether one went to the heroes of history, he would find in either case that the first prerequisite was the willingness to work and sacrifice for an ideal. Self-sacrifice would be necessary in India's cause, as he himself had learned. He retaught the great Vedic lesson in writing:

Whatever a man does, must be taken to have been done by him for the purpose of the *yajana* (sacrifice)... Inasmuch as the Vedas themselves have enjoined the performance of the *yajnas*, any action done for the purpose of the *yajna* cannot of itself be a source of bondage to man.[15]

By the example of his own life, Tilak proved that courage and self-sacrifice could create a new spirit in nation.

Along with *Dharma* of action he taught the *Dharma* of unity. The unity of India, the unity of the civilization, is the *Bharatdharma*, the spiritually based and spiritually-dedicated way of life. The spirit of orthodoxy had done injustice to that way of life. It had compartmented and placed men in segregated and exclusive caste communities that were inimical to the feeling of common heritage and common cause. The true spirit of the *Varnashrama-dharma* was harmony and cooperation and unity, and this spirit Tilak sought to reawaken through religious education. He wrote, 'It is possible to unite the followers of Hinduism by the revival and growth of the Hindu religion', for 'the Hindu religion does not lie in caste, eating and drinking'.[16] He explained his *Dharma* of unity by relying on classical concepts:

'The word *Dharma* means a tie and comes from the root *dhri*, to bear or hold. What is there to hold together? To connect the soul with God, and man with man. *Dharma* means our duties towards God and duty towards man. Hindu religion as such provides for a moral as well as social tie. This being our definition we must go back to the past and see how it was worked out. During Vedic times India was a self-contained country. It was united as a great nation. That unity has disappeared bringing on us great degradation

and it becomes the duty of the leaders to revive that union...The gist of *Dharma* does not lie in rivalry, but it lies in effective union.'[17] Nothing must be allowed to stand in the way of the reassertion of that effective union. He struck hard at the divisiveness of caste: 'Communal jealousies and caste rivalries are the weak points in our armour, but we must strengthen our position by sinking all ourselves'.[18] He emphasized that national unity transcended all communities, that the unity of India was greater than the interests of any sects.

The Ganapati and Shivaji festivals served the purpose of bringing people together. People who worship a common deity, people who recognize a common ideal in his mind, be able to stand historical tradition will, in his mind, be able to stand together, to overcome the disunity of social form and to work together for the common good. Tilak envisioned a unity of India, united among themselves and united with their traditions, united to face the future by the common ideals they held. In this way, through common, united effort, social evils could be corrected by the people themselves; and, moreover, the spirit of national revival, the restoration of national essential for gaining self-rule, depended upon the restoration of national unity and mutual respect. His friend, Kelkar, wrote in *The Mahratta,*

'The rousing of a sense of self-respect in the Indian people, the creation of a hope of a bright future before the assertion of their full national rights and the infusion of a spirit of proud and even defiance of anything that may stand in the way of this—that was the main theme of all his idealism and realism.'[19]

This was Tilak's reply to the westernized reformers who would disregard their own civilization in order to ape the West, and who would employ the force of an alien state to bring about social change. This was also Tilak's reply to the dead spirit of orthodoxy which had nearly destroyed the vital spirit, the self-respect and sense of unity of great common purpose, of the people. In his personal life, in his writings and his philosophy, and in all his message to India, Tilak emphasized this *Dharma* of action and this *Dharma* of unity. It is all too easy for us today to minimize tremendously, this seemingly simple teaching. Village India at the end of the nineteenth century slumbered, un-remembering the greatness of its past and unaware

of the promise of its future. The people were weighted down by negation and passivity, they were disunified by communal rivalries and the compartmentation of Act that India no longer slumbers disunited and inert, is in large measure a testimony to the effectiveness of Tilak's teachings. Tilak and the Nationalist leaders brought about the reawakening of India.

The Beginnings of the Battle with the Bureaucracy

As editor of *Kesari* and *The Mahratta*, Tilak became the acknowledged 'awakener of India'. In this position he also became active in political affairs. After he left the Deccan Education Society in 1889, he joined the Indian National Congress hoping that it would be instrumental in further uniting the nation and in securing political reforms. He held a post in the Congress as early as 1892, as Secretary of the Bombay Provincial Conference. At the same time he actively participated in public affairs, holding Public office, elected a Fellow on several occasions. In 1894, he was elected a Fellow of Bombay University, and next year he held a post in Poona municipality. For two years he was a member of the Bombay Legislative Council, but he called the completely circumscribed powers and the work of this body a 'huge joke'. He did not seek public office because he desired a political or governmental career but rather because it was one means among several which he chose to utilize to further the causes in which he believed. But he soon realized that holding public office was one of the least effective way of promoting his ends, and, more important, he soon realized that public office under the alien *raj* was self-defeating. With time he also began to be disillusioned of the programmes and policies of the Moderate-dominated Congress. His fighting spirit was antagonized by the predominant Congress attitude of pleading for reform and passing mild resolutions of protest against the abuses of the administration. The Congress was not coming to grips with the real problems of the people. In 1896, he publicly announced his disagreement with the policies of the Congress in writing.

'For the last twelve years we have been shouting hoarse, desiring that the Government should hear us. But our shouting has

no more affected the Government than sound of a gnat. Our rulers disbelieve our statements or profess to do so. Let us now try to force our grievances into their ears by strong constitutional means. We must give the best political education possible to the ignorant villagers. We must meet them on terms of equality, teach them their rights and show how to fight constitution ally. Then only will the Government realize that to despise the Congress is to despise the Indian Nation. Then only will the efforts of the Congress be crowned with success. Such a work will require a large body of able and single-minded workers, to whom Politics would not mean some holiday recreation but everyday duty to be performed with strictest regularity and utmost capacity.[20]

As he had relied on democratic social action through religious education, he now relied on political education to rally the people behind the cause of political reform.

Tilak again practised what he preached. In the Crawford case he had opposed governmental favouritism in his role as editor. In 1896, a severe famine struck Maharashtra. Tilak early foresaw the imminent danger the famine brought to the peasants. As the leading editor of the province, he called upon the Government to take those measures of relief which were provided for under law in the Famine Relief Code. In accordance with the provisions of this law he urged the Government to omit the collection of land tax during the famine, to permit the free use of jungle land, to pay wages to people doing famine relief work in the villages, and to assist in providing free meals in poor houses. The Government officials hesitated, refused to believe that a major famine was impending and were reluctant to take his suggestion on any of these measures, instead, the bureaucrats remonstrated that until the famine was sweeping the land and the people demanded these relief measures, they would not be provided. Naturally, therefore, Tilak began, through the pages of the *Kesari* and through an organization of volunteer famine relief workers, to inform the poverty-stricken peasants of their legal rights. He urged the people to protest against governmental inaction. He sent out volunteers to collect detailed information on the devastation in rural areas. which he then forwarded to the Government to support his case. He printed and distributed a leaflet explaining the provisions

of the Famine Relief Code to the people and, urged them to take their case to the Government. His efforts informed and aroused the people and alienated the bureaucracy. On the heels of the famine, Poona was stricken by an epidemic of plague. The city panicked. Tragically, many of the educated, many of the leading social reformers fled the city; Tilak did not. He offered his services to the Government and went through the plague-infested districts of the city with the Government sanitation teams. He opened and managed a hospital for plague victims when Government facilities proved inadequate. He established a free kitchen, and did everything within his power to alleviate the tragic condition of the people. If social reform meant anything, it meant tireless work on behalf of the people in the time of their greatest need. His famine and plague work marked Tilak as the greatest social reformer of them all.

The British official in-charge of plague relief was a man named Rand, who was undoubtedly a sincere, hard-working Government official, but he was unimaginative, and appeared to lack the sympathy, warmth and understanding towards the plague and panic-stricken people which were so necessary in a position such as his. He freely used soldiers to segregate real and presumed plague victims, to herd them into camps, and, to the best of his ability with the medical science of his day, to contain, forcibly the spread of the disease. He paid little regard to personal feelings. Many people objected to his high-handed measures, and Tilak felt that his position required him to protest on behalf of the people about the abuses, real or imaginary, which they felt emanated from Rand's headquarters. As editor, Tilak was the only spokesman of the people. Years later he was questioned about his role as critic of the Government, and he succinctly explained his attitude towards the duty of editorship in replying, 'We have to criticize the acts of Government; there is no constitutional body to do it, and the Press have to do it. They [the Indian press] have the place of a permanent opposition in India.[21] But the British officials represented his outspoken opposition to their procedures. Both his protests and his recommendations went unheeded.

The British bureaucracy and the Anglo-Indian press recognized that Tilak was an emerging leader of the people and of a new spirit

in India. Those who lacked foresight began to fear him. When the tense atmosphere of famine and plague racked Poona, a young man assassinated Rand, and many of those who feared him were quick to blame Tilak for the death, going as far as to hint at his complicity in a conspiracy for political assassination. Tilak was, of course, innocent of any knowledge of or collaboration in this crime. He had publicly disagreed with Rand, he had condemned the humane aspects of the British anti-plague campaign, but had never contemplated or encouraged the assassination of the British official in-charge. Tilak, nevertheless, was brought to trial in 1807, not as an accessory to assassination nor as being involved in the plot to commit murder, but rather on the charge of sedition. The court allowed the prosecution to argue that he had written seditious matter and his criminal sedition constituted, in effect, 'disaffection' with the British Raj. 'Disaffection' was demonstrated by the prosecution in showing that Tilak was not positively 'affectionate' for British officialdom. This was one of the most unusual interpretations of 'sedition and disaffection' in the annals of British justice. Nevertheless, Tilak was convicted and sentenced to two years' imprisonment. The British had miscalculated both the effect of this sentence on Tilak and on public opinion. As N.C. Kelkar explained,

"His arrest and prosecution in 1897 was a sensation that nearly pulled the mind of the country by its roots, as political prosecutions were then extremely rare, and Tilak was, in himself, a man big enough to mark an epoch by his personal misfortune."[22]

This was not to be Tilak's last imprisonment. The British Indian Government endeavoured to convict him of perjury in connexion with the well-known *Tai Maharaj Case* in 1904. They did not succeed as he was acquitted by the High Court. In 1908, he was sentenced to six years' imprisonment, again for sedition; but in 1916, he was acquitted of a similar charge. For two decades he was prosecuted by the British Indian Government because they saw in him the greatest challenge to their rule over the Indian Empire.

Tilak emerged from prison in 1899 after serving eighteen months of his sentence. His health had been broken. But he was a national hero. Through his dedication and willing self-sacrifice, he had become the first all-India national leader. Earlier, he had been persecuted

for his political opinions, he was now the acknowledged political leader of the nation, and the nation was prepared to heed his opinions. He had begun as an awakener of the people and as a critic of bureaucratic abuses. He emerged from prison with the responsibility of leading the Nationalist cause to political self-determination (*Swatantra*). He was acclaimed the 'Lokmanya', the honoured and respected by people.

His knowledge and love of the great classical Indian values had prepared him with a personal philosophy and a frame of reference for his battles with social reformism and with the spirit of orthodoxy. It also provided him with the foundation of his emerging political philosophy. He had fought against injustice, as argued against the placating policies of the Moderates, and he now began to put forward a positive political programme centred around the concept of *Swaraj*, self-rule for India. As early as 1895, he had to preach the necessity for *Swaraj*. He came to realize that self-rule must precede meaningful social reform that the only enduring basis for national unity and national self-respect must be national self-rule. In 1895 he had reminded the people that Shivaji had recreated *Swaraj* as the necessary foundation of social and political freedom and progress and morality. His historical and philosophic frame of reference is clearly in his writing.

'One who is a wee bit introduced to history knows what is *Swarajya* (people's own government) and *Swadharma* (people's own religion), knows the extraordinary qualities that are needed for the founder to establish *Swarajya* and *Swadharma* when both of them are in a state of ruin for hundreds of years, knows the valour, courage, guts and brains of Shivaji Maharaj by the dint of which he saved the whole nation from bitter ruin.[23]

The Westernized reformers, in their desire to better the conditions of life in India, had failed to comprehend this great truth which Tilak had learned from India's past. They saw only reform while Tilak knew that 'we want freedom. We must have in our hands the right of carrying on our affairs. If you do not get these things, no reform would be fruitful for you. That is the root of all reforms.'[24] To Tilak, *Swaraj* was a philosophic and historical necessity. To gain *Swaraj*, he knew that he must battle against the

might of the British bureaucracy. He now firmly understood the lesson of the Indian tradition that without *Swaraj* there can be no *Dharmarajya*, that without *Dharmarajya* there can be harmony neither in the state nor the society and the individual cannot fulfil the purpose of life. *Swaraj*—self-rule—became the objective of Tilak's political battle. As Shivaji before him, he set about to 'establish *Swaraj* and *Swadharma* when both of them are in a state of ruin'.

His insistence on *Swaraj* was completely consistent with his personal, social and political philosophy. He approached all issues as a realist. He had the example of his own Maharashtrian history and the categorical imperative of his nation's philosophy. As Aurobindo Ghose has written,

"To found the greatness of the future on the greatness of the past, to infuse Indian politics with Indian religious fervour and spirituality, are the indispensable conditions for a great and powerful political awakening in India.

Other writers, thinkers, spiritual leaders, had seen truth. Tilak was the first to bring it into the actual field of practical politics."[25]

Unlike the westernized social reformers and the political moderates, the leaders of nineteenth-century India, Tilak was a leader of the twentieth century. He advocated an integrated programme based on an integrated political philosophy, and by teaching the *Dharmas* of action and unity, he foresaw the reawakening of an integrated, self-governing nation.

REFERENCES

1. *Kesari*, 19 September 1905.
2. Bapat, S.V. (ed.), *Gleanings from Tilak's Writings and Speeches* (Poona: S. V. Bapat), 1926, p. 111.
3. Tilak, B.G., *Gita Rahasya* (Poona: Tilak Brothers), 1925, p. 93.
4. Ghose, Aurobindo, *The Foundations of Indian Culture* (New York: The Sri Aurobindo Library),1953, pp. 22-23.
5. Ghose, Aurobindo, *The Ideal of the Karmayogin* (Pondicherry: Sri Aurobindo Ashram),1950, p. 25.
6. *The Mahratta*, 20 September 1896.
7. *Kesari*, 8 September 1896
8. Tilak, B.G., *His Writings and Speeches* (Madras: Ganeshan & Co.), 1922, p. 73.

9. Athalye, D.V., *The Life of Lokmanya Tilak*, op. cit., p. 54.
10. *Kesari*, 21 January 1904.
11. Tilak, B.G., *His Writings and Speeches, op. cit.*, p. 263.
12. Kelkar, N.C. *Landmarks in Lokamanya's Life* (Madras: Ganesan & Co.), 1924, p. 10.
13. Tilak, B.G., *His Writings and Speeches*, op. cit., p. 49.
14. *Ibid.*, p. 277.
15. Tilak, B.G., *Gita Rahsya, op. cit.*, p. 72.
16. Bapat, S. V. (ed.), *Gleanings from Tilak's Writings and Speeches, op. cit.*, p. 342.
17. Tilak, B.G., *His Writings and Speeches, op. cit.*, pp. 13-14.
18. *Ibid.*, p. 353.
19. *The Mahratta*, 8 August 1920.
20. *Kesari*, 12 January 1896.
21. *The Legal Proceedings in the case of Tilak* Vs *Chirol and another*, Vol. I (London: Oxford University Press), 1919, p. 304.
22. Kelkar, N.C. *Landmarks in Lokmanya's Life, op. cit.*, p. vi.
23. *Kesari*, 2 July 1895.
24. Tilak, B.G., *His Writings and Speeches, op. cit.*, p. 165.
25. Ghose, Aurobindo in Introduction to Bal Gangadhar Tilak, *His Writings and Speeches, op. cit.*, p. 7.

3

NATIONALISM

Lokmanya Tilak's unparalleled popularity could not be adequately accounted for by his high education, urbane culture, keen intellect, learned scholarship, versatile genius, journalistic enterprise, powerful eloquence, purity of character, steadfastness of friendship, magnetic personality, material selflessness or even his towering patriotism. Some of these eminent qualities he shared with this or that leader in every province of India. All these qualities together no doubt made him great, but what made him a hero among his people is something else. Heroism is described as a military attitude of the soul towards external evil, and the stout affirmation of one's ability to cope single-handed with an infinite army of enemies. This attitude characterised Lokmanya Tilak throughout his life; and the particular form of external evil that he chose to fight against was the political domination of his country by foreigners. "It is no use mincing matters here," writes N.C. Kalkar, "and I, for one, am prepared to accept the choice epithets showered on him by government and its minions as only tributes of praise in disguise to Lokmanya Tilak. Sir Valentine Chirol rendered a signal service to Lokmanya Tilak by describing him as the 'Father of Indian Unrest' and I am quite sure that Tilak would not have sued Sir Valentine if the latter had stopped at that, and not vilified him by reflections upon his private character."[1] '*The Father of Indian Unrest' indeed!*[2] A simpler and yet a pithier description of such a patriot as Tilak was can hardly be imagined. The rousing of a sense of self-respect in the Indian people, the creation of a hope of a bright future before them, the assertion of their full natural rights as a nation, and the infusion of a spirit of

proud and even reckless defiance of anything that may stand in the way of all this—that was the main theme of all his idealism and realism. This theme he held in a relentless grip throughout his life, and like a consummate General, concentrated all his powers and energies in life upon that single objective. That is why the Government hated him, that is why those who differed from him disliked him, and that is also why the people in every part of the country loved him. In him they knew they ever had a stout and faithful champion.

Heroism like this naturally took time to receive its recognition. But it came at last. Says Emerson:

"Heroism works in contradiction to the voice of mankind and in contradiction for a time to the voice of the great and good. Heroism is an obedience to a secret impulse of an individual's character. Now to no other man can its wisdom appear as it does to him. Therefore, just and wise men take umbrage at his acts until after little time be past they see it in unison with their acts. All prudent men see that the action is clean, contrary to a sensual prosperity; for every heroic act measures itself by its contempt of some external good. But it finds its own success at last, and then the prudent also extol".[3] And so it was also with the heroism of Lokmanya Tilak.

Nationalism and Revivalism

Tilak's nationalism had to some extent a revivalistic orientation. He wanted to bring to the front the message of Vedas and the Gita for providing spiritual energy and moral enthusiasm to the nation. A recovery of the healthy and vital traditions of the old culture of India was essential. He said:

"A true nationalist desires to build on old foundations. Reform based on utter disrespect for the old does not appeal to him as constructive work. We do not want to anglicise our institutions and so denationalise them in the name of social and political reforms."[4]

Hence he pointed out that the Shivaji and the Ganapati festivals had been encouraged by him because they served to link contemporary events and movements with historical traditions.

Nationalism is essentially a psychological and spiritual conception. It is the modern version of the old deep sentiments of tribal patriotism which we find since prehistoric and ancient times. The feelings of affection and attachment which people felt for the tribe or the gang or the polis or the civitas or the desha has now been extended to cover the entire nation. It is true that nationalism flourishes best when there are objective entities which create sentiments of unity. A common spoken language, belief in common descent from an actual or a mythical race, habitation on the same territory and profession of a common religion are very important objective factors which generate the feelings of nationalism. But the subjective psychological factor is dominant. There must be the presence of a psychological unity fostered by the heritage of historical tradition. In spite of racial and linguistic diversities, this psychological bond of nationalism has been important in India. The overflowing continuity of the stream of Indian culture since olden times has contributed to produce this fundamental psychological unity in India. Besides the subjective experience of this psychological unity, another feature of nationalism is a spiritual (soulish or relating to soul) phenomenon. Not only the economic grievances against an alien imperialism and the political desire for autonomous self-determinate existence but the evolution of the soul of a culture is demonstrated in the phenomenon of nationalism. In India this spiritual side of nationalism has been stressed by Bankim Chandra, Vivekananda, Tilak, Aurobindo Ghose, Bipin Chandra Pal and Gandhi. On the other hand, a more secularistic conception of nationalism was emphasised by Dadabhai Naoroji, Pherozeshah Mehta and Gokhale. But although essentially based on the subjective experience of the common psychological and spiritual bonds of unity, nationalism also needs its objective adjuncts. Festivals are symbolical adjuncts of nationalism. On one side, they are expressions of some deep bond of unity permeating those who are participants in them, and on the other hand, they reinforce and accentuate these feelings of unity which can be canalised into creative forces by wise and discerning leadership. Flags, celebrations of independence days and observance of festivals are thus the symbolisations of deep sentiments. Symbolisation in this sense is an advance in civilisation, being

demonstration of cultural growth because it shows that man is rising above his mere physical self and can feel the exhilarations and thrills of some super-personal entities like the nation. The nature and the physical appearance of the symbol is not important. Some of the symbols may appear crude to a refined aesthetic sense, but the point of utmost importance is the power of the symbol to evoke common response. As a leader, Tilak wanted to create a solid nationalistic following in Maharashtra and for the purpose he wanted to symbolise the permanent religious and historical traditions of the people. The Ganapati and the Shivaji festivals were the symbols of the rising nationalism in Maharashtra, and later on to some extent in other parts of India also.

The Ganapati Utsava was an old institution and is traditional in Maharashtra. In former times the great chiefs and Sardars of Maharashtra used to give donations for its celebration. The ingenuity of Tilak and his colleagues consisted in giving a public character to a festival which was so long celebrated on a private basis. This public aspect could intensify the bonds of nationalism because there would occur the reinforcement of feelings evoked by participation in a common religious festival. It is also true that the public orientation was imparted to the Ganapati festival after the Hindu-Muslim riots in the Bombay Presidency. The idea of the public celebration of the Ganesh festival originated in a private discussion between Tilak and some of his colleagues like Namjoshi. The Hindu-Muslim riots had demonstrated the utter necessity of the strengthening of the foundations of Hindu solidarity and the Ganesh festival could be of great service in this connection. Both Brahmans and non-Brahmans participated in the celebrations. The idea of a public Ganesh festival, spread in the Indian states, and by 1896-97 it began to be celebrated all over Maharashtra. Hence Tilak deserves the credit of having renovated and reinterpreted the Ganapati festival and thus, the mere mechanical conception of a political movement was transformed into an almost civil religion. By inaugurating the public Ganesh festival, Tilak tried to bring nationalism to the masses. The Indian National Congress in those days was more or less an academic movement, moving on occidental lines and quoting Burke, Mill and Spencer and their arguments for

liberty and individualism. But the Ganapati festival was an experiment and a very successful one in mass nationalism and to this extent it has successfully influenced the psychological orientation of the people of Maharashtra over several decades.

Just as it was a European who was responsible for the birth of the Indian National Congress so also the first impetus to the reconstruction of the grave of Shivaji came from Europeans. Since 1885 several newspapers stressed the necessity of rebuilding the tomb of Shivaji at Raigarh. Some high government officials visited the place and recommended that it should be repaired. Lord Reay also recommended that the grave should be saved from its dilapidated condition. The *Kesari* in an article on 23rd April, 1895, called upon the people of Maharashtra to vindicate the honour of the historic name of Shivaji. Tilak regarded Shivaji as a *vibhuti* in the language of the *Gita*. A *vibhuti* is a man gifted with creative powers of divine nature.[5] After Tilak's release from prison, after the first sedition imprisonment, a magnificent Shivaji festival celebration was held in 1900 at Raigarh. In the early years of the twentieth century the Shivaji festival movement spread even to Bengal and Japan. Sakharam Ganesh Deuskar took the lead in the Shivaji celebrations in Calcutta and was supported by Motilal Ghosh and Bipin Chandra Pal. Before Tilak's arrival in Calcutta in June 1906, the Shivaji festival was celebrated on Western lines by summoning a meeting for delivering speeches. But after Tilak's arrival in June 1906, a Hinduisation process began. Now for three days the worship of Bhawani was celebrated and even the statue of Ramadas Swami was put in the *mandap*.

The *Kesari* of the 21st April 1896, reported a speech of Tilak wherein he had stated that in the Shivaji festival, there was no disloyalty of any kind whatsoever.[6] According to him, it was the duty of every Hindu to celebrate the Shivaji festival. On the 1st September, 1896, the *Kesari* published another article by Tilak on the necessity of national festivals. It referred to the historical examples of the Olympian and the Pythian festivals. It also mentioned the great *Yajnas* in ancient India when huge number of people assembled at the *Ashwamedha* and the *Rajasuya Yajnas*.[7] In another article on the 8th September in the *Kesari* Tilak criticised

the isolationism and the intellectualism of the social reformers who used to keep themselves separate from the masses.[8] National festivals, according to him, provided opportunities of cofraternity amongst the educated and the uneducated multitude. This congregational activity would reinvigorate and educate, and would liberalise and enlighten the masses. He even went to the extent of saying that Justice Ranade mixing up with the people and taking part in the festival of Ganesh, Shivaii and Ramadas would be a more magnificent sight than Ranade absorbed in the contemplation of an abstract metaphysical concept or entity. In some of these articles and speeches after 1898, Tilak had discussed in great details the sociology of the Shivaji festival. He had a sacred conception of the festival. He felt that it was an imperative duty of posterity to pay respects to the ancestors and heroes and it was as ridiculous and superficial to enquire into the advantages to be derived from it as from the *shraddha* of the ancestors. Another very important point stressed by Tilak, in an article in the *Kesari* of the 9th April, 1901, was that while the Congress movement aimed at the immediate acquisition of some specific rights, the Shivaji festival was like an invigorating tonic which strengthened the foundations of the body politic.[9] Nationalism, according to Tilak, is not a visible and concrete entity but is a kind of sentiment and idea, and in generating this idea the historical memories of the great figures of a country play a significant part. Shivaji had in his mind the sentiments of the good of the people and he did not think in narrow terms of local subdivisions and social segments, and in virtue of his great achievement it was not an exaggeration to say that he was a *vibhuti* and even an incarnation of the divine being. To say that Shivaji was an incarnation appeared crude and demagogic to the social reformers but Tilak was a fearless man and he would not hesitate to tell the truth that was in his mind. It is true that behind the scheme of the propagation of the Shivaji festival, Tilak had a systematic philosophy of nationalism. He rightly felt that the roots of Indian nationalism must lie not in the mere intellectual appeals to the theories of the western liberal writers but in the sentiments and emotions of the Indian masses and hence he felt that the memories of Shivaji would serve to reinvigorate nationalistic emotions of the common people. Shivaji

was the symbol of resentment and resistance of the people against oppression and injustice. Tilak tried several times to refute the charge of anti-Muslimism against this festival. He was very careful and emphatic in pointing out that he wanted neither the resumption nor the actual revival of the specific methods and techniques of Shivaji, but of his fundamental spirit. In the seventeenth century he fought the Muslims because they were the oppressors. Now there was no question of fighting the Muslims. During anti-partition days, Tilak said that both Hindus and Muslims should assert their rights against the bureaucracy that was trying to crush all legitimate and oppressive measures.

But because Tilak was partly a revivalist, it must not be thought that he was a mere Hindu nationalist. As a person, he had intense pride in Hindu religion and culture. As a political leader, he wanted to preserve the legitimate interests of the Hindu people and would not approve cowardice and surrender. But it is wrong to say that he was a mere Hindu nationalist and was opposed to the Muslims. Zacharias says that Tilak was the spokesman of an anti-Muslim retaliation.[10] A British historian, Powell Price says, "The Muslim, League was an answer to the Indian National Congress, necessary because the possibility of self-government raised the spirit of separation which the intolerance of Tilak had emphasised."[11] Chirol says that due to Tilak's extreme orthodoxy the Muslim members of the Poona Sarvajanika Sabha resigned from that body. Palme Dutt blames Tilak and Aurobindo Ghosh because their identification of national awakening with the revival of Hinduism cut off the Muslim masses from the national movement.[12] But all these propositions are partial and even incorrect interpretations of the political thought and action of Tilak. Jinnah, M.A. Ansari and Hasan Imam have praised the nationalistic sentiments and spirit of compromise of Tilak because due to his wise counsel and moderation the Lucknow Pact of 1916 could be achieved. Shaukat Ali and Hasrat Mohani regarded Tilak as their political Guru. Shaukat Ali says:

"I would like to mention again for the hundredth time that both Mohammed Ali and myself belonged and still belong to Lokmanya Tilak's political party."[13]

Hasrat Mohani says: "I even at that early age, chose the Lokmanya as the ideal leader for me... During that period I had ample opportunities of appreciating the thought and ability of almost all Indian political leaders and basing my remarks on that close personal study, I can state without the 'least fear of contradiction, that I found the Lokmanya greater and superior to every other leader in every respect... When I declare that all through Tilak's life I was both intellectually and practically a blind follower of his, anyone can well judge thereby, of that love that I cherished towards him."[14]

Furthermore, Tilak had promised to support the Khilafat movement if the majority of the Muslims were behind it. He had also proposed the Congress resolution for the release of the Ali brothers. If Tilak would have been anti-Muslim he could never have commanded the confidence of the great Muslim leaders. Hence it can be said, that with the profoundest regard for Hinduism in private life, as a political leader Tilak had a broad policy, calculated to lead to national emancipation.

He did want to substantiate the nationalistic movement in India by a strong cultural and religious revival of Hinduism. But he also accepted the economic arguments for nationalism. Dadabhai Naoroji made famous the 'Drain Theory' in Indian economics. Both Tilak and Gokhale accepted that foreign imperialism resulted in the enormous 'drain' of India's resources. In 1897, Tilak wrote three articles in the *Kesari* at the time of the Diamond Jubilee celebrations of Queen Victoria. In the article written on 22nd June, he stated that India's arts and industries had declined under the British rule. He wrote that the various economic enterprises and investments in India, of the foreign capitalists, only created a delusion of prosperity. He referred to the evidence given by Dadabhai before the Welby Commission wherein that patriarch of Indian politics had shown that during the imperialistic sway of Great Britain.[15] India had become impoverished and economically ruined. He referred to the economic 'drain' of India also in the interview he gave to Nevinson (1856-1941) in 1907. He also emphasised the economic dimension of the Swadeshi movement which indicates his awareness of the economic roots of Indian nationalism. The *Swadeshi* movement in

India assumed a spiritual and a political character. It became a movement for the liberation of the spiritual energies of the nation for the sake of the political emancipation of the land. But in its economic roots it was the movement for the growth and expansion of early capitalism in India. Gokhale had admirably pointed out in his presidential speech at Benaras that the *Swadeshi* movement was a patriotic movement for the expansion of production by the rational harnessing of capital enterprise and skill. The growing destruction of small industries in India and the forcing back of the people only upon one resource agriculture had been the consequences of England's economic policy in imposing upon India the policy of free trade. Tilak recognized that with an alien government in the political control of the country, state protection was not possible here, but still people could work towards the spirit of protection on their own initiative. In a speech in January 1907 at Allahabad, Tilak pleaded for a protective tariff of our own by the boycott of foreign goods. He acknowledged that the British Government had given to the country peace and a certain degree of liberty, but it was essential to make further progress if the nation was to survive. The salvation of the country could be attained not by waiting on the bureaucracy and sending petitions to them, containing appeals to logic and reason but only by the concerted efforts of the people themselves. He, therefore, exhorted the nation to work for the concrete realisation of the resolutions on *Swadeshi*, boycott and national education which had been passed at the Congress session of 1906 at Calcutta.

It is a known fact that Tilak was a Vedantist in his metaphysical views. His conception of freedom as a divine instinct in man and of *Swarajya* as inner self-realisation indicate his Vedantic views. His belief in human fellowship also followed from his Vedantism. In a way, he pleaded for the reconciliation between the ideal of nationalism and the Vedantic conception of human unity. In a speech, he once said:

"If the Vedantic ideal is higher, it necessarily includes the national ideal which is lower. The two are not irreconcilable if you know how to reconcile them. The two are not opposed to each other. One includes the other much in the same way as a thousand includes

five hundred. The two ideals are mutually consistent and both of them demand a kind of self-control. Both of them demand in addition to self-control and self-sacrifice, a kind of higher altruistic feeling by which man is impelled to ignore selfish considerations and to work for persons and for objects which do not in the least savour of any egotistic aim. The feeling is one of love for humanity, for the equality of man before God, and it is the spirit of that feeling that governs the two ideals, Vedantic and national."[16]

The Foundations of Indian Extremist Nationalism

Lord Curzon was an arch-imperialist who had the vision of the glorious expansion of the power and prestige of the British empire. But unknowingly he succeeded in intensifying the nationalist agitation in India. He became the unconscious instrument of *weltgeist* (the world-spirit) in creating the foundations of the new nationalist party in India which was committed to extremist political ideals. It was inevitable that Tilak should appear as a bitter critic of the administrative policy of Curzon. He denounced the policies of Curzon in a series of articles in the *Kesari*. On the 15th March 1904, he wrote in the *Kesari* regarding the new educational policy of the government.[17] He thought that the new educational policy would be opposed to the educational growth of the country. In another article in the *Kesari* on the 15th April 1904, he admitted that Curzon was persevering, able, and astute, but he lamented that all his wisdom and diplomacy were being used for the purpose of perpetuating the slavery of the Indians under the British.[18] The *Kesari* of April 1904, categorically asserted that Curzon had attempted to impose rigorous control over universities and colleges. On the 21st February 1905, Tilak wrote a biting criticism of the allegations made against Indians in Curzon's convocation address. The cult of "efficiency" led Curzon into many unpopular adventures.[19] The supreme example of his Machiavellian diplomacy was revealed in the partition of Bengal. The partition was intended at the destruction of the homogeneity and solidarity of the over eighty millions of the Bengalee population. The metropolis of Calcutta being the intelligentsia was gradually becoming the centre of political radicalism. It was essential to limit

this influence in the interests of imperialism. The growth of political radicalism could be chocked by fomenting communalism. The now province of Eastern Bengal was to be a predominantly Mohammedan province which could become the source of permanent hostility to the rest of Bengal. Hence, Curzon decided upon the partition of Bengal. On December 3, 1903, there appeared the resolution of the Government of India proclaiming the intention of the government to revive the question of the transfer of the entire Chittagong division and the two districts of Dacca and Mymensing to Assam. On July 20, 1905, the news of the proposed partition of Bengal was published in the official Gazette and on October 16, 1905, the partition scheme was carried into execution. From December 1903 to October 1905, more than two thousand public meetings were held in Bengal where the population of Bengal protested against the partition. On November 18, 1905, Curzon sailed for England. Due to controversies with Kitchener he had already resigned his viceroyalty, but he insisted on the partition being concretely effected in practice before he left India.

The partition of Bengal was apparently the simple example of territorial redistribution for administrative purpose. But the agitation against it carried on under the leadership of Tilak, Pal, Aurobindo and Surendranath Benerjea developed into a struggle for the liberation of the country. Just as the Indian movement of 1857 has to be understood in the perspective of world political events, for example, the Revolution of 1448, the Crimean War of 1856, and the beginning of the Italian unification movement about that time, so also the anti-partition movement in India has to be analysed in the light of the growing intensification of the Asiatic political consciousness as manifested by the Boxer movement of China, the victories of Japan over Russia, and the growth of national movements in Persia and Turkey. Tilak was a student of international politics and as early as 1805, commenting on the Sino-Japanese War of 1894-95, he had written in the *Kesari* that the condition of Japan was representative of the revolution proceeding in Asia. He had predicted that the defeat of China would lead to a patriotic awakening of that big country. In several articles in the *Kesari*, Tilak candidly acknowledged the great inspiration received by the Asiatic youth

from the political triumphs of Japan over Russia. Japan's signal victory was a standing refutation of the myth of the Asiatic inferiority. Some inspiration to Indian youth was also provided by the boycott-campaign of the Chinese against the exclusivist orientation of the immigration policy of the United States.

From 1899 to 1904, Tilak could not get the necessary opportunity to carry on dynamic political agitation because his following in the Congress was small. The anti-partition agitation gave him the much sought opportunity of intensified political action. Tilak now emerged as an all-India leader of the new nationalist party. It was the insight of Tilak that turned an agitation for territorial change into an all-India movement for national consolidation. Due to his efforts Bengal and Maharashtra and partly also the Punjab were united by the bond of common political-affiliations. The personality and actions of leaders like Tilak, Lala Lajpat Rai, Bipin Chandra Pal, and Aurobindo Ghose transformed the anti-partition movement into crusade for the regeneration of a fallen nation. The technics of repression and coercion followed by the bureaucracy worked as aids and instruments of the national movement. The political genius of Tilak was now revealed. He attempted to transmute the anti-partition agitation into a movement for the *Swaraj* of the country. This movement of Swaraj had four technics—*Swedeshi*, boycott, national education and passive resistance. At times, some of the theorists of the New Party identified boycott with passive resistance. If so, then there would be counted only three technics of the Extremists (New Party). During the period from 1905 to 1909 we find various movements—for national education, for temperance, attempts to raise up the depressed classes and for the establishment of many nationalist newspapers like *Bande Mataram*, the *Rashtramat* etc. This movement of *Swaraj* and *Swadeshi* was to supplement the work of the Congress. The Congress had confined itself to the educated classes; the *Swadeshi* movement attempted to bring not only the lower middle-classes but also the masses into some sort of political and economic action. Thus Tilak and the other lieutenants of his, in Bengal and Maharshtra, were trying to change the prevailing conceptions of politics. The *Swadeshi*-boycott movement was an attempt at vindicating the rights of the people to self-government

and hence it used several technics of political agitation as mass processions, big public meetings, strikes, picketings, etc., which have been followed by later Indian leaders in their political movement. The *Swadeshi*-boycott movement was an organized attempt for the assertion of democratic principle that the predominant political opinion of the inhabitants of a country must not be transgressed by the rulers. The partition had been a gigantic wrong and a great blunder. The movement that developed against it has to be understood from the general sociological standpoint of the genesis and growth of modern Indian nationalism since the seventies and eighties of the last century. Indian capitalism was rising and the new bourgeoisie of Calcutta and Bombay financially helped the movement of *Swadeshi* because it made a passionate propaganda for things made in India. The growth of nationalism in India, however, was not a mere consequence of the rise of capitalism. Nationalism in India manifested itself also as a spiritual and religious phenomenon. In Bengal especially, the teachings of Aurobindo and Pal gave to nationalism a religious character. Aurobindo regarded nationalism as *Sattvika* religion, with God as its captain and the great goddess Kali as its executive force. Even a messianic consciousness manifested itself at this time and the Bengal leaders spoke of the spiritual mission of India. Tilak, however, stressed more on the political side of the problem and spoke in terms of organizing strong agitation so that the bureaucracy could be made to part with power. His was the main genius in solidifying the new nationalist party that carried on the anti-partition agitation.

In his speech at the Banaras Congress (1905), Tilak dwelt on the problems of famine, poverty and land revenue, and analyzed the economic roots of the Indian malady. He stated that Digby's book had amply emphasized the immense poverty of the Indian masses. The letters of Mr. R.C. Datta to Lord Curzon had also pointed out the defects in the system of land revenue. The Government resolution issued by Curzon in 1902 attempted to reconsider these points. In their turn Khare and G. Subramanya Aiyer had expressed their opinion on the Government resolution. It was not necessary to provide further statistics to corroborate the proposition that India was poor and was subjected to excessive

land revenue charges. The Swadeshi movement was spreading in the country. Tilak humorously remarked that even famine and plague were claiming to be *Swadeshi* and wanted to make their permanent say in this country. But against them a boycott had been launched which had to be carried on. The Government of India disowned responsibility for the economic malady in the country and said that if nature did not provide rains what could it do. It also confessed that in spite of its preventive measures plague had spread. It boasted that it had provided to India peace and had improved the transportation system through the railways. Tilak, on the other hand, stated that it is the duty of a government to provide prosperity to the country. It only could initiate significant administrative measures. To do so was its duty. According to Tilak's political philosophy, the function of the government was not merely to provide peace but also to secure prosperity to the country. Thus he was formulating, of course, in a rudimentary way, the philosophy of what had been later called a welfare or a positive state. He also pointed out that financial and economic questions could not be dealt with by individuals. If nature provided adequate raft every year and if plague did not break out and if there was no disease, it would be possible to dispense not only with government but also with physicians. Tilak categorically remarked that it was the function of the government not to grumble at the deplorable situation whether created by climatic or by economic factors, but to find out remedies so that the whole of the country could become prosperous.

He cited the case of England where the soil does not yield adequate food for the consumption of the Country even for three or four months in the year. But the British government would not say that since the soil is not productive it was helpless to provide food for the people for eight months. If the government were to maintain such a point of view, the English people would certainly go against that government and would demand the resignation of the ministry. They would say that they find another ministry and another Parliament. The situation in India was also similar. If there were not adequate rains, the government had to adopt such measures as would counteract the niggardliness of nature. They had to devise measures for provision of supply of water by irrigational and other

methods. Furthermore, Tilak pointed out that if the wealth which was produced in the country did not remain here but was drained away, it was the function of the government to take such steps as would prevent the operation of this drain. If there was a plague in the country and if it was clearly shown that it was due to poverty and starvation, it was the clear duty of the government to remove poverty and starvation and not to adopt techniques of repression. The Government of India had neglected the discharge of its clear economic duties. Tilak emphatically pleaded, hence, that the Government should be forced to do its duty. In his political philosophy, it was not sedition to force the government to perform its duty. Sedition meant subversion of the Government. The Congress was only asking the Government to initiate such measures as would secure prosperity to the country. All these matters had been placed before Lord Curzon but he took no steps to revive the decadent industries of the country nor did he take any step to stop the economic drain. He only allotted more money for irrigation. Tilak said that he was not going to thank Lord Curzon for this and his reason was simple. Indians had to work even for twelve or twenty-four hours in a day but even that amount of hard work was not enough to provide them sufficient food. Tilak wanted the Viceroy to stop the economic drain of the country and also to revive the industries which had been killed by competition from foreigners. Instead of initiating a big industrial policy, Curzon only took up the question of agricultural improvement and allotted more money for irrigational purposes. But unless the drain was stopped mere allotment of additional funds for agricultural improvement would only mean that the bleeding was to be kept up while a little tonic was to be given to the people so that they might be "bled the more, more for England and more for Manchester."[20] It is clear that Tilak was showing economic realism and vision in his speech. He was not satisfied with a mere tinkering or mere provision of certain irrigational facilities. He felt that unless there was industrial growth of the country, its economic malady could not be stopped. He also stated that the economic and administrative policy of the Government of India had killed Indian industries and although the process might not be apparent to most people, nevertheless, it was a patent fact that the Government of

India's economic policy during the past hundred years had completely destroyed the industries of weaving and other industries of the country. In the past, India was certainly, never a purely agricultural country. But due to the British policy it had been reduced to the position of an agricultural country. The types of clothes which people were getting from Manchester were previously manufactured in India. India even exported manufactured clothes to other countries. Due to the destruction of Indian industries, land had become the only source of subsistence of the people. To make the malady worse, even the profits of the land were drained away by the government in such a way that agriculture also was not prosperous. The people were being subjected to increasing payments at every revisional survey. The reasons that were given for this were that now there were more railways and other amenities. But really speaking, the railways, roads and channels were there to take away the produce of India to England. The prices were also rising in the country and people had to pay more to the Government. Tilak categorically stated that this state of affairs could not last long and India could not be permanently drained in this way. The resolution which he had proposed at the session of the Congress demanded an economic inquiry into every village. The Government had before it facts and figures. Either the Government had to contradict them or regard them as correct. If the Government would institute an inquiry of its own, the two types of statistics might be compared. Tilak was emphatic in pointing out the great evils of the killing of Indian industries and the increasing demand of the Government on land. Thus the economic dimensions of the growingly extremist nationalism were defined by him.

At the Calcutta Congress of 1906, Tilak supported the *Swadeshi* resolution and spelled out the economic foundations of Indian nationalism. He hailed Calcutta for being the home of the *Swadeshi* Movement and paid tributes to leaders like Surendranath Banerjee who had trained and inspired the people in the path of *Swadeshism*. Other parts of India had to learn the lesson of *Swadeshi* from Bengal. He also stated that the Congress had been able to formulate a resolution which reconciled the points of view of the two groups in it. The Anglo-Indian leader had predicted that the Calcutta

Congress was going to be the last Congress and it would meet premature death but the reconciliation arrived at under the leadership of Dadabhai Naoroji had falsified these ominous predictions. All the differences had been settled and both Hindus and Muslims had co-operated in arriving at an amicable and impartial settlement. Tilak further stated that it was a mistake to suppose that the Mussalmans lent no support to the *Swadeshi* movement. It was also incorrect to suppose that the *Swadeshi* movement demanded sacrifice from the poor people. He accused the middle classes as the greatest offenders because it was they and not the poor villagers who required consumer articles from foreign countries. The Government of India was not prepared to stop the economic drain of the country by imposing a protective duty. Hence it became essential for the people to pursue a policy which the Government should have categorically followed but had refrained from pursuing. 'Self-help' and 'determined will' were necessary. If the people were prepared for making sacrifices, they were sure to succeed. He also pointed out that Dadabhai Naoroji's presidential address had stated that *Swadeshism* was a forced necessity in India in view of the "unnatural economic conditions in India."[21]

Tilak was an acknowledged extremist and there were several factors responsible for that. Temperamentally, he was buoyant and represented the vigorous spirit of manhood. He had been inspired by the careers and exploits of Shivaji and other Maratha heroes who represented struggle and fight and successful victories. His extremism had also been influenced by his growing disillusion at the coercive and repressive technics of the bureaucracy. But, although an extremist, he believed in legal methods of agitation. For example, he was twice elected to the Bombay Legislative Council. He contemplated election also a third time. He formed the Congress Democratic Party in 1920 for contesting elections. But although Tilak accepted the framework of the existing law, he wanted to use the areas of action left free by the law of the British government to intensify the nationalist movement in the country. Ranade, Pherozeshah Mehta and Gokhale went to the extent of regarding the British rule in India as part of divine dispensation[22], but the leaders of the extremist party always believed in the independent

destiny of India. In a speech in 1909, Gokhale defended passive resistance; but although Tilak and Gokhale might at times have used the same words and might have put them within the same political objectives, still there was fundamental difference in their political technics. The activities of Tilak in the famine agitation of 1896, in the movement of 1905 to 1908, and during the Home Rule days were calculated to train the people in organized action. He wanted to infuse a spirit of dynamic assertiveness among the people who had grown enervated and prostrate. His advocacy of no-rent campaign in 1896, his stress on national education, his advocacy of picketing for the purpose of stopping the sale of liquor and his firm support of *Swadeshi* and boycott definitely showed that he wanted that the national movement should have its strong roots in co-ordinated and united action by Indian people. Before Tilak came into prominence as a leader, the Indian nationalist movement was committed to a philosophy of intellectual discussion on occidental lines. He, on the other hand, taught the gospel of Indianisation of the nationalist movement. Hence his technics of political action and his philosophical defence of the nationalist movement were oriented to the historical heritage of the people of India. If some of the important moderate leaders looked only to Burke, Mazzini and Spencer for intellectal inspiration, Tilak also looked to Shivaji and Nana Fadnavis and the *Bhagavad Gita.* Tilak's attempts to Indianize the policy and orientation of the nationalist movement brought to him the support of Lajpat Rai who in several respects closely associated himself also with Gokhale. It was unfortunate for the country that Tilak and Gokhale could not co-operate in their work and activities. Both were Chitpavan Brahmans and had extraordinary gifts of intellect and character. Both were patriots and utterly selfless. But while Gokhale appealed to the intelligentsia, Tilak was the idol of the masses. Gokhale was a champion of the cult of connexion between England and India, Tilak was irrevocably attached to the concept of *Swaraj* and would not be satisfied with mere administrative changes. Gokhale was a polished debator and speaker in the halls of the legislative council but Tilak made a profound appeal to the hearts of his countrymen. Since 1888, Tilak and Gokhale thought and acted differently and it can only be speculated as to

what might have been the good fortune of the country if these two colossal political geniuses could work together. The tributes that Tilak paid to Gokhale show the magnanimity of the former. On 23rd February, 1915, Tilak wrote an article in the *Kesari* on the death of Gokhale. Therein he paid glorious tribute to the spirit of devotion to the cause of the country which Gokhale manifested.[23] The later history of Indian nationalism, however, showed the efficiency of the methods of Tilak. The advocacy of the economic theory of *Swadeshi* and boycott of foreign goods showed also that extremist nationalism was slowly becoming a vehicle of the rising Indian middle-classes.

As a national leader, Tilak adhered to the concept of the economic emancipation of all sections of Indians from the exploitationist technics of an alien imperialism. But he did not worship at the shrine of Marxist historical materialism or the dialectics of surplus value. He stood for the rights of the peasants, the labourers, the artisans, and as yet the immature capitalists. He did not think in terms of socio-economic polarization, nor could he do so in the era of undeveloped capitalism. Although Tilak's great grandfathers had once enjoyed semi-feudal Khoti right in his ancestral village of Chikhalgaon, Tilak himself was no champion of agrarian feudalism. He wanted the mobilization of the energies of all sections of the people for the work of *Swaraj*. He was deeply concerned with the miseries and the abject destitution of the villagers and labourers. He wanted to provide relief to those people. He exposed the dire distress on the economic front in the pages of the *Kesari* and the *Mahratta*. But he was never a ruralist nor an advocate of peasantism. He favoured the growth of industrialization. On the issue of industrialization, both Ranade and Tilak agreed, but of course, these were quantitative differences. Ranade favoured more intensive and more diversified industrialization than Tilak. The controllers of the decision making processes in the contemporary Indian political system were bent upon fostering the interests of British industrial and finance capital and this inhibited the growth of Indian capitalism. Furthermore, the growing "immiserisation" (*Verelendung* or making poor) of the labourers did not leave them enough purchasing power to demand industrial goods. Hence the Nationalist party passionately

championed the concepts of *Swadeshi* and boycott during the anti-partition agitation. Tilak advocated both economic and political *Swadeshi*.

On January 2, 1907, Tilak delivered a historic speech on "Tenets of the New Party." In a sense, in 1896, two factions had come to the front in Maharashtra. But the years 1905-1906 erected the solid foundations of a new party which was not content with the old passive policy of representation of views, appeals and petitions. Tilak was the acknowledged leader of the new party. His erudition, his vast sacrifices and his unimpeachable patriotism had naturally fitted him in an eminent measure to lead the new party. Temperamentally, he believed in self-help.

He also justified the political doctrine of self-help by the philosophy of the *Atman* as formulated in the *Bhagavad Gita*. Tilak pointed out in his speech that the terms 'Moderates' and 'Extremists' were relative to time. An extremist of today becomes the moderate of tomorrow. When the Congress was started, Dadabhai Naoroji was regarded as an Extremist but later he began to be considered a Moderate. Tilak prophesied that with the lapse of time even his views would be regarded as moderate. Dadabhai was now disillusioned of the bureaucracy and he had given vent to his grave disappointment in his presidential speech in 1906. But although Dadabhai was disillusioned, Gokhale still had faith in the British administration. "Mr. Gokhale, I know, is not disappointed. He is a friend of mine and this is his honest conviction. Mr. Gokhale is not disappointed but he is ready to wait another eighty years till he is also disappointed like Mr. Dadabhai."[24] But although Gokhale was not disappointed, Lajpat Rai who also had gone with him in the Congress deputation of England was disappointed.

The New Party had no belief in educating and convincing the British electorate in favour of India. It would be a long-tem, complicated and even futile process. It was true that both the old and the new parties had lost faith in making appeals to the bureaucracy at Home, but the old party believed in appealing to the British nation and the new party did not. Tilak outlined a realistic conception of politics. Politics did not mean speculative fancy or utopian sentimentalism or idealistic norm-preaching. It was a game

where the rival side must be prepared to fight for their points. He cited the example of Krishna who had worked desperately hard to make the Kauravas yield. But although the Pandavas wanted a compromise to be arranged, they did not renounce their preparations. "This is politics. Are you prepared in this way to fight if your demand is refused?" Tilak categorically stated that Englishmen were spreading the myth that they were strong and the Indians were weak, only to strengthen the psychological foundations of their own political power. But again, "this is politics".[25]

In thundering words, Tilak defined self-government as the goal of the New Party:

"The point is to have the entire control in our hands. I want to have key of my house and not merely one stranger turned out of it. Self-government is our goal; we want a control over our administrative machinery. We do not want to become clerks... At present we are clerks and willing instruments of our own oppression in the hands of an alien government."[26]

Besides defining the goal, Tilak also outlined certain specific technics of political struggle, in case the political demands of the Indian People were accepted. He said that we should not give assistance to the government to collect revenue and keep peace. He formulated the dynamic methods of passive resistance. He said:

"What the New Party wants you to do is to realize the fact that your future rests entirely in your own hands. If you mean to be free you can be free; if you do not mean to be free, you will fall and be for ever fallen. So many of you need not like arms; but if you have not the power of active resistance, have you not the power of self-denial and self-abstinence in such a way as not to assist this foreign Government to rule over you? This is boycott and this is what is meant when we say, boycott is a political weapon. We shall not give them assistance to collect revenue and keep peace. We shall not assist them in fighting beyond the frontiers or outside India with Indian blood and money. We shall not assist them in carrying on the administration of justice. We shall have our own courts and when time comes we shall not pay taxes: Can you do that by your united efforts? If you can, you are free from tomorrow. Some gentlemen who spoke this evening referred to half bread as against

the whole bread. I say I want the whole bread and that immediately. But if I cannot get the whole, don't think that I have no patience. I will take the half they give me and then try for the remainder. This is the line of thought and action in which you must train yourself. We have not raised this cry from a mere impulse. It is a reasoned impulse."[27]

Tilak did not cherish the spirit of fanaticism and irreconcilable intransigence in politics. He would take what he would get and then carry on the struggle for the remainder. This was the essence of his political method. Hence the dominant ideology of the New Party was the concept of self-help understood in terms of *Swadeshi* and boycott. Boycott, however, was to be interpreted not merely in the passive and static sense of economic boycott but was regarded as the dynamic science of passive resistance. Tilak said:

"Are you prepared in this way to fight if your demand is refused? If you are, be sure you will not be refused; but if you are not, nothing can be more certain than that your demand will be refused, and perhaps, for ever. We are not armed, and there is no necessity for arms either. We have a stronger weapon, a political weapon, in boycott."[28]

Evidently Tilak was sounding a new note of strengthened political consciousness to be manifested through the capacity to struggle and suffer. The Calcutta Congress was a landmark in the evolution of the Indian national movement. Tilak said:

"The Congress has now in effect laid down that *Swaraj* or Self-government is the goal to be ultimately and gradually attained by the nation and that, while the nation may pray and petition to the Government as part of the constitutional agitation and seek the redress of grievances or the fruition of political aspirations, the nation will mainly rely on its own endeavours to accomplish the object. *Swadeshi*, boycott and national education are the three most potent weapons given into our hands by the National Congress, and with these we must establish *Swaraj*."[29]

It is evident that since 1904, and especially since 1905, a new nationalist party had grown up under the leadership of Tilak. It was committed to the philosophy of national emancipation to be attained by *Swadeshi*, boycott and national education. But the old party of

the Moderates which had been in control of the structure of the Congress still believed in the resuscitation of the love of liberty and justice among the British politicians. Only the venerable personality of Dadabhai could prevent an open rupture between the two parties in 1906. But since the beginning of 1907, it became clear that the compromise at Calcutta had been more external and mechanical than organic. In a speech at Lucknow, Gokhale tried to minimize the significance of the boycott resolution passed at Calcutta. He said that the positive aspect of boycott was included in *Swadeshi* while boycott was such that according to him (Gokhale), it had also a sinister and vindictive meaning. He argued that a strict boycott of foreign goods was not possible in the present industrial condition of India and hence he remarked that "we only make ourselves ridiculous by talking of resolution which we cannot enforce." Referring to the goal of Indian nationalist aspirations, in a speech delivered on February 4,1907, Gokhale said that "he was glad to see that one of the leaders of what was known as the New Party—Mr. Tilak had stated in a recent issue of his paper that self-government on colonial lines sufficed for him as a thing to work for."[30] Throughout the early months of the year 1907, Tilak and Gokhale were engaged in a controversy about the meaning and implications of the various resolutions passed at Calcutta. Tilak said:

"We do not believe in philanthropy in politics. There is no instance in history where a foreign nation has ruled another without any expectations of profit. We believe in Lord Morley and in the genuineness of his professions as a philosopher. The old school thinks that politics could be governed by the dictates of philosophy, we hold that these are quite different things and ought not to be mixed up together. The old school thinks that concessions could be secured by logical persuasion. Mr. Gokhale believes in sacrifice. He calls upon the people to be up and doing. He accepts even passive resistance as a constitutional weapon. He admits that the bureaucracy here is callous and the democracy at home is indifferent. He allows that our efforts have not yet borne sufficient fruit. He declared that the situation is critical. In all this he is at one with the New Party. But when it comes to action he will say, 'My friends, let us still wait a little. No use flouting the Government. They will

suppress us.' It therefore, comes to this. Mr. Gokhale belongs in theory to the New Party, and in practice to the old one."[31]

The meaning of the phrase "constitutional agitation" was also a bone of contention between Tilak and Gokhale. Gokhale stressed that the Indian political agitation should be constitutional. But Tilak pointed out that India did not have any constitution in the sense of fundamental law, as it was used in countries of the western civilization. The Proclamation of 1858 was not exactly a constitution and even this had been flouted several times. He humorously said that Indians had no constitution except the Penal Code. India's political agitation could not be exactly legal because the changing whims of the bureaucracy reflected itself in legal fluctuations and the existing legal structure and system could be changed without any protest from the people who were affected by that. Hence Tilak presented justice, morality and history as the guides in political agitation. There was one point of cardinal significance, however, in Tilak's political action and policy. He never wanted to break a law. He wanted to work within the framework of the existing legal structure. He had subtle penetration into the complexities of law and he said that he could carry on his political propaganda within the bounds of law, however, narrow they be. But he said, at the same time, that the Government must maintain the principle of fair play, and not amend the law according to its changing whims and fancies. But although Tilak wanted to work within the existing legal framework, there was a fundamental disparateness between him and Gokhale. Tilak wanted to interpret the existing law in such a way that the extremist political agitation of India could be carried on. Gokhale, on the other hand, pleaded conformity to the existing legal system. Tilak even favoured extension of boycott and the withdrawal of co-operation from the Government, but these ideals could never find favour with Gokhale who in the preamble to the Constitution of the Servants of India Society accepted the British connection as ordained by providence, But Tilak was devoted to the creed of *Swarajya* and always regarded the bureaucracy as alien.

Tilak's trial in July 1908, which led to his Mandalay imprisonment for six years demonstrated the confrontation of two philosophies of

public law. The Advocate General and the agents of the British Government emphasized the letter of the Penal Code. They wanted to find out if the incriminated articles in the *Kesari* came under the purview of sections 124-A and 153-A of the Indian Penal Code. For them the attendant environmental circumstances in which the articles were written were immaterial. If the articles could be incriminated on the basis of the letter of the law that was sufficient. Thus they were concerned with the purely formal and technical aspects of criminal law. Tilak, on the other hand, viewed the whole thing from the standpoint of constitutional law and political rights. He wanted that the Indian citizens should have the same liberty of the press as the British in England or the Anglo-Indian citizens in India had. For him, the safeguarding of the liberty of the press was a very great consideration. Liberty of the press was a key-factor in the maintenance of a political system that could claim to be civilized. He had enough historical sense to recognize that the protracted fight for obtaining the liberty of the press which the British citizens had offered to the absolutist system in their country had not been waged in India. The right which the British citizens were enjoying as a result of their long struggles could, however, very well be granted to the Indian subjects of the British Empire in India. Thus, indirectly, Tilak was implying and emphasizing that the British policy was discriminatory. It denied to the Indian people the essential political rights which had been granted to the British citizens at home. His insinuation became still more glaring when he referred to the discriminatory practice of the British between their Anglo-Indian subjects and the rest of the population. In terms of jurisprudence, thus, Tilak was maintaining that the British policy amounted to a negation of the rule of law. According to the exponents of the rule of law, it is an essential proposition that all citizens regardless of race, sex, etc., should be treated equally and impartially in the ordinary courts of the land.

A second point emphasised by Tilak was that the adequate consideration of political circumstances prevailing then in the country was also important in judging whether the articles were seditious in their nature. A bomb had been thrown in Muzaffarpur. Tilak definitely considered the throwing of the bomb as outrageous, illegal, immoral

and felonious. He wanted, nevertheless to warn the government not to indulge in excessive repression. The supporters of the British system were advocating a determined policy of repression and coercion. Newspapers like, *The Pioneer, The Times of India, The Statesman, The Englishman* etc. were of the opinion that the bomb incident was a consequence of the seditionist teachings of the Nationalist Party. In order to controvert this point of view, Tilak emphasized that the present policy of the ruling bureaucracy was not suited to the demands of the hour. He claimed that what he had been writing was in legitimate reply to the points of view sponsored by the Anglo-Indian and British newspapers in India. He quoted excerpts from the above-mentioned newspapers to stress that they had been advocating a policy of unmitigated repression. During the course of his trial speech, he repeatedly harped on the point that the articles in the *Kesari* could not be properly judged unless qualitatively and circumstantially evaluated in the context of what the other newspapers belonging to the bureaucratic camp were saying. The circumstantial points, in his opinion were fundamental. Unless it was seen that he was engaged in a polemical controversy with the Anglo-Indian newspapers, it was likely that he might be denied justice.

Although Tilak did not say so expressly, he was upholding some basic elements of constitutional law. He was pleading for the right of the newspaper editor to voice public opinion and to create a public opinion as a legitimate function in a democratic system. He said that as a newspaper editor it was his duty to present public opinion and even to create and mould public opinion. He could not be negligent towards that kind of responsibility. He suggested that what made him appear for his defence personally was that the jury could get a chance of seeing the man and through physical proximity and communication understand his point of view. He could, thus, get a chance of convincing them of the justness of his cause.

Tilak was, throughout his trial speech and especially in the last part of his address, very conscious of the fact that he was identified with a cause and his was not an isolated case. It was linked up with the political struggle going on in the country. More than once, he reminded the jury that later generation would be interested in the verdict that they returned.

REFERENCES

1. Saggi, P.D. (ed.), *Life and Work of Lal, Bal and Pal* (New Delhi: Overseas Publishing House), 1962, p. 121.
2. Chirol, Valentine, *Indian Unrest* (London: Macmillan), 1910.
3. Saggi, P.D. (ed.), *Life and Work of Lal, Bal and Pal, op. cit.*, p. 122.
4. *Tilak's Letter to the Mahratta*, 13 December 1919.
5. *Kesari*, 23 April 1895.
6. *Ibid.*, 21 April 1896.
7. *Ibid.*, 1 September 1896.
8. *Ibid.*, 8 September 1896.
9. *Ibid.*, 9 April 1901.
10. Zachaias, H.C.E., *Renascent India* (London: Allen), 1933, p. 121.
11. Price Powell, *A History of India* (London: Thomas Nelson and Sons Limited), 1955, p. 599.
12. Dutt, R., Palme, *India Today* (Delhi: People's Publishing House), 1955, p. 383.
13. Bapat, S.V. (ed.) *The Reminiscences and the Anecdotes of Lokmanya Tilak*, Vol. II (Poona: S.V. Bapat), 1925, p. 32.
14. *Ibid.*, Vol. III, pp. 36-37.
15. *Welby Commission Report*, 2 Volumes
16. *Tilak, B.G., His Writings and Speeches, op. cit.*, pp. 15-16.
17. *Kesari*, 15 March 1904.
18. *Ibid.*, 15 April 1904
19. *Ibid.*, 21 February 1905.
20. Varma, V.P., *Modern Indian Political Thought* (Agra: Luxmi Narain Aggarwal), 1961, p. 225.
21. *Ibid.*, p. 226.
22. Zaidi, A.M. and others, *The Encyclopaedia of Indian National Congress*, Vol. I (New Delhi: S. Chand), 1980, pp. 422-437.
23. Jog, N.G., *Lokmanya Bal Gangadhar Tilak, op. cit.*, pp. 184-185.
24. Tilak, B.G., *His Writings and Speeches, op. cit.*, pp. 40.
25. *Ibid.*, p. 65.
26. *Ibid.*
27. *Ibid.*
28. *Ibid.*, p. 69.
29. *Ibid.*
30. *Speeches and Writings of Gopal Krishna Gokhale* (Bombay: Asia Publishing House), 1966, Vol. II, p. xxx.
31. *Tilak, B.G., His Writings and Speeches, op. cit.*, p. 48.

4

CONCEPT OF SWARAJ

Tilak's connotation of the concept of *Swaraj* needs to be analysed a little more carefully. The interpretation and analysis made so far is either too narrow or superficial. This may be due to the fact that scholars have paid more attention to Tilak's role as an Agitator than as a Philosopher of *Swaraj*. It has thus become necessary to review and assess afresh the contribution of Tilak.

The main difficulty that any student of nineteenth century Indian Political thought faces is the time in which the main political thinkers were functioning. This applies not only to Tilak, but probably to all Indian political thinkers. Most of them were primarily political activists, and not pure academicians secluded from the main currents of their times. This was more true of Tilak who, practically for all his life, was mainly concerned with the mission of mobilizing people for *Swaraj*. Therefore, it is difficult to expect any kind of coherent political philosophy from Tilak. This becomes even more difficult as one has to rely mainly on Tilak's occasional writings in *Kesari* and many speeches he delivered in the long span of his political life. Many scholars, therefore, can cite evidences from such kind of writings in support of contradictory inferences.

Politically, the twentieth century seemed to begin calmly enough for the British Raj. Virtually all political activities were centred in the Indian National Congress, and the Congress was firmly controlled by the Moderates. The leading Moderates, such as Dadabhai Naoroji, Gopal Krishna Gokhale, Sir Surendranath Banerjea, and Sir Pherozeshah Mehta, retained their deep conviction of British justice and based their hopes for political reform on their ability to persuade their British rulers to reform the British Raj. They firmly

believed in the political theories of nineteenth-century British liberalism, and their programme was chiefly concerned with the presentation of their case to the British Government with the expectation that the British Indian administration would be reformed to bring it into accord with the theories of British liberalism which filled the British textbooks, But no reforms had been forthcoming. The Viceroyalty of Lord Curzon had proved anything but liberal. Whereas once the British administration had at least been willing to listen to the opinions of the Moderates, it now looked upon the Congress as a somewhat antagonistic organization. The pleas and petitions of the Moderates fell on deaf ears.

Among the younger generation, there was a growing dissatisfaction with the inadequacy of the Moderate programme to bring about meaningful political reforms. Moreover, there was a growing conviction that reforms of the British administration in India might not be the really important political objective young India should seek. In Bengal, in the Punjab, and in Maharashtra, the Nationalists had begun to distinguish themselves from the Moderates in the Congress, and they had begun to talk about self-rule for India. More important, perhaps, the people had begun to listen to them. Two events were to take place in 1904 and 1905 that would give impetus to the cause of the Nationalists. First, the young Japanese nation defeated the forces of Imperial Russia in the Russo-Japanese War. As though it were a common signal, nationalist movements sprang to life in many colonial and semi-dependent areas in Asia. Historians date the so-called 'revolt of Asia' from this Japanese victory. The second vital event was directly related to nationalism in India. It was the partitioning of the province of Bengal.[1]

The Partitioning of Bengal

The capital of British India was Calcutta. Bengal was one of the first states to be governed by the British, and having become the capital province, it was probably the most politically conscious area of India. Suddenly, the Viceroy, Lord Curzon, proposed that the province of Bengal was too large to be administered with ease and economy. He, therefore, set about to partition it without regard to

the culture, linguistic homogeneity, or feelings of the people. The long-smouldering resentment of the people crystallized around the issue of partition. It was almost universally unpopular. As protests were of no avail, on 16 October 1905, Bengal was partitioned. However, the issue of Bengal became the focal point of Indian dissatisfaction with the British Indian Government.

The Moderate leaders of the Congress, especially Surendranath Banerjea, were shocked that the British would take so autocratic a step with so little justification. The Nationalist condemned Curzon's action. To them this was the crowning example of what an irresponsible alien government could do regardless of the wishes of the people or the good of the country. Many believed that the real reason for partitioning Bengal was to divide the articulate spokesmen of that advanced province and to weaken the pressure they were able to bring upon the Government. If they were correct that this was the true motive of the Government, then few political manoeuvres in history have been more grossly miscalculated. The portioning of Bengal became that cause which the young Nationalists all over India had needed to rally their forces and to challenge the administration. The cause inflamed the people. The Moderates' cherished belief in the good faith of British actions was resoundingly disavowed. The partition of Bengal was the awakening of modern political India. The Nationalists aroused wide support for their thesis that alien rule would always be arbitrary and autocratic; only self-rule could be just. The days of placation and petition were ended. The Indian Independence Movement was begun. As T.L. Vaswani movingly wrote on a later date:

'For over a generation we were groping in the dark, begging at the bureaucracy's doors, beseeching England to grant us what no nation can grant to another, what every nation must achieve for itself—Swaraj. After a weary wandering for 30 years and more, the truth has dawned upon us! A people must work out its own salvation! That is the meaning of the New Movement, as I understand it. It is a Movement of India's return to Herself, to Her own Culture, Her own Civilization, Her loyalty to the Law of Her own History, Her own Genius, Her own Individuality, the God-given Inspiration of Her own life.'[2]

The nation was prepared to follow the lead of those who could provide a more dynamic and more helpful programme than the Moderates had been able to put forward. The Nationalists presented India with such a programme, based on the God-given Inspiration of Her own life.

The Foundations of the Political Programme

The Moderates had based their political programme on the political philosophy of nineteenth century European liberalism. Long before the partition of Bengal, the new Nationalists recognized that this Moderate programme was ineffective and, perhaps more important because it was based on foreign ideas of the political order; it was alien to the philosophy of life and the spirit of the people of India. They had begun to examine the political problems of their day in the light of the 'God given Inspiration' of India's civilization. With the urgency of the situation arising out of the partition and the need for an effective programme of political action they began to present their programme to the nation.

They initiated mass political education in terms understandable to the people. Tilak sounded the keynote in saying, 'To spread our Dharma in our people is one of the aspects of the national form of our religion', because in his opinion, 'Politics cannot be separated from religion.'[3] The reason for political education and political action was not merely injustice of foreign rule, not merely the arbitrary partitioning of Bengal. Self-rule was moral necessity, the achievement of self-rule was the Dharma of all self-respecting men. As he later wrote in the *Gita-Rahasya,* 'The Blessed Lord had to show the importance and the necessity of performing at all costs the duties enjoined by one's Dharma while life lasts.'[4] And for Tilak and the Nationalists, '*Swaraj* is our *Dharma.*' In partitioned Bengal, Bepin Chandra Pal reiterated Tilak's conviction: 'There can be no reform—social, economic or political—that can be got from outside'.[5] Political action would alone accomplish the national *Dharma*. In order that India solve her own destiny, the first essential, as in the case of the awakening of India, was the call for action, for a new spirit of courage and self-sacrifice. Only a pride in history

and the values of India's own civilization could inspire men to the task ahead. As Tilak movingly wrote:

'To succeed in any business with full self-control and determination in spite of our valour does not generally happen unless a firm conviction is engendered in our minds that we are doing good work and God is helping us and that the religious instinct and the blessings of saints are at our back.'[6]

How well the Nationalists knew that India's unity was spiritual unity, the divinely-ordered way of life, the *Bharat dharma*.

It was with this firm conviction that the Nationalists set out to arouse the nation to political action for the creation of its own destiny. By their personal example the leaders were able to capture the imagination of the long-silent people. Like the Founding Fathers of the American Republic, with a deep faith in God, they had pledged 'their lives, their fortunes and their sacred honour 'to the cause' in which they believed.

The sense of united action, the feeling of common cause throughout the land underlying common action, also had to be developed. The Nationalists taught that the partition of Bengal was not just the problem of Bengal, but represented the problem of the whole of India, in all the provinces, and in all walks of life. Throughout, the Nationalists relied on the classical values of the *Bharat dharma* to emphasize the great common bonds that united all India. Tilak wrote, for example, one common religion becomes a great means to create mutual affinity and sympathy among people.[7] The people came to know that far more than isolated political events stimulated the new movement, that the battle with the bureaucracy involved a way of life. In order to make this way of life most meaningful, the Nationalists symbolized it in the nation and taught the almost forgotten ideal of love of country.

History and tradition, religion and philosophy, action and unity were all made meaningful in the concept of love of country. Tilak wrote, 'God and our country are not different. In short, our country is one form of God.'[8] The love of nation, like the love of God, had to transcend narrow provincialism, communalism and sectarianism, it had to be the first cause for both action and for unity. While Tilak wrote of God and country, Lala Lajpat Rai in Punjab spoke of

Dharma and duty growing out of love of country. The *Punjabee* of 27 March 1907 reports the conclusion of the famous speech for which he was subsequently deported:

'Ye Hindus! Ye Mahomedans! in the name of your *Dharma*, in the name of your ancestors, be firm in these vows you take. You were once the rulers of this land. All that is vanished. You have now become dumb creatures. Why! Because you have forgotten to preserve the self-respect of your forefathers.'[9]

All Indians, the Nationalists taught, regardless of their religion, province, sect, language, caste or profession must become united around love of country. This sentiment, and the mystic overtones the Nationalists gave it, was perhaps best expressed by the rallying cry of *Bande Mataram*, 'Bow down to the Mother [India]'. This was the fiery and devotional love of nation that the Nationalists stressed. India, the faithful mother to all her sons—India, which needed the sacrifice of all her sons in her time of trials became the object of the highest reverence, the image for which her sons would willingly fight and, if need be, die. From Bengal the cry surged across the subcontinent—*Bande Mataram*! All the greatness, the wisdom, the heritage and the heroism of India were united in the words of a prayer—*Bande Mataram.* As her sons bowed down, India arose.

The Programme: Boycott, *Swadeshi* and National Education

With this foundation securely laid, the Nationalists presented the nation with a threefold programme for effective and, practical political action. The three principles were Boycott, *Swadeshi* and National education. Originally, they were designed for use in Bengal, as the most effective way to bring the British administrators to their senses over the issue had all along been bigger than merely the inglorious partitioning, but this was the first cause, the immediate need for direct political action. It was soon decided, however, that the entire nation could well cooperate with Bengal in following this threefold programme and thus increase tremendously the pressure on the British. And it was further taught that the great wrong, the significant evil, was not alone, that an alien raj had partitioned the

province of Bengal, but actually that Bengal was only a symbol, that an alien *raj* ruled autocratically over the whole nation of India, and that it was to alleviate this wrong that the programme was to be employed.

Boycott initially involved the refusal of the people to purchase British-manufactured goods. It was started as a measure designed to bring economic pressure on the British business interests both in India and abroad. If British business could be moved, then business could be counted on to move the British Raj. But soon the boycott movement took on far more significant aspects than merely economic pressure. The Nationalists saw whole superstructure of the British, Indian administration, that the British system of rule over India, was based upon the willing, or at least unthinking, cooperation of the Indian people. Tilak was one of the first to discern this, and he realized that boycott could be expanded to the point of jeopardizing the foundation of the whole British administrative machinery in India. In a speech at Poona, as early as 1902, he urged,

"You must realize that you are a great factor in the power with which the administration in India is conducted. You are yourselves the useful lubricants which enable the gigantic machinery to work so smoothly.

Though down-trodden and neglected, you must be conscious of your power of making the administration impossible if you but choose to make it so. It is you who manage the railroad and the telegraph, it is you who make settlements and collect revenues, it is in fact you who do everything for the administration though in a subordinate capacity. You must consider whether you cannot turn your hand to better use for your nation than drudging on in this fashion."[10]

Boycott became a political weapon. Its effective use demanded courage and a measure of self-sacrifice. Tilak emphasized this in a speech at Calcutta:

'If you have not the power of active resistance, have not the power of self-denial and self-abstinence in such a way as not to assist this foreign Government to rule over you? This is boycott and this is what is meant when we say, boycott is a political weapon.'[11]

Boycott moved from the economic into the political; it moved from the arena of as an all-India political weapon, and was the first of the programmes of the Nationalist leaders. Boycott foreshadowed non-cooperation.

Swadeshi initially began as a primary economic counterpart to the programme of economic boycott. Swadeshi meant self-help to rely upon Indian-made goods rather than to patronize the retail outlets of the manufactured produce of Birmingham and Manchester. Beginning in Bengal, bonfires of European clothing lit the night sky, and the people turned to local Indian production of *swadeshi* goods. *Swadeshi* was the first great impetus to industrial development in India. Local Indian production was given the stimulus for its natural growth. But like boycott, *Swadeshi* soon came to mean a great deal more than simple economic self-sufficiency. If there could be self-help in the economic sphere, then there most certainly could be self-help in all spheres of life. The *Dharma* of action had taught self-respect and self-reliance, and *swadeshi* extended self-reliance to self-help in all things. *Swadeshi* was a tangible way in which to demonstrate the new spirit the Nationalists had been teaching the people. As Tilak later explained:

'The object…is to bring about the spread of *swadeshi* (i.e., country-made things), visible and invisible, to bring about the gradual disappearance of visible foreign things, and to bring about the gradual disappearance of foreign ideas also.'

And he added, 'Like the bodies our minds also should become *swadeshi*... *Swadeshi* thoughts should always reign in our hearts.'[12] *Swadeshi* was the first assertion of the spirit of independence. It could no longer be popularly argued that India could claim its rights through transmitting resolutions to the Government and requesting reforms. The Nationalists had taught India to become self-reliant, independent in all things, and thereby to earn all those privileges and rights of free men. The *swadeshi* movement quickly became a movement of national regeneration. *Swadeshi* was a practical application of love of country. As Tilak said, 'To recognize the land of the Aryas as mother-earth is the *swadeshi* movement.'[13] It was an economic, political and spiritual weapon. *Swadeshi* was *Bande Mataram* in action.

The third element in their threefold programme, for effective political action was 'national education'. If it was clear to anyone in India, it was clear to the Nationalist leaders that the Western education begun by Lord Macaulay and pursued in all the Government-supported schools was ruinous to the future health and well-being of the nation. The younger generations were being educated away from not only their families and the great majority of the Indian people, but also away from the value system of India's civilization. Government supported Western education, uprooted the youths from their ties to the past, and made them Indians-in-name only. The Nationalist leaders had received Western education themselves, but they had fought their own way back to the sense of meaning and value of their traditions. Western liberal arts education especially was not a productive kind of education for young India. Moreover, Western education was available only to the relative few, to those who could afford to go to Western schools; and the great bulk of the people of India were left untouched by any kind of formal education. National education was the Nationalists' answer.

The programme for national education was a logical outgrowth of boycott and *Swadeshi* movements. The plan involved the establishment of schools throughout the country dedicated to giving young India a truly national educational background. The useful lessons of Western education were not to be ignored but rather supplemented with the lessons of India's own great culture. Mrs. Besant and the Theosophists had founded the Hindu University at Banaras to reteach the classical values and to prepare the younger generation for fruitful participation in the affairs of national life. Tilak and the other Nationalists wanted the Congress to support with all its assets the establishment of schools and colleges throughout the country to provide inexpensive and wholesome education, emphasizing the new spirit of self-respect and self-reliance, which young people could not expect to receive in the Government-supported institutions. Writing of Tilak's initial resolve to become an educator and his work for the establishment of the Poona School, N.C. Kelkar has commented, 'The idea of national education was implicit in the starting and conducting of this school, though it was not known by that name in those days'.[14] National

education became an integral part of the Nationalist programme for the India of the twentieth century.

This threefold programme of boycott, swadeshi and national education was presented to the country by the Nationalist leaders and was also presented to the Indian National Congress for its approval and adoption. The programme began primarily as an economic weapon but quickly its political importance was realized and became predominant. The impetus behind the programme was initially a reaction to the British portioning of the Bengal, but it soon developed an all-India momentum. The first reason for its use was to cause the Government to reunify Bengal, but it soon became a programme for national reawakening and national liberation—*Swaraj*. Thus, an economic programme became a political programme; a locally-centred agitation became a national issue; the cause of altering a specific British policy evolved into the cause of gaining India's self-determination. The goal of the Nationalists, relying upon this threefold programme of action, became *Swaraj*.

The Goal: *Swaraj*

Swaraj became the reason and justification for the entire programme and movement led by the Nationalists. Usually *Swaraj* is translated to mean 'self-rule' or 'independence' from foreign political domination. Actually, *Swaraj*, while being literally 'self-rule', meant far more than European usually associated with the concept. In the context of the Indian independence movement, *Swaraj*, the goal of all efforts, was a moral national necessity. This greater meaning was clearly understood by the Nationalist leaders. As Aurobindo Ghōse wrote in his Calcutta paper, *Bande Mataram*,

'*Swadeshi*, Boycott, Arbitration, National Education, are all doomed to failure if pursued separately and for their own sake; but as part of a single co-ordinated attempt to attain an organized independence they are the necessity of the present time. They are merely component parts of *Swaraj*, which is made of all of them put together and harmonized in a single whole.'[15]

To understand this necessity of *Swaraj*, we must go back to the importance *Swaraj* played in the political philosophy of the Indian

value system. We must remember that Tilak and the Nationalists viewed the political struggles for their day from the frame of reference of these classical values.

The classical meaning of Swaraj referred both to the self-rule of the individual and to the self-rule of the political community. *Swaraj* was a part of both—the Philosophy and Politics. The term is perhaps as old as the Aryan civilization; it is found in Rig Veda and the *Shastras*. As Tilak often reminded the people, 'The idea of *Swaraj* is an old one.' For the individual *Swaraj* meant the exercise of his freedom lawfully. It meant the choice of cosmos over chaos, and the regulation of all actions morally in accordance with the individual's *Swadharma*. Unless there was *Swaraj*, conscious, lawful living of *Swadharma*, the individual could not live in his True Nature, could not attain and fulfill the purpose of life. In like manner, *Swaraj* was meaningful in the classical philosophy of politics for the political community. *Swaraj* meant the lawful exercise of the community's freedom. For the community it also meant the choice of cosmos over chaos, and the regulation of all community activities morally in accordance with *Dharmarajya*, the rule of *Dharma*. Unless there was *Swaraj*, the conscious, lawful living under *Dharmarajya*, the right ordering of the community could never be attained, individual life-situations could not be morally profitable, men could not live in their True Natures, and the Purpose of life and creation could not be fulfilled. The political community existed only to preserve and promote the *Dharma*, and without *Swaraj* this was not possible. *Swaraj*, therefore, in the classical value system was a moral imperative for both the individual and community. Without *Swaraj* life was not worthwhile. Because Tilak viewed the world from the perspective of this value system, he insisted that 'our life and our *Dharma* are in vain in the absence of *Swarajya*.'[16]

The truth of this is apparent when we remember what the loss of *Swaraj* for a thousand years did to the preservation and harmonization of the Indian social system. The evils of the nineteenth and twentieth centuries were largely the result of the weakening of the Indian social order because of its long struggle to preserve the *Dharma* in the absence of *Swaraj*. For the Nationalists, it was self-evident that the only lasting remedy of social evil was the

re-establishment of lawful self-rule, *Swaraj*. Life could have no moral purposefulness unless there was *Swaraj* to protect and promote the *Dharma*. This was the essence of Tilak's argument with the social reformers as to which had precedence—political reform or social reform. Political reform, defined as absolutely essential for meaningful social reform.

The restoration of *Swaraj* was a moral imperative. The laws, the institutions of government, the use of power and the ordering of political community could only be moral under *Dharmarajya* and *Dharma* could only rule if the people had *Swaraj*. The Nationalist believed that democratic control over government, popular self-rule, was essential for this kind of moral rule. Tilak defined *Swaraj* in this way in writing, 'People's rule instead of that of bureaucracy is *Swarajya*'.[17] This was the essence of Tilak's argument with the social reformers when they sought to have the British Government legislate and enforce social reform measures. Tilak held that unless the people supported the reforms, in effect, unless the people exercised self-rule to legislate and enforce the reforms, the reforms were not only meaningless but also undemocratic and without moral significance. Aurobindo Ghose, in his Introductory Appreciation to *Tilak's Writings and Speeches*, repeated Tilak's thesis: 'Let us first have liberty and the organised control of the life of the nation, afterwards we can see how we can use it in social matters; meanwhile let us move on without noise or strife'.[18] There must be popular control over the power of government, for otherwise there can be no moral use of that power. *Swaraj* must be democratic.

But social progress was only one aspect of the future greatness of the nation that was dependent upon the achievement of *Swaraj*. Tilak believed all progress, all hope for national advancement, rested in *Swaraj*; no issue had precedence over *Swaraj*. In his public addresses, he often said,

'If we do not get *Swarajya*, there will be no industrial progress, if we do not get *Swarajya* there will be no possibility of having any kind of education useful to the nation, either primary or higher. If we do get *Swarajya* it is not merely to advance female education or to secure industrial reform or social reform. All these are parts of *Swarajya*. Power is wanted first.'[19]

Swaraj was a moral imperative, for 'There is no question which is not dependent upon *Swarajya*'. Or, as continually emphasised, 'We demand *Swaraj*, as it is the foundation and not the height of our future prosperity.'[20]

Swaraj was the goal of Nationalists because it had a deeper meaning than Western concepts of national independence. *Swaraj* was a concept integrally related to the values of the Indian civilization. And though Tilak spoke of democratic *Swaraj*, democracy, too, had a different meaning to the Nationalists than is usually associated with it in the Western philosophy of politics. As Bepin Chandra Pal explained,

'The ideal of *Swaraj*, that has revealed itself to, is the ideal of divine democracy.... There is a higher message still: men are gods and the equality of Indian democracy is the equality of divine origin, the divine nature, the divine possibilities and the divine destiny of every individual being.'[21]

Democratic *Swaraj* was the opportunity for spiritual *Swaraj* for all the people. This was a great restatement of the classical philosophy of life, relating that philosophy to the philosophy of politics of the independent and to the goal of that movement—*Swaraj*. Such a goal could not be reconciled with the aspirations for merely reform of the administration and the inclusion of more educated Indians in the civil service. Tilak was little interested in securing government posts for deserving Indians, and he repeatedly would say, 'To get posts of big salaries is not the meaning of *Swaraj*.'[22] *Swaraj*, as Pal explained, was not based on the Western concept of man in the political community. The ends of the Indian state were distinctly different, because they were related to the Indian theory of right ordering. *Swaraj* meant a total change in political theory. This Tilak clearly stated in unequivocal terms: 'It is true that what we seek may seem like a revolution in the sense that it means a complete change in the "theory" of the Government of India as now put forward by the bureaucracy.'[23] This complete change in the theory of the Government, in the philosophic basis of the state, involved a reapplication of the state as it would be modified in its forms to meet the changed circumstances of the twentieth century. This change in the theory of the Government was obviously far

more radical than simply an Indian use of the British forms of the state. It meant a revolutionary recasting of those forms to accord with Indian civilization's value system; it meant the remaking of the state so that it would fulfil the purposes and become the embodiment of Swaraj as it was in the Indian civilization. Swaraj was the restoration of the political order so that it would accord with the cosmic order, and so that individual lives might be assisted in attaining to the purpose of life. Tilak always insisted, '*Swaraj* is the Foundation.'

From the Nationalists' classical frame of reference, the restoration of *Swaraj* under *Dharmarajya* was the moral imperative. Only under *Dharmarajya* could national and individual lives be fulfilled. Sri Aurobindo clearly defined this as the meaning of the goal in his speech at Jhalakati:

> 'What is it that we seek? We seek the fulfillments of our life as a nation. This is what the word "Swaraj" which is a bugbear and terror to the Europeans, really means...Swaraj is not the colonial form of Government nor any form of Government. It means the fulfilment of our national life. That is what we seek, that is why God has sent us into the world to fulfil Him by fulfilling ourselves in our individual life, in the family, in the community, in the nation, in humanity. That is why He has sent us to the world and it is this fulfilment that we demand, for this fulfilment is life and to depart from it is to perish.'[24]

This is the revolution that is *Swaraj*; this is the recreation and fulfilment of the purpose of life.

For India, there could be no such thing as partial *Swaraj*. Self-rule under *Dharmrajaya* either existed fully or did not exist at all. Partial *Swaraj* was a contradiction in terms. Only the Westernized few, who could not understand this, could talk in such contradictory terms, could agree to settle for administrative reforms, could not see that '*Swaraj* is India's birth-right'. Through *Swaraj*, the revolutionary change in the theory of Government, and through *Swaraj* alone meaning when he wrote '*Swaraj* is our *Dharma*'. Before the people of the nation the Nationalists set this goal. Next

they set about to make it a political realty, to implement the programme to bring about the goal.

The Implementation

Tilak has taught that morally, '*Swaraj* is the natural consequence of diligent performance of duty'.[25] But to assist this process of moral evolution, the Nationalists devised a three-part campaign, relying upon boycott, Swadeshi and national education, to implement *Swaraj*. Since there was to be democratic *Swaraj*, since all the people were to share in self-rule, all the people should be brought into the movement for gaining it. The first part of the campaign, therefore, was the enlistment of broad popular support for the national cause. As Tilak had objected that the social reformers sought exclusiveness rather than contact with the people, and that exclusiveness was unproductive, so also did he teach in matters of political education and action. The Nationalist went to the people. They taught the *Dharma* of action and the *Dharma* of unity to found their programme on united popular action. In Bengal, Pal emphasized the common goal in saying, "You and I, the meanest of men, to whatever caste, to whatever community or denomination, the Indian may belong, we all form an organic element of the big *Swa* whose *raj* we desire to set up and attain in this country."[26] Unified popular action, properly led into the proper channels, could bring about *Swaraj*.

Briefly, the following summarises Tilak's connotation of the concept of *Swaraj*:

To Tilak, the concept of *Swaraj* does not have only a negative meaning, that is only to be free from the foreign yoke. Tilak recognised the possibility of a native government turning tyrannical. He observed that under such circumstances the people naturally become hostile to such a regime and at times may not regret even the loss of political independence.[27]

Tilak's concept of *Swaraj* was not a product of romantic nationalism nor spiritual nationalism. The thrust of his argument in favour of *Swaraj* was basically not emotional. He preferred to elaborate the adverse moral and material effects of British rule,

and then render a rational explanation of this phenomenon, namely that the British Government was failing in its duties as a government because it was foreign in character. It also needs to be mentioned here that Tilak used the word *dharma* only with a view to emphasise that *Swarajya* is not only a natural right of a people, a nation, but also its 'bounden duty, a sort of moral obligation. It does not have any religious implications. Tilak's concept of *Swaraj* has a positive content. This aspect has been neglected by the academicians so far.

Tilak looked upon freedom as the *elan* vital (Chaitanya) of a nation and as such essential for the existence of a society as oxygen is for the existence of the human body. Once the vital spark has extinguished, a nation is reduced to a vegetative life. He observed that the loss of political freedom hampers the vitality and moral grit of any society; foreign rule truncates the development and curbs the growth of a subjected nation and deprives it of the chance of attaining excellence in any field of life. A subject nation comes to lose the very necessary human qualities which make social and individual living meaningful. Tilak perceives that adverse consequences of political subjection are bound to be reflected in the economic field as well, and more so in the post-industrial revolution world. His articles make it quite evident that Tilak was aware of this dimension of modern European imperialism. Tilak concluded that it was essential for a subject nation to strive for freedom for its salvation.

At this juncture, Tilak raised a basic question: Can a subject nation rely on the imperial power for help and guidance towards the attainment of its freedom? This question is all the more significant as the then prevailing conditions in India had overshadowed the true character of the relationship between India and Britain. Though convinced of the necessity of self-rule, the moderates had chosen to rely on the foreign rulers and they looked to Britain for inspiration and guidance. To them Britain was their political guide and moral preceptor. For the moderates, the British Government was a God-sent institution meant for the promotion of the highest interests of India. Tilak realised the need of going behind the facade of the benevolent British rule. To start with, Tilak was concerned with

deteriorating Indian conditions under foreign rule. But once he applied his mind to the Indian issue he tried to sort out and analyse the Indo-British relationship only as an illustration of a colonial relationship model. He gathered that historical experience conclusively proved that there was an inherent contradiction between the interests of the imperial nation and the subject nation; and hence it would be political folly naively to expect that the foreign power, however liberal and progressive otherwise, would come to the rescue of the subject nation. Tilak was not ready to make a distinction between British liberals and British conservatives as the same constraints wouid operate with both of them. The uniqueness of Tilak's approach is his awareness of this phenomenon. Foreign domination to Tilak, was the foremost and all pervading obstruction in the way of true development of any nation towards ultimate freedom. Demand for freedom to Tilak, thus became imperative on the part of a subject nation. Hence Tilak gave top priority to and advocated total concentration of all efforts to end the foreign rule.

But to be free from the foreign rule is not the logical end of *Swaraj* to Tilak. He was unequivocal in stating that the society must be governed by the people for the interests and welfare of the people, then only could it be called free. Attainment of freedom thus represents, simply, the removal of a foremost, powerful obstruction towards ultimate freedom. Though it is a necessary prerequisite of the next stage, substitution of foreign rule by native rule does not, according to Tilak, amount to real *Swaraj*.

In advocating the cause of *Swaraj*, Tilak had relied mainly upon rational argument. He had sought to enlighten the people on their rights as *praja* and asked them to judge the performance of the British rulers on the criterion of *Praja-hita*, that is, good of the people. Tilak added, there was a time when it was believed that whatever a king, a ruler, did was just; but now they feel that he who rules justly can legitimately be called a king. He not only emphasised that he who tramples on the interests of the subjects cannot be called a king in the true sense of the term, but also reminded that those who allow their interests to be so trampled are not also the real *praja*. He thereby clearly indicated that "an unjust regime would soon lose its legitimacy in the eyes of the people."

It is against this background that Tilak knowingly and deliberately raised the question: "What is *Swaraj*?" Giving the literal meaning of *Swaraj* as rule by the natives, Tilak pointed out that an inquiring mind would not be satisfied with this explanation. Real *Swaraj*, to Tilak was rule by the people according to the wishes of the people. '*Swa*' (self) in '*Swaraj*' (self-rule) meant people's (*Praja's*) rule, and hence self-rule, or *Swaraj* should, therefore, mean people's rule or democracy. He maintained that according to this criterion neither Russia under the Czar nor Germany under the Kaiser could boast of enjoying *Swaraj* in the true sense of the term, though both of them were politically independent and were governed in the larger interests of the nation state.

The main point of Tilak's criticism against foreign domination was that it stagnates the growth of an individual, deprives him of the opportunity of attaining excellence in any field of life. The purpose of *Swaraj* was to remove this obstacle; it would not be meaningful otherwise. Hence under an undemocratic political set-up people do not feel that they are enjoying *Swaraj*.

Tilak prophesied that ultimately the people under such conditions would strive for the attainment of true *Swaraj*, that is, democratic self-rule. All. people, at least the knowledgeable ones, cherish liberty and as such are not happy under an authoritarian political set-up. Tilak explained that the Socialist movement in Germany was an illustration of this trend. The same logic was true of the democratic movement in Russia also. According to Tilak, people should not rest over their oars unless and until they are granted the right of participating in and of influencing the decision-making process.

It may be pointed out here that Tilak conceded that a democratic political set-up may at times be lacking in the discipline and efficiency of a dictatorial regime. But he maintained that it would be gratifying because there is nothing more important man than his liberty. He compares life in such regimes to the life in jail, which is also well-disciplined and even well-protected but fails to bring happiness to its inmates. Tilak urged that the famous adage, "self-government is better than good government", should be understood in this context. He asked the people always to keep in mind this meaning of the *Swaraj*. Tilak hoped that with increasing political awareness people

would come to identify the idea of self-rule with that of democratic rule, and would realise that the emergence of good government would not be possible in the absence of a democratic set-up.

Tilak maintained that with the spread of modern education demand for democratic form of government would become universal. To support his inference Tilak cited democratic agitations in various countries like China, Japan and Iran. Tilak claimed that the Indian nationalists also wanted to secure the same rights for their people, and when they implored the people to strive for *Swaraj*, they had in mind democratic rule only.

More importantly, Tilak set and prescribed certain guidelines for action in an undemocratic, unconstitutional political set-up. Proper cognizance of his article 'Legal or Constitutional'—*Kayadesheer ki Sanadsheer* (in Marathi) is very rarely taken. This article is not merely incidental, it is rather the fountain of Tilak's thoughts on *Swaraj*. It is quite evident that he was concerned not only with the compulsions and constraints in a subject country agitating to secure freedom, but also with the prevailing political conditions and the consequent popular demands in the undemocratic political set-up.

Tilak, first of all examines the term 'constitutional', that is, the concept of constitutionalism, and explains in quite simple words the substance of constitutionalism. In its literal sense, any regime, even the most arbitrary and authoritarian one, can be classified as constitutional. But the spirit of constitutionalism does not approve of such an interpretation. In political science the term constitutional has a definite connotation; it refers to a limited government. Tilak also explains the *raison d'etre of* such political arrangement, that is provision for limited government. It is in human nature to attract concentrated power in one's hands. As a corrective, therefore, in all developed countries, controls are exercised over the government on behalf of the people and the rulers are made accountable to the people. Citing the Russian experience, Tilak further stated that once this aspiration for 'true *Swaraj*', that is constitutional political set-up is aroused in people's mind, no amount of repression or suppression would succeed in quenching their desire.

Tilak, consequently, raised the basic question regarding the constitutionality of the methods of political agitation in an

unconstitutional set-up. He asked whether the people who are leading such an agitation can claim with any validity that their agitation is carried within the bounds of the constitution. To him such a claim is quite meaningless in the absence of any constitution. The only valid claim can be to press the legality of their efforts. Even this claim has very little significance when in an arbitrary political set-up it is up to the government to decide whether the particular agitation is legal or otherwise, There is every likelihood that this sanction would be arbitrarily applied even when the people's efforts are in accordance with common usage, natural rights principle or morality. Tilak declared that whatever is legal is not necessarily just and that when there is discrepancy between what is legal and what is just, the people have no other alternative but to resist the arbitrary, oppressive law, even at the peril of suffering. The people need only consider whether their efforts have the support of justice, morality, historical tradition and progress and need not worry as to whether their efforts are branded as legal or otherwise. Violating (disobeying) the law will result in punishment, but one must accept punishment, and still resist. This is inevitable. The word of the rulers may become law but it cannot be necessarily equated with morality. When the law becomes oppressive, it is the duty of the individual to break it. Tilak feels that in this regard, to act as per the dictates of one's conscience is the essence of humanity. The rulers in any dictatorial regime tend to invoke articles of the law on treason in order to suppress the rightful efforts of a people to ventilate their grievances and articulate their just demands. This would mean that the rulers are not at all concerned with justice, morality and resistance to evil. Tilak asserted that if the true end and strength of the regime is the welfare of the people, then it automatically follows, as a corollary, that it is a duty on the part of the people to resist any injustice, and this is commensurate with the real spirit of government.

Tilak further stated that it is the people who are to judge the actions of the government and to decide as to whether the government is unjust, unfair, oppressive or otherwise. If a government does not feel any compunction in validating its act as legal then the people should exercise their natural right of passing a verdict that the government is oppressive and ought to perform their moral duty

of resisting any such action on the part of the government. Tilak, thus, not only explained the core of constitutional government but claimed that to have it was the natural right of the people.

Tilak juxtaposed the concept of *Praja-Droha* (treason by the subjects) against the tendency on the part of the rulers to invoke articles of the law on sedition to suppress even the just demands of the people. Tilak explained that the rulers and the ruled have mutual obligations. Tilak's definition of *Praja-Droha* is quite simple. If the rulers fail to fulfil their obligations towards the people and behave with the people unjustly, it amounts to *Praja-Droha*. Referring to this mutual relationship, Tilak observed that the existing penal code might not have incorporated an article on *Praja-Droha*, but surely it must have been mentioned in the Divine Code, and proper provision for a punishment in the divine court must also have been made. By using the term *Praja-Droha*, Tilak conveyed to the people who had so far heard only about *Raj-Droha*, that in the modern age the real sovereign was the people and not the king or a coterie of rulers who were holding formal power. In a society brought up on traditional norms, this approach of Tilak was of course novel. Referring to the old adage, "King is Vishnu, i.e. God" (ना विष्णु पृथिवी पतिः), he commented that by the same logic '*Praja* is also God', and as such *Praja* should not suffer injustice at the hands of the rulers.

Tilak openly and frankly told the people that even under self-rule people cannot hope to win political rights merely by sweet persuasion of the rulers, but would have to agitate for them. if the people want to secure their just and valid rights they have to do so through their own valour and self-endeavour. At times, they may have to resort to obstructive measures. Tilak's advocacy of this concept of *Praja-Droha* should thus be evaluated in this context. It must be appreciated that to prove his point, Tilak cites instances from the British history and histories of other countries enjoying self-rule in the limited sense of the term. This clearly shows that Tilak was not concerned only with conditions in India, that is, conditions and compulsions in a subject country, but that his observations had relevance and were valid wherever people did not enjoy real *Swaraj*.

To sum up, it may be said that to Tilak "*Swaraj* is birthright and I will have it" was no expression of his mere patriotic emotions, but of well-knit logical argument.

REFERENCES

1. Shay, Theodore, *The Legacy of Lokmanya* (London: Oxford University Press), 1956, p. 88.
2. Vaswani, T.L., *India in Chains* (Madras: Ganesan & Co.), 1920, pp. 56-57.
3. *Gleanings from Tilak Writings and Speeches, op. cit.*, p. 112.
4. Tilak, B.G., *Gita Rahasya*, op. cit., p. 37.
5. Pal, Bepin Chandra, *His Life and Utterances* (Madras: Ganesan & Co.), 1925, p. 91.
6. *Gleanings from Tilak Writings and Speeches, op. cit.*, p. 121.
7. *Ibid.*, p. 112.
8. *Ibid.*, p. 322.
9. Shay, Theodore, *The Legacy of Lokmanya, op. cit.*, p. 93.
10. Tilak, B.G., *His Writings and Speeches, op. cit.*, p. 77.
11. *Ibid.*, p. 65.
12. *Tilak* Vs *Chirol*, Vol. I, op. cit., pp. 376-79.
13. *Gleanings from Tilak Writings and Speeches, op. cit.*, p. 322.
14. Kelkar, N.C. *Life and Times of Lokamanya Tilak*, Vol. I, op. cit., p. 94.
15. *Bande Matram*, 30 June, 1907.
16. *Gleanings from Tilak Writings and Speeches, op. cit.*, p. 333.
17. *Ibid.*, p. 329.
18. Ghose, Aurobindo's Introduction to *Bal Gangadhar Tilak, His Writings and Speeches*, p. 15.
19. *Tilak, B.G., His Writings and Speeches, op. cit.*, p. 164.
20. *Ibid.*, pp. 187 and 278.
21. Pal, Bepin Chandra, *His Life and Utterances, op. cit.*, p. 93.
22. *Gleanings from Tilak Writings and Speeches, op. cit.*, p. 331.
23. *Tilak, B.G., His Writings and Speeches, op. cit.*, p. 276.
24. Ghose, Aurobindo's 'Introduction' to *Bal Gangadhar Tilak, His Writings and Speeches*, pp. 85-86.
25. *Tilak, B.G., His Writings and Speeches, op. cit.*, p. 276.
26. Pal, Bepin Chandra, *His Life and Utterances, op. cit.*, p. 94.
27. *Tilak, B.G., Samagra Lokmanya Tilak*, Vol. IV (Pune: *Kesari* Prakashan), 1974, p. 60.

5

SOCIAL PHILOSOPHY

Several critics have lamented the alliance between the political extremism and social orthodoxy of the Tilak school of thought. This line of approach was originated by Chirol and has been later on repeated by several critics and historians. It is true that Tilak was definitely opposed to social change on western lines. But he was not opposed to social change as such. He was a nationalist and he put the primacy on political emancipation. His idea was that the social and religious solidarity of the people must be preserved in order that successful struggles could be fought against the bureaucracy. His discerning eye saw in the teachings of social reform the tendency towards social disruption and that he regarded as unfortunate at that time. Mere social advancement was no criterion for political emancipation. His experiences in Burma, in 1899, confirmed his standpoint. In Burma there was more social freedom than in India but still the political condition of Burma was not better than that of India.[1]

Tilak was opposed to the fact that a foreign bureaucratic government should make interference in the field of social and religious reforms. The foreign state represented the concentration of force and its ways of operation were mechanical, externalistic and alien. Hence, Tilak did not want to surrender the social field—an area hitherto under the control of the people—to the control of the bureaucracy. He argued that those leaders and people who had strong Moslem political domination in India in the sixteenth and seventeenth centuries did not clamour for social reform. Hence he stated these two propositions. First, social reform should not be

given priority. The prime need of the hour was concentration of energy for the attainment of political rights. Social reform would naturally and necessarily come after political rights had been obtained. Secondly, whatever reforms were necessary should be introduced gradually through a process of education. Tilak, thus believed in the organic conception of society. He resented that those councils where elected Indian members did not have the majority, should be entrusted with the decision of the social fate of India.[2]

He was opposed to untouchability. In the Ganapati celebrations, the men of the lower caste were allowed to take their statues of the God Ganesha in procession along with the statues belonging to the higher castes. In 1918, at the time of Lonavala District Conference Tilak had a discussion on the problem of untouchability with V.R. Shinde of the Depressed Classes Mission. Tilak agreed to offer his co-operation in his own way.[3] The First Depressed Classes Conference was held in Bombay near the French Bridge, on 24th and 25th March 1918. Shinde had organized this conference. While addressing the meeting Tilak declared that untouchability should go. He said that all Indians were children of the same motherland. There could be no spiritual and moral deference of untouchability. He said in thundering words: "...if a God were to tolerate untouchability, I would not recognize him as God at all."[4] But he confessed that political activities consumed all his energies and hence in adherence to the principle of division of labour he was devoting all his time to political work. He wanted others to take up social work. In July 1920, he attended a Kirtan party organized by the members of the depressed classes of Poona.

Tilak was certainly a conservative but he did adapt himself to the changing situation. He was opposed to marriage among the various castes but had no objection to marriage among the various sub-sections of the same caste. He held that remarriage of widows was against the Shastras but he also held that those who were remarried did not lose their caste although they might occupy a somewhat inferior position. Some of the non-Brahmans in Maharashtra, especially under the leadership of the Maharaja of Kolhapur, tried to overadvertise the Brahmanistic leanings of Tilak. We have to bear in mind that social situations are changing and it

will not be proper to apply the standards of modern social egalitarianism to a leader of a tradition-bound country, who had to carry behind him the vast masses, in the years 1880 to 1920. A martyr can do and utter whatever he likes. But a leader has to act with great caution and moderation. If he wants to have a continued following among the masses for a number of years, he can only go a few paces ahead of them. Tilak was a democrat and he wanted the people to follow him. Hence he believed in organic and gradual growth in matters of social change.

Social Reforms

Tilak has elaborated his philosophy of social change in various articles contributed by him to the *Kesari*. He was not opposed to social reform as such but was hostile to a total and immediate programme of social revolution. He adhered to an organic, evolutionary and spontaneous conception of social change brought about by progressive education and growing enlightenment. Any system of reform imposed from the top under the sanction of legal punishment appeared to him mechanical and, hence, likely to subvert the pattern of existing life and society. He did not want to disrupt the cohesiveness of the community as an evolving organism by creating sections and factions on the question of social reform. His principal aim was a nationalistic upsurge and hence he was opposed to creating confusion in the mass mind by holding up before them divergent social philosophies. He did not want to incorporate corrosive influences in the social body by creating schisms. He felt that progressive social change should be gradually introduced but it should be under the inspiration and leadership of those who had reverence for Hindus ideals. People who had lost faith in the primacy of the spiritual principle and were more or less outcast intellectuals had no moral right to impose their ill-digested notions of social reform borrowed from a rather fragmentary acquaintance with the complexities and intricacies of western social history. He wanted gradual and peaceful change in society and refused to believe that the salvation of India lay in the blind social imitation of the West. He wanted progress but he had sufficient appreciation of what

Hegal calls the *Volksgeist*—the spirit of the people, not to rush into the blind alley of hasty social legislation conceived in utter disregard of the history and evolution of the Hindu society.

Tilak refused to be hoodwinked by the outbursts of the reformers that social reform was the necessary antecedent to political progress. The reformers said that it was imperative to modify the Hindu social structure before the solid fruit of political development could be obtained. Tilak was opposed to the proposition that social reformism was the necessary antecedent for obtaining political right from the British rulers. He pointed out the case of Ireland in those days. Ireland had almost realized the scheme of social reforms which were advocated by the Indian social reformers but still she was politically prostrate. During 1898-99, Tilak visited Ceylon and Burma and in those countries he found a far greater degree of social freedom than in India but still those areas were politically very backward. By these examples he tried to reveal the inadequacy of the logic which pointed to the inevitable precedence of social reform to political progress and emancipation. He seriously and tenaciously clung to his conviction that political right being primary and utterly and absolutely important, the acquisition of more and more political right was the supreme necessity for India. Social questions could taken be up after that.

In his later life, Tilak often used to refer to the concept of 'division of labour' among the personnel concerned with problems of the country. Tilak was that he was concentrating on the question of political rights and felt that some other people should take up the question of social emancipation of the depressed classes. Hence it is a mistake to interpret Tilak as a social obscurantist or a conservative apologist of old creeds and dogmas.[5] Time and again in his speeches and writings he asserts that he is not opposed to social reform. In concentrating upon political emancipation as the supreme need of the nation, Tilak gave evidence of his political insight into how to build up the strength of the nation. Any introduction of social schism would have disrupted the cohesiveness of the nation, however, palatable it might have been to the fancies of the social reformer and idealist. The life of a nation is a psychological and historical continuum. Instead of creating ruptures in this

continuum, Tilak felt that the necessity of the hour was the realization of the unity of this continuum and he wanted to galvanize its life in a channel which could finally lead to the enshrinement of the concept of political self-determination. Hence it is a mistake to think that Tilak's demagogic ethics cleverly permitted the union of political extremism and social reaction. This view was made fashionable by Tilak's arch-opponent, Sir Valentine Chirol, and since the publication of the latter's *The Indian Unrest*, it has been repeated by many uncritical students of Indian nationalism. If we study the history of nationalism in the west, we find that nationalism is built not upon cold mechanical reason but upon the community of emotions generated by participation in the common memories of historical sufferings and victories. Hence the accumulation of the cultural *ethos* and values goes a great way to create the foundations of nationalism.[6] Renan has also regarded the nation as a psychological concept. In the process of the onward advance of a nation it is necessary to preserve cultural continuity. Tilak wanted to preserve the dominant moral and spiritual values of the Hindu culture. But at the same time, he felt that without the acquisition of political right, cultural autonomy could not be maintained. Hence this advocate of the perennial values of Hindu philosophy became also a stalwart of Indian nationalism. He wanted political rights because only after obtaining them the proper atmosphere could be created for the development of comprehensive activities of the nation. Meantime, by the teachings and precepts, the consciousness of the nation was to be gradually prepared for the acceptance of social transformation.

Another vital element in Tilak's attitude to social reform was that he was opposed to bureaucratic interference in social and religious matters. The making of any social law would also involve the necessity of its execution as well as the judicial settlement of disputes regarding the transgression of the law. This meant the extension of the power of the British rulers and judges. 'Tilak was opposed to the increase of the area of bureaucratic power. He did not look with favour upon the possibility of bureaucratic inroads and invasion upon a sphere which had so for been autonomous and immune. The alien rulers professing the values of a different civilization should not be made the judges and legislators in social

matters because these were suffused with the collective emotions and sentiments of the Hindu population. It was unwise to trust the so-called omniscience of an alien bureaucracy attempting to look at the Indian social situation from almost Olympian heights. Tilak almost felt it humiliating that the Hindus should go supplicating to the bureaucracy and request them to make social laws because the former (the Hindus) had fallen so low that they could not even manage their social problems.[7] Such a supplicating mood, according to Tilak would weaken the moral and intellectual foundations of *Swaraj*. He on the contrary, asserted that the Indians were politically able and had vast organizational and administrative achievements to their credit in the past. Hence there was no rationale for an imposition of social reform from above. If the government would have been composed of democratically elected representatives of independent India, his attitude would have been different. Thus, in Tilak's radical opposition to bureaucratic social legislation we may find sentiments of deep-seated patriotism and not the demagogic desire to strengthen his leadership by making appeals to the fetishes, dogmas, religious passions and social prejudices of the people of the Hindu society.

It is true that Tilak did not like the attitude of the social reformers. They had received western education and wanted to introduce western social notions in Hindu society. They had the scoffing and ridiculing attitude towards Hindu religious codes and scriptures. Philosophically speaking, Tilak did believe that with the change in times there were bound to be changes in the interpretation of the scriptures. Even new social laws were bound to be made. But so long as the majority was sticking to the teachings of the religious codes, it was not proper according to Tilak, to deride their notions and conceptions. In Indian history it is found that social reformers have also been saints. Nanak and Kabir were spiritual souls. But the modern self-styled reformers, who were at best intellectual, and some of whom even did not hesitate to bask in the sunshine of bureaucratic favours, had no moral right to sit in judgement upon the social codes, which according to the Hindu cultural orientation, were associated with religion. The social reformers had purely secularistic notions of social reform conceived

in the western fashion. They were social positivists believing in the judgement of political authority in the social and moral spheres. Tilak, on the other hand, was a conservative historicist believing in the gradual evolution of the social consciousness. He did accept the need for social change and reform but felt that these should be carried on under the leadership of men of eminent moral and spiritual character living as the embodiment of the Hindu way of life and not by mere intellectuals pouring the vials of their wrath on the contemporary society in newspapers. Hence it is clear that Tilak's attitude to social reform was dictated by his comprehensive conception of politics and culture.

Tilak and Agarkar

G.G. Agarkar was a rationalist. He wanted to play the part of an ardent champion of social reform. Once in the *Sudharak* he stated his social philosophy thus:

"We have as much right to inaugurate new customs and usages as the ancient *Rishis;* we enjoy the same favour of God as the ancient Acharyas; we are endowed with the same, if not greater, fault of discrimination between right and wrong as they; our hearts melt with pity for the depressed classes much more than theirs did; our knowledge of the universe and its cause is greater, not less than theirs; hence we shall observe only those injunctions laid down by them which we deem beneficial, and replace those which we think harmful by others. It is on these lines that reform must be made, it is useless to quote one sage against another and try to reconcile them all."[8]

Agarkar being a champion of social enlightenment, advocated progressive and liberal social legislation. He had advanced social views and like Ram Mohun Roy had a burning passion for the eradication of the social evils of contemporary Hindu society. He was opposed to child marriage and marriage in old age. He thoroughly accepted a positive philosophy of the state. His attitude partly bears resemblance to Plato's ideas which are formulated in the Republic and the Laws. Plato wanted the state to make laws about marriage and other related social problems. To Agarkar the

essential problem was the eradication of social evils and he did not see any harm or injury in the foreign state making laws for social and martial regulation. The Kesari was not the paper of any single individual, and though up to 1887 Agarkar was mainly in charge of the Kesari, he could not transform it into an instrument for the propagation of his own reformist social views. Hence some sort of a compromise was arrived at. If Agarkar had to write anything which referred to advocacy of advanced social reforms, he could put that article under separate columns, under his own signature, or could put that under the general heading "contributed". However, this compromise did not work for a long time.[9]

Tilak was a member of the conservative group. He was not quite opposed to social reform but was opposed to the way social reforms were being advocated. He was a believer in the *Shastras*, and acknowledged that the religious scriptures are the creations of persons whose minds have attained discriminatory vision and who have obtained equanimity. Hence he did not like to give a rough treatment to the *Shastras*. On the other hand, he did acknowledge that the *Shastras* could be changed with reference to the demands of space and time. Svetaketu is a significant example in this connexion. It was he who (Svetaketu) introduced the custom of regular marriages. Tilak did not like that an alien bureaucratic political and administrative system should make innovations in the social and religious affairs of the subject peoples. He would have rejected the political theory of Hobbes which advocates the control of the state over the church. According to Tilak, progressive enlightenment of the people into a reform-accepting type of social consciousness, and not alien imposition from the top, was the true method of social reform. Since their college days, Tilak and Agarkar had been engaging in sophisticated discussions about the relative priority of social reform and political emancipation. Agarkar wanted the immediate social enlightenment of the people. He felt that if rationality was introduced in the social process, political problems would not prove baffling. Tilak, on the other hand, was convinced that the fundamental requirement of the country was the reduction, if not the total elimination, of the foreign bureaucratic pressure. Once the political soul of India was free, the Indian Councilors could decide

upon the problems of social change in an atmosphere of free criticism. Hence Tilak did not see any justification for inviting people of a different culture and civilization to pronounce upon the Hindu social situation. Neither Tilak nor Agarkar was ready for any compromise. Both were powerful personalities and hence a break between them lay in the logic of their psychological structure.

The differences between Tilak and Agarkar which had their fundamental roots in their divergent attitudes towards social reform became more acute with the passage of time. Most of the members connected with the *Kesari* did not appreciate the advanced social philosophy of Agarkar. Hence the rift between Tilak and Agarkar progressively widened. A series of immediate events, like the case of Rakambhai, provided the opportunity for the accentuation of the conflict.[10] The examples of the growing hostility between the group of Tilak and the party of the social reformers under the leadership of Ranade may be seen in the articles of the *Kesari* of those years. On the 9th June 1885, the *Kesari* published a bitterly sarcastic article against Ranade.[11] Due to the mounting differences between the two groups, Agarkar severed his connexion with the *Kesari* in 1887, in the month of October. Henceforth, Tilak, Vasudeorao Kelkar and H.N. Gokhale became the proprietors of the *Kesari* and the *Maharatta.* Since October 1887, Tilak became the declared editor of the *Kesari.* After severing his connexion with the *Kesari,* Agarkar started a new paper of his own—the *Sudharak,* in October 1888. It was an Anglo-Marathi paper and for some years Gopal Krishna Gokhale was the editor of its English section. Gokhale and Agarkar set new ideals in the history of political and journalistic asceticism by accepting only Rs. 4/- per month in the first year of the establishment of the paper. With the inception of the *Sudharak* began a period of criticisms and recriminations both in the *Kesari* and the *Sudharak.* The *Sudharak* once made a concealed attack on Tilak. It condemned those leaders who refused to expose the voices of the people for the sake of maintaining their leadership over them. Such leaders, according to the *Sudharak,* lead to the eventual disaster of the people. A famous source of controversy between the *Kesari* and the *Sudharak* was the difference over the question of curriculum in the Female High School of Poona.

Tilak's view was that girls should be educated but he was opposed to extravagant westernization.

(a) The Age of Consent Act, 1891. On the 9th January 1891, the Age of Consent Bill was formally introduced in the Imperial Legislative Council at Calcutta. It was stated that the aim of the bill was only to raise the age of consent from ten to twelve. Hence it was clear that for the present the government had only taken up for consideration the first point in the Malabari's corpus of social reforms. Ramesh Chandra Mitter strongly opposed the bill. The Viceroy Lansdowne pointed out, however, that the proposed bill did not go against the Proclamation of 1858 of Queen Victoria. In a leading article on the 20th January, the *Kesari* emphatically argued that the proposed bill was bound to interfere in Hindu religious practices, and hence the people ought to oppose the passage of the bill.[12] For about three months the *Kesari* published articles and notes against the bill. But although, in spite of Tilak's opposition, the bill had been passed, he protested against it even after enactment of the Bill. The Fourth Bombay Provincial Conference was held in Poona in May 1891, under the Presidentship of Govindrao Limaye. Tilak said in the conference that public opinion had been opposed to the enactment. There was some opposition to Tilak's standpoint but still the provincial conference passed a resolution protesting against the action of the government in not giving sufficient recognition to public opinion. Tilak was not satisfied just with the passing of a proposal as he had contemplated some action as well in the British Parliament and wanted that a bill be moved therein. However, though Tilak did not succeed in getting the bill rejected, still he emerged as a leader of opposition to the government, and to the group of social reformers.

But Tilak must not be considered only as an uncompromising champion of orthodoxy. At the fourth Social Conference held in Calcutta in December 1890, R.N. Mudholkar moved a resolution, condemning child marriage and advocating adult marriage. Tilak supported the proposal, but the Sanskrit scholar that he was, he wanted to delete an incorrect reference to the *Shastras*. Tilak also attended the fifth Social Conference held in 1891 at Nagpur under the presidentship of G.S. Khaparde. There a resolution was

introduced, advocating the remarriage of widows, and it exhorted the people to help the movement. Tilak moved an amendment suggesting that the sympathisers of the movement of widow-remarriage should not merely attend the celebration of the marriage but should be prepared to demonstrate their sincerity. But this was putting the reformers to a difficult test and they got out of the vulnerable position, adding the words "so far as possible" to "help the movement". Tilak's presence was a source of acute discussion in the meeting of the subjects' committee of the Nagpur Social Conference. By a series of pointed questions Tilak made Ranade acknowledge that there were some irregularities in the constitution of the subjects committee. Tilak was a bold personality and realising that he was asking searching questions, the reformers even threatened his expulsion from the conference. We can anticipate the march of events a little and refer to two questions which bring about Tilak's attitude to social reform very clearly. In 1914, Shastri introduced a bill in the Madras Council for the extension of the age for marriage. In the *Kesari*, Lokmanya wrote a strong criticism of it. In 1918, Vithalbhai Patel introduced the Hindu Marriage Bill in the Imperial Council. Tilak was opposed also to this bill. But in a letter to the *Mahratta* on the 13th December 1919, he pointed out that his opposition to the bill was not based on social and religious grounds. He was opposed to the bill only because it would interfere with economic law of succession.[13]

(b) *Tilak and the Tea-party Incident*. The 4th October 1890 became an important day in the social history of Poona as forty-two persons, including Tilak, Ranade and Gokhale had taken tea at the house of a missionary. It was scandalous in the eyes of the orthodox sections and a case was launched in the ecclesiastical court of Shankaracharya. Sardar Natu who posed as the champion of extreme Hindu orthodoxy took the initiative in the religious case against Tilak and Ranade. Tilak's knowledge of the Hindu legal and religious code stood in good stead now. He urged that the *Shastras* prescribe *prayaschitta* for such occasions and by undergoing these expiation-ceremonies people could become purified. Tilak showed his readiness to accept the award of Shankaracharya. But the award of Shankaracharya given by his deputies was not equally acceptable

to all the defendants. A second award was given but this time the deputies of Shankaracharya did not agree on were not agreed the controversy about the Punch Howd Mission Tea-party, and the dispute in the court of Shankaracharya illustrate Tilak's spirit of compromise. He would neither yield to the dictates of orthodoxy of the extreme type nor would he throw overboard existing social conventions. Compromise does not mean weakness but is the secret of long-continued leadership over men. Tilak wrote in the *Kesari* on the 7th June 1892:

"There is considerable resemblance between our difficulties in the political field and those in the social one, neither the political administration nor the structure of our society completely satisfies us. We want to reform both. The English administration as well as the Indian society have solid foundation. We are, therefore, bound to proceed with caution. Now, if people are willing to accept political reforms in a spirit of conciliation and compromise, we fail to understand why we should like to proceed with social reform in an arrogant and defiant manner. If we are prepared to make compromise when the Parliament passes the Council's Act 1892, why should we not do so with respect to questions like widow remarriage? Fanatical opposition might occasionally be successful but as a rule, in political as well as social matters, fanaticism is suicidal."[14]

This adherence to the concept of gradualism and compromise made, in the eyes of opponents, Tilak's attitude to social reform look inconsistent. Tilak was opposed, for example, to child marriage but would not want a bureaucratic law or decree to stop it. He decried the remarriage of widows but also condemned the remarriage of men and wanted widowers to dedicate themselves to the task of the emancipation of the country. From his own standpoint and from the standpoint of the needs and demands of the time and place amidst which he had to fight against the entrenched ramparts of a foreign bureaucracy, he could not but uphold the views that he did. Moreover, we must never forget that he was a Sanatanist Hindu and it is illogical to judge his action from a radically different standpoint.

(c) *The Sarda Sadan Controversy*. Soon after her return from America, in 1889, Ramabai started the *Sarda Sadan* as a home for widows in Bombay and later on at Poona. This residential school had been started with American financial support. Tilak did not favour the idea of a girls' school established by missionaries because he felt that it was bound to become a centre for proselytization, however loudly its secularistic orientations were preached. Nevertheless, when full assurances were given, Tilak enrolled himself as a sympathiser. In the *Illustrated Christian* Weekly of 21st December 1889, Tilak got a distressing piece of news. There appeared the news that two out of the seven child-widows residing in the *Sarda Sadan* had voluntarily expressed their willingness for being evangelized into the Christian religion. It was also stated that four Indian girls were studying Christianity and some had been even attending Christian prayers. There was also a covert suggestion that the *Sarda Sadan* was in several senses Christian organization because it was supported by money from an American Christian organization.[15] The *Kesari* warned the people to be cautious. But Ramabai tried to explain away the matter in a rejoinder. The advisory committee consisting of Bhandarkar and Ranade also made some mild protest, and for a while it appeared that the Christianizing process had stopped. But while the *Kesari* had been throughout suspicious of the designs of Ramabai, Ranade and Bhandarkar felt that there should be no legitimate ground against accepting educational grants even from Christian sources. The tone of the *Kesari* was bitter against the reformers of the school of Ranade and Bhandarkar and soon the rightness of the attitude of the *Kesari* was vindicated. The argument of Ramabai was that she had to accept Christian help simply because of the fact that the Hindus would not subsidize her educational enterprises. On the 13th August 1893, the controversy which had been growing for two years ended. Ranade and Bhandarkar tendered their resignation from the advisory committee of the *Sarda Sadan*.

The *Sarda Sadan* controversy was an unmistakable indication that Tilak was opposed to the conversion of Hindu women to Christianity by non-spiritual inducements. He was not opposed to the institution *Sarda Sadan* as such, provided it confined itself to

the work of imparting secular education. He was never opposed to female education and to the emancipation of widows but he could not reconcile himself to the game of Christian conversion carried on by subtle and devious means. Tilak's *Kesari* could not view with favour the proselytizing zeal of Ramabai and that accounts for the bitterness and the sarcasm which it sometimes manifested against the social reformers who appeared to be helping the designs of Ramabai. But in this controversy Tilak was not acting as an orthodox conservative. He had an austere national instinct. He rightly saw that conversion is a matter of emotional transformation and it should not be made to subserve petty mundane ends. Hence although apologists of Pandita Ramabai and especially her Christian biographer Macnicol, have regarded Tilak as a demagogue behind this controversy one can discern the national instinct of the latter.

The controversy about the *Sarda Sadan* widened the split between Tilak and the social reformers which was growing ever since 1886 and 1887. Tilak's argument was that once the real proselytizing motivation behind the Sadan had been revealed, Ranade and Bhandarkar should have severed their connexions with that institution and exposed the designs of Ramabai. The bitter newspaper controversy only confirmed the mutual antagonism of the two groups. However, the resignation of Ranade and Bhandarkar served two purposes. First, it vindicated that Tilak's perceptions about the real intention of the founder of the Sadan were correct. Secondly, the resignation definitely pointed out that, at the most, Ranade and Bhandarkar were social-reformers and men of comprehensive toleration but certainly they were not anti-Hindu. They could not reconcile themselves to the game of the conversion of the Hindus.

The Caste System and Industrial Functionalism

In 1892 Tilak had written and presented before the Poona Industrial Conference a paper entitled "The Hindu Caste System from an Industrial Point of View." In this paper, which he wrote in the early part of his political career, he being only thirty-six at that time, he analysed the industrial aspects of the Hindu social structure.[16] He

stated that the caste system owed its origin to the peculiar historical situation of ancient times (But he would certainly have repudiated any implication that the ascription of a divine origin to it, as has been done in the Hindu Shastras, was wrong, baseless and incorrect). He stated that the caste system had served three purposes: (i) It had preserved the knowledge of industrial arts, (ii) It had checked the abuse of despotic political power, and (iii) It had kept up feelings of morality, self-respect and superiority amongst the people.[17] Possibly, he was implying that the Vaishyas have preserved industrial arts and crafts. Perhaps he also might have in mind the notion that in days when associational structures were not differentiated in the country, the caste system inculcated the sentiments of pride and self-esteem amongst the people and thereby checked their demoralization in periods of strains and political predicaments. Tilak shows a historical perspective in maintaining that all Hindu castes, except the lowest castes, were based on the criterion of difference in occupation, trade, profession and calling. Hence caste was a secular and a social organisation and its aim was the preservation of the pattern of hereditary occupations. He compared the Indian caste structure to the social and economic guilds in medieval Europe. These guilds sprang to safeguard the interests of the workers when the government failed to provide them adequate protection. Tilak quoted Dr. Brentano on this point. According to the latter, when the state failed to provide safeguard to the workers, and there was social and economic disorganization, the workers had to form their unions against the aggressive designs and activities of the leaders of the manufacturing industries. In still earlier times, the old freeman had formed their Frith-guilds against the tyranny of the medieval magnates. Free handicraftsmen had also formed their craft-guilds against the aggression of the old burglers. Tilak compared the caste structure to these Frith-guilds, Craft-guilds and trade unions. He wrote that the institutions of Mahajans and Panchayats did serve important social and judicial purposes in former times. They regulated the forms of trade and dispensed justice in petty cases and their decisions were speedy and satisfactory. Tilak further pointed out that these ancient and medieval organisations of India acted as preservers and protectors

of social and sexual morals and prevented the use of alcohol. He quoted Mr. Elliot who had admitted that with regard to some moral matters, the Indian workmen were superior to their European counterparts. This important regulative function with regard to social morality was performed by the caste structure through its rules, norms and conventions.[18]

So far, Tilak is historically correct in pointing out the advantageous functional role which the caste system performed in social system-maintaining, but he failed to realise that an expansive environment of the industrial system cannot but be the greatest destroyer of the dogmatic rigidity of the caste structure and is bound to expose its low legitimacy for an egalitarian society. He had hoped that the existing institution of caste might be utilized to improve the material and moral conditions of the working-classes in modem India just as it had performed such a task in previous ages. Tilak was categorical in his belief that the caste system could perform such a regulatory function with regard to the morals of industrial workers. But it appears to me that he failed to appreciate that in a complex industrial civilization it was absolutely impossible to formulate a scheme of caste panchayats as sub-cultural entities for the regulation of social morals. Tilak may be correct in his historical interpretation of the role of the caste in the Hindu social system, but it appears that he failed to consider some of the dysfunctional and mal-integrative aspects of caste. In ancient and medieval times, the caste system was, to a considerable extent, a mechanism for the perpetration of exploitation of the lower classes and castes. The caste system did provide some kind of harmony but it was a harmony based upon subordination of the backward sections. It did not provide any channel of genuine responsive feedback from the side of the suppressed sections. There was, it is true, no organization of alienation and revolt on the part of the backward sections in those days, but the reason was that the radical social philosophies had not permeated their consciousness. Nevertheless, it will be historically incorrect to maintain and reiterate only the brighter side of the caste system. It must, however, be stated that in a sociological study of the caste system, the regulatory role of the old caste panchayats should not be lost sight of.

REFERENCES

1. Varma, V. P., *Modern Indian Political Thought, op. cit*., p. 213.
2. *Ibid.*
3. Cashman, Richard I., *The Myth of Lokmanya* (Berkeley: University of California Press), 1975, p. 55.
4. Pradhan, G. P. and A.K. Bhagwat, *Lokmanya Tilak: A Biography* (Poona: J.S. Tilak), 1963, p. 306.
5. Ray, M.N., *India in Transition* (Bombay: Nachiketa), 1971, p. 186.
6. Varma, V.P., *Modern Indian Political Thought, op. cit*., p. 206.
7. *Ibid.*
8. *Ibid.*, p. 207.
9. Parvate, T.V., *Bal Gangadhar Tilak* (Ahmedabad: Navajivan Publishing House),1958, pp. 56-60.
10. Jog, N.G., *Lokmanya Bal Gangadhar Tilak, op. cit*., p. 31.
11. *Kesari*, 9 June 1885.
12. *Ibid.*, 20 January, 1891.
13. *Mahratta*, 13 December 1919.
14. *Kesari*, 9 June 1885.
15. *The Illustrated Christian Weekly*, 21 December 1889.
16. Kulkarni, A.V., *Lokmanya Tilak* (Bombay: Inderprakash Steam Press), 1909, pp. 195-96.
17. *Ibid.*
18. *Ibid.*

6

LEGACY OF TILAK

Tilak's activities were, like the featureless Brahman, self-luminous. Straightforward, lucid, never turning aside from the point which they meant to hammer in or wrapping it up in ornamental verbiage, they read like a series of self-evident propositions. And Tilak himself, his career, his place in Indian politics are also a self-evident proposition, a hard fact, baffling and dismaying in the last degree to those to whom his name had been anathema and his increasing pre-eminence figured as a portent of evil. The condition of things in India at that time, the one possible aim for political effort resulting and the sole means and spirit by which it could be brought about, this man had to come and, once in the field, had to come to the front. He could not but stand in the end where he stands today, as one of the two or three leaders of the Indian people who are in their eyes the incarnations of the national endeavour and, the God-given captains of the national aspiration. His life, his character, his work and endurance, his acceptance by the heart and the mind of the people were a stronger argument than all the reasonings in his speeches, powerful as these are, for *Swaraj*, Self-government, Home Rule, by whatever name it is called, the sole possible aim was, the freedom of the life of India, its self-determination by the people of India. Sir Aurobindo has very aptly said, '...arguments and speeches do not win liberty for a nation; but where there is a will in the nation to be free and a man to embody that will in every action of his life and to devote his days to its realisation and where the will of the nation has once said, "This man and his life mean what I have in my heart and my purpose," that is a sure signpost of the future which no one has any excuse for mistaking.'[1]

That indomitable will and that unwavering devotion had been the whole meaning of Tilak's life ; they were the reasons of his immense hold on the people. For he did not owe his pre-eminent position to any of the causes which had usually made for political leading in India, wealth and great social position, professional success, recognition by Government, a power of fervid oratory or of fluent speech ; for he had none of these things to help him. He owed it to himself alone and to the thing his life had meant and because he had meant it with his whole mind and his whole soul. He had kept back nothing for himself or for other aims, but had given himself to his country.

Yet Tilak was a man of extraordinary gifts. Though he had never practised, he had a close knowledge of Law and an acute legal mind which, had he cared in the least degree for wealth and worldly position, would have brought him to the front at the bar. He was a great Sanskrit scholar, a powerful writer and a strong, subtle and lucid thinker. He might have filled a large place in the field of contemporary Asiatic scholarship. Even as it was, his Orion and his Arctic Home had acquired at once a world-wide recognition and left as strong a mark as could at all be imprinted on the ever-shifting sands of oriental research: His work on the *Gita*, no mere commentary, but an original criticism and presentation of ethical truth, is a monumental work, the first prose writing of the front ranking weight and importance in the Marathi language, and has already become a classic. This one book sufficiently proves that had he devoted his energies in this direction, he might easily have filled a large place in the history of Marathi literature and in the history of ethical thought, so subtle and comprehensive is its thinking, so great the perfection and satisfying force of its style. But it was psychologically impossible for Tilak to devote his energies in any great degree to another action than the one life-mission for which the Master of his works had chosen him. His powerful literary gift had been given up to a journalistic work, ephemeral as even the best journalistic work must be, but consistently brilliant, vigorous, politically educative through decades, to an extent seldom matched and certainly never surpassed. His scholastic labour had been done almost by way of recreation. Nor could anything be more significant

than the fact that the works which had brought him a fame other than that of the politicians and patriot, were done in periods of compulsory cessation from his life-work, planned and partly, if not wholly, executed during the imprisonments which could alone enforce leisure upon this unresting worker for his country. Even these byproducts of his genius had some reference to one passion of his life, the renewal, if not the surpassing of the past greatness of the nation by the greatness of its future. His Vedic researches seek to fix its pre-historic point of departure; the *Gita-rahasya* takes the scripture which is perhaps the strongest and most comprehensive production of Indian spirituality and justifies to that spirituality by its own authoritative ancient message the sense of the importance of life, of action, of human existence, of man's labour, for mankind which is indispensable to the idealism of the modern spirit.[2]

The landmarks of Tilak's life were landmarks also in the history of the country. His first great step associated him in a pioneer work whose motive was to educate the people for a new life under the new conditions, on the one side, a purely educational, movement of which the fruit was the Ferguson College, fitly founding the reawakening of the country by an effort of which co-operation in self-sacrifice was the moving spirit, on the other, the initiation of the *Kesari* newspaper, which since then had figured increasingly as the characteristic, and powerful expression of the political mind of Maharashtra. Tilak's career has counted three periods each of which had an imprisonment for its culminating point. His first imprisonment in the Kolhapur case belongs to this first stage of self-development and development of the country for new ideas and activities and for the national future.

The second period brought in a wider conception and a profounder effort. For now it was to reawaken not only the political mind, but the soul of the people by linking its future to its past; it worked by a more strenuous and popular propaganda, which reached its height in the organisation of the Shivaji and, the Ganapati festivals...His separation from the social reform leader, Agarkar, had opened the way for the peculiar role which he has played as a trusted and accredited leader of conservative and religious India in the path of democratic politics. It was this position which enabled

him to effect the union of the new political spirit with the tradition and sentiment of the historic past and of both with the ineradicable religious temperament of the people of which these festivals were the symbol. The Congress Movement was for a long time purely accidental in its mind, character and methods confined to the English-educated few, founded on the political rights and interests of the people, read in the light of English history and European ideals, but with no roots either in the past of the country or in the inner spirit of the nation. Tilak was the first political leader to break through the routine of its somewhat academic methods, to bridge the gulf between the present and the past and to restore continuity to the political life of the nation. He developed a language and a spirit and he used methods which Indianised the movement and brought into it the masses. To his work of this period we owe that really living, strong and readily organised movement which has shown its energy and sincerity in more than one crisis and struggle. This divination of the mind and spirit of his people and its needs and this power to seize on the right way to call it forth, prove strikingly the political genius of Tilak; they made him the one man predestined to lead them in a period when all had to be discovered and all had to be reconstructed. What was done then by Tilak in Maharashtra has been initiated for all India by the Swadeshi Movement.[3] To bring in the mass of the people, to found the greatness of the future on the greatness of the past, to infuse Indian politics with Indian religious fervour and spirituality, are the indispensable conditions for a great and powerful political awakening in India. Others—writers, thinkers, spiritual leaders—had seen this truth. Tilak was the first to bring it into the actual field of practical politics. The second period of his labour for his country culminated in a longer and harsher imprisonment which was, as it were, the second seal of the divine hand upon his work; for there can be no diviner seal than suffering for a cause.

A third period, that of the Swadeshi Movement, brought Tilak forward prominently as an All-India leader; it gave him at last the wider field, the greater driving power, the larger leverage he needed to bring his life-work rapidly to a head, and not only in Maharashtra but throughout the country. From the inception of the Boycott to the

Surat catastrophe and his last and longest imprisonment, which was its sequel, the name and work of Tilak are a part of Indian history. These three imprisonments, each showing more clearly the stuff and quality of the man under the test and glare of suffering, have been the three seals of his career. The first placed him among pioneer workers; it establishing him as a strong and inflexible leader of a strong and sturdy people. The second made him the inspiring power of a great reawakening of the Maratha spirit; it left him an uncrowned king in the Deccan and gave him that high reputation throughout India, which was the foundation-stone of his commanding influence. The last gave him the status of a leader of an All-India party, the foremost exponent and head of a thorough-going Nationalism: it sent him back to be one of the two or three foremost men of India, adored and followed by the whole nation.[4]

The qualities which had supported him and given him his hard-earned success, had been comparatively rare in Indian politics. The first is his entirely representative character as a born leader for the sub-nation to which he belonged. India is a unity full of diversities and its strength as well as its weakness is rooted in those diversities; the vigour of its national life can exist only by the vigour of its regional life. Therefore, in politics as in everything else, a leader, to have a firm basis for his life-work, must build it upon a living work and influence in his own sub-race or province. No man was more fitted to do this than Tilak. He was the very type and incarnation of the Maratha character, the Maratha qualities, the Maratha spirit, but with the unified solidarity in the character, the touch of genius in the qualities, the vital force in the spirit which make a great personality, readily the representative man of his people. "The Maratha race, as their soil and their history have made them", in the words of Sri Aurobindo, "are a rugged, strong and sturdy people, democratic in their every fibre, keenly intelligent and practical to the very marrow, following in ideas even in poetry, philosophy and religion, the drive towards life and action, capable of great fervour, feeling and enthusiasm, like all Indian peoples, but not emotional idealists, having in their thought and speech always a turn for strength, sense, accuracy, lucidity and vigour, in learning and scholarship patient, industrious, careful, thorough and penetrating,

in life simple, hardy and frugal, in their temperament courageous, pugnacious, full of spirit, yet with a tact in dealing with hard facts and circumventing obstacles, shrewd yet aggressive diplomatists, born politicians, born fighters."[5] All this Tilak had with a singular and eminent completeness, and all on a large scale, adding to it all a lucid simplicity of genius, a secret intensity, an inner strength of will, a singlemindedness in aim of quite extraordinary force, which remind one of the brightness, sharpness and perfect temper of a fine sword hidden in a sober scabbard. As he emerged on the political field, his people saw more and more clearly in him their representative man, themselves in large, the genius of their type. They felt him to be of one spirit, and the greatmen who had made their past history, almost believed him to be a reincarnation of one of them returned to carry out his old work in a new form and under new conditions.

On the wider national field also Tilak had rare qualities which fitted him for the hour and the work. He was in no sense what his enemies have called him, a demagogue; he had not the loose suppleness, the oratorical fervour, the facile appeal to the passions which demagogy require; his speeches were too much made up of hard and straight thinking, he was too much a map of serious and practical action. None more careless of mere effervescence, emotional applause, popular gush, public ovations. He tolerated them since popular enthusiasm expressed itself in that way but he had always been a little impatient of them as dissipative of serious strength and will and a waste of time and energy which might better had been solidified and devoted to effective work. But he was entirely a democratic politician, of a type not very common among our leaders, one who could both awaken the spirit of the mass and respond to their spirit, able to lead them, but also able to see where he must follow the lead of their predominant sense and will and feelings. He moved among his followers as one of them in a perfect equality, simple and familiar in his dealings with them by the very force of his temperament and character, open, plain and direct and though capable of great reserve yet, wherever necessary, in his speech, admitting them into his plans and ideas as one taking counsel from them, taking their sense even while enforcing as much as possible his own view of policy and action with all the great strength

of quiet will at his command.[6] He had that closeness of spirit to the mass of men, that unpretentious openness of intercourse with them, that faculty of plain and direct speech which interprets their feelings and shows them how to think out what they feel, which are pre-eminently the democratic qualities. For this reason he had always been able to unite all classes of men behind him, to be the leader not only of the educated, but of the people, the merchant, the trader, the villager, the peasant.

It is equally a mistake to think of Tilak as, by nature, a revolutionary leader; that is not his character or his political temperament. The Indian peoples generally, have very little of the revolutionary temper; they can be goaded to revolution like any and every people on the face of the earth, but they have no natural disposition towards it. They are capable of large ideals and fervent enthusiasm, sensitive in feeling and liable to gusts of passionate revolt which are easily appeased by even an appearance of concession; but naturally they are conservative in temperament and deliberate in action. Tilak, though a strong-willed man and a fighter by nature, had this much of the ordinary Indian temperament, that with a large mind open to progressive ideas he united a conservative temperament strongly in touch with the sense of his people. In a free India, he would probably have figured as an advanced Liberal statesman eager for national progress and greatness, but as careful of every step, as firm and decided in it and always seeking to carry the conservative instinct of the nation with him in every change. He was besides a born Parliamentarian, a leader of the Assembly, though always in touch with the people outside as the constant source of the mandate and the final referee in differences. He loved a clear and fixed procedure which he could abide by and use, even while making the most of its details of which the theory and practice would always be at his finger tips to secure a practical advantage in the struggle of parties. He always set a high value on the Congress for this reason; he saw in it a centralising body, an instrument and a first, though yet shapeless, essay at a popular Assembly. Many after Surat, spoke of him as the deliberate breaker of the Congress, but to no one was the catastrophe so great a blow as to Tilak.[7] He did not love the do-nothingness of that Assembly, but he valued it

both as a great national fact and for its unrealised possibilities and hoped to make of it a central organisation for practical work. To destroy an existing and useful institution was alien to his way of seeing and would not have entered into his ideas or his wishes.

Moreover, though he had ideals, he was not an idealist by character. Once the ideal was fixed, all the rest was for him 'practical work', the facing of hard facts, though overcoming them when they stood in the way of the goal, the use of strong and effective means with the utmost care and prudence, consistent with the primary need of as rapid an effectivity as will and earnest action could bring about. Though he could be obstinate and iron-willed when his mind was made up as to the necessity of a course of action or the indispensable recognition of a principle, he was always ready for a compromise and would take willingly half a loaf rather than no bread, though always with a full intention of getting the whole loaf in good time. But he would not accept chaff or plaster in place of good bread. Nor did he like to go too far ahead of possibilities, and indeed had often shown in this respect a caution highly disconcerting to the more impatient of his followers. But neither would he mistake, like the born Moderate, the minimum effort and the minimum immediate aim for the utmost possibility of the moment. Such a man is no natural revolutionist, but a constitutionalist by temper, though always in such times necessarily the leader of an advanced party or section. A clear constitution he may use, amend and enlarge which would have suited him much better than to break existing institutions and get a clear field for innovations which is the natural delight of the revolutionary temperament.[8]

This character of Tilak's mind explains his attitude in social reform. He was no dogmatic reactionary. "The Maratha people, writes Sri Aurobindo, were incapable of either unreasoning or too much reasoning rigid, conservatism or of the fiery iconoclasm which can exist side by side—they are often only two sides of the same temper of mind in other parts of India. It is attached to its social institutions like all people who live close to the soil, but it has always shown a readiness to adapt, loosen and accommodate them in practice to the pressure of actual needs.[9] Tilak shared this general temperament and attitude of his people. But there have also been

other reasons which a strong political sense has dictated; and first, the clear perception that the political movement could not afford to cut itself off from the great mass of the nation or split itself up into warring factions by a premature association of the Social reform question with politics. The proper time for that, as a politician would naturally feel, is when the country has a free Assembly of its own, which can consult the needs or carry out the mandates of the people. Moreover, he had felt strongly that political emancipation was the one pressing need for the people of India and that all else not directly connected with it must take a second place; this had been the principle of his own life and had held that it should be the principle of the national life at the present hour. Let us have first liberty and the organised control of the life of the nation, afterwards we can see how we should use it in social matters; meanwhile let us move on without noise and strife, only so far as actual need and advisability demand and the sense of the people is ready to advance. This attitude may be right or wrong but Tilak being what he was, and the nation being what it is, he could think no other way.

If, Tilak had throughout his life been an exponent of the idea of radical change in politics, and during the *Swadeshi* agitation the head of a party which could be called extremist, it is due to that clear practical sense, essential in a leader of political action, which seizes at once on the main necessity and goes straight without hesitation or deviation to the indispensable means. There are always two classes of political mind: one is pre-occupied with details for their own sake, revels in the petty point of the moment and puts away into the background the great principles and the great necessities, the other sees rather these first and always and details only in relation to them. The one type moves in a routine circle which may or may not have an issue; it cannot see the forest for the trees and it is only by an accident that it stumbles, if at all, on the way out. The other type takes a mountain-top view of the goal and all the directions and keeps that in their mental compass through all the deflections, retardations and tortuosities which the character of the intervening country may compel them to accept; but these they abridge as much as possible. The former class arrogate the name of statesman in their own day; it is to the latter that posterity concedes

it and sees in them the true leaders of great movements. Tilak, like all men of pre-eminent political genius, belongs to this second and greater order of mind.[10]

Moreover in India, owing to the divorce of political activity from the actual government and administration of the affairs of the country, an academical turn of thought is too common in our dealings with politics. But Tilak had never been an academic politician; he was action-oriented and moved forward accordingly. It was impossible for him to view the facts and needs of current Indian politics of the nineteenth century in the pure, serene or the dim, religious light of the Witenagemot and the Magna Carta and the constitutional history of England during the past seven centuries, or to accept the academic sophism of a gradual preparation for liberty, or merely to discuss isolated or omnibus grievances and strive to enlighten the darkness of the official mind by luminous speeches and resolutions, as was the general practice of Congress politics till 1905.[11] A national agitation in the country which would make the Congress movement a living and active force was always his ideal, and what the Congress would not do, he, when still an isolated leader of a handful of enthusiasts in a corner of the country, set out to do in his own strength and by his own hand. He saw from the first that for a people circumstanced like ours there could be only one political question and one aim, not the gradual improvement of the present administration into something in the end fundamentally the opposite of itself, but the early substitution of Indian and national for English and bureaucratic control in the affairs on India. A subject nation does not prepare itself by gradual progress for liberty—it opens by liberty its way to rapid progress. The only progress that has to be made in the preparation for liberty, is progress in the awakening of the national spirit and in the creation of the will to be free and the will to adopt the necessary means and bear the necessary sacrifices for liberty. It is these clear perceptions that have regulated his political career.[12]

Therefore, the whole of the first part of his political life was devoted to a vigorous and living propaganda for the reawakening and solidifying of the national life of Maharashtra. When the *Swadeshi* agitation gave him the first opportunity of a large

movement, he seized it with avidity, while his past work in Maharashtra, his position as the leader of a small advanced section in the old Congress politics and his character, sacrifices and sufferings, at once fixed the choice of the new party on him as their predestined leader. Tilak adopted the four major points whch had emerged in the Bengal agitation, these were *swaraj*, *swadeshi*, National education and boycolt. He introduced them into the resolutions of the Congress at the Calcutta session—much to the detriment of the uniformity of safe and dignified impotence which had characterised the august proceedings of that temperate national body. The four resolutions were for him the first step towards shaking the Congress out of its torpid tortoise-like gait and turning it into a living and acting body.

Swaraj, complete and early self-government in whatever form, had the merit in his eyes of making definite and near to the national vision, the one thing needful, the one aim that mattered, the one essential change that included all the others. No nation can develop a living enthusiasm or accept great action and great sacrifices for a goal that is lost to its eye in the mist of far-off centuries; it must see it near and distinct before it, magnified by a present hope, looming largely and actualised as a living aim whose early realisation only depends on a great sustained and sincere effort. National education meant for him the training of the young generation in the new national spirit, to be the architects of liberty; *Swadeshi* meant actualisation of the national self-consciousness and the national will and the readiness to sacrifice which would fix them in the daily mind and daily life of the people. In boycott, which was only a popular name for passive resistance, he saw the means to give to the struggle between the two ideas in conflict, bureaucratic control and national control, a vigorous shape and body and to the popular side a weapon and an effective form of action. As a man of action with organising skills, he knew well that by action and not by thought and speech alone, can the will of a people be vivified, trained and made solid and enduring. To get a sustained authority from the Congress for a sustained effort in these four directions seemed to him of capital importance; this was the reason for his inflexible insistence on their unchanged inclusion when the programme seemed to him to be in danger.[13]

Yet also, because he was a practical politician and a man of action, he had always, so long as the essentials were safe, been ready to admit any change, in name or form or any modification of programme or action dictated be the necessities of the time. Thus during the movement of 1905-1910, the *Swadeshi* leader and the *Swadeshi* party insisted on agitation in India and discouraged reliance on agitation in England, because the awakening and fixing of a self-reliant national spirit and will in India was the need of the hour. In England, no party or body of opinion existed which would listen to the national claim, nor could exist—as anybody with the least knowledge of English politics could have told—until that claim had been unmistakably and insistently made and was clearly supported by the fixed will of the nation. The leader of men in war or politics always distrust petty and episodical gains which, while giving false hopes are merely nominal and put off or even endanger the real issue, but will always seize any advantage which brings decisive victory definitely nearer. It is only the pure idealist—but let us remember that he too has his great and indispensable uses—who insists always on either all or nothing at all. Not revolutionary methods or revolutionary idealism, but the clear sight and the direct propaganda and action of the patriotic political leader on the one thing needful and the straightway to drive at it, had been the sense of Tilak's political career.

The Vision of Free India

Beyond the attainment of *Swaraj*, which was always the goal, Tilak saw a higher vision of free India. He visualized an emerging India, self-respecting and free, an India leading the world to an even higher destiny. This is why Tilak repeatedly said, '*Swaraj* is the foundation and not the heights of our future prosperity.'[14] Free India would fulfil its destiny because they created that foundation.

In the economic sphere, with complete freedom to control trade and manufactures, India could build her own industries and create her own economic life. Western science and technology, industrialization and modernization were all to be studied and applied to the material advancement of India. The nation was great and

potentially rich, needing only development by her own people for her own benefit. The boycott of foreign goods, the development of Indian manufacturers under the impetus of *swadeshi*, were the first steps in the economic reawakening of India. The welfare of the peasant and the worker, the merchant and the professional man was all bound together in the welfare of the nation and national welfare could not be based on class warfare but on the Indian ideal of community cooperation. The spirit of independence, unity and self-help, which were cardinal to the programme of the Nationalists, would lead to the regeneration of India.

Regarding social reform, Tilak urged the removal of all the disabilities that had grown up in the social order during more than a thousand years of warfare and alien rule. He never opposed social reform but battled against the Westernized social reformers. Tilak's plan for reform involved three necessary steps: popular education for the need for reform which would come from the people making it moral and democratic; basing the reforms on the Indian civilization's own ideals of cooperative social organization, not on merely the imitated pattern of social organization of some alien culture; and concentration on the political goal for *Swaraj* was the basis of all meaningful reform, whether social, economic, educational or political. With the attainment of *Swaraj* the necessary steps for social reform might be taken, supported by education and popular consent, based on the classical values and the ideals of India's own way of life. Tilak was a realist. Meaningful and effective reform was dependent upon self-rule.[15]

Tilak, Ghose, Rai and Pal were all educators. They knew, perhaps better than any other members of their generation, the value of education and the need for the spread of education throughout the land. Education, according to them was not be confined to the schoolroom, but the everyday task of all the people, led by the press of India, and supported and encouraged by all those who had received the benefits of education. They conceptualised national education that would take the best from both the West and from India's own past and resynthesize these into the intellectual tools for the growth of the people and the nation.

After *Swaraj*, when India could develop her own system of education, the renaissance of India could be brought to its fulfilment.

Tilak had a vision of India moving forward under the banner of freedom, prepared to meet all the challenges of national life, both internal and external, building a new nation because the people were willing to stand united in all their actions. Spiritual unity is the fundamental unity of India. In planning the details of his political programme, Tilak presented the country with his plan for the constructive programme of the Congress which could be relevant for India even after attaining *swaraj*. As a realist he understand that it was more important to prepare the nation for self-rule, to equip the people with the ability to rule themselves, than to set forth doctrine as to the details of the ordering of the political community. He was convinced that, if his legacy to free India provided the nation with the broad outlines of a philosophy of a political order, then the people could rely upon that philosophy to guide them in applying it to the specific needs, situations, the detailed legislation, the day-to-day administration of the free state of India. This is why the greatest legacy of the Lokmanya is the political philosophy that he and the Nationalists developed in the course of the long struggle for *Swaraj* as a guide and inspiration to free India.

His philosophy of the right order of the political community was a part of the total theory of the right order of man and the universe. His political philosophy was integrally part of the philosophy of life of India. Aurobindo Ghose foresaw the future of his nation, 'The right order of human life as of the universe is preserved according to the ancient Indian idea by each individual being following faithfully his *svadharma*, the true law and norm of his nature and the nature of his kind and by the group being, the organic collective life, doing likewise.'[16]

The duty of the individual came first; the duty of the society and the state was to assist the individual to fulfil his duty and to attain the moral purpose of life. Individual well-being was the basis of social and political obligation. The *raison d' tre* of the state in the political philosophy of Tilak was *Dharma*. The state existed for a spiritual end, and it was because only the free state could perform its spiritual duties that *Swaraj* was a moral imperative.

But this does not mean that he had a vision of a theocratic state. The Sanatana Dharma was not meant to be rigid, exclusive, dogmatic, but rather eternal and universal, open, tolerant and flexible. In the classical theory of the state, the secular state protected and promoted all *Dharmas*, assisted men on all paths to the attainment of the Purpose of life. Tilak agreed completely with this meaning of the purpose of the state. Tilak was emphatic on this point. 'The government of a country, where different religions are followed by the people, must render proper assistance and give concessions to the people to follow their respective religions.'[17] The state must build the spirit of tolerance and of unity, must rest upon the common need of all men for the attainment of the common goal. Sister Nivedita beautifully expressed it in writing, '...side by side must work brothers of all shades of opinion, of all forms of energy, for recreating of the *Dharma*, for the building anew, in the modern world, of *Mahabharata*, Heroic India'.[18]

Redemption or salvation or liberation or realization or *Moksha* is the birthright of every *Karma*-bound soul. The state should never deny this ultimate right as its very reason for existence is to assist man in this fulfilment. This is why free India was the glorious goal for which so many fought, sacrificed and died. Shortly after his release from prison in Alipore bomb case, Aurobindo Ghose reminded his nation that 'it is for the *Dharma* and by the *Dharma* that India exists. To magnify the religion means to magnify the country.'[19]

And Tilak's vision and hopes were not restricted to India alone. He foresaw a great destiny for his nation, a destiny which was not merely political. First he saw free India as a bastion of freedom and justice in the world, as a source of strength, material and moral, in the affairs of the world. Tilak believed that 'from the point of view of the peace of Asia and the world, it is absolutely necessary that India should be self-governed internally and made a bulwark of liberty in the East.' But more than this Tilak foresaw India's role in the world as a messenger of a world reawakening, or a world rediscovery of spiritual values. He knew and loved the philosophy of life of his civilization; he knew Sanatana *Dharma* was not solely India's possession but that it belonged to the world, that it was

eternal and that that which is eternal is universal; and he saw in it the answer to the prayers of mankind for guidance, for peace and for justice. Free India was to be *guru* to the world, for he believed the day would come when we shall see our preachers preaching the Sanatana Dharma all over the world.[20]

After *Swaraj*, free India, living in peace and advancing to meet her destiny, guided by the eternal and universal philosophy of life, would be the greatest positive force in the world. Aurobindo Ghose summarized this higher destiny of free India when he wrote,

'We shall devote ourselves not to politics alone, nor to social questions alone, not to theology or philosophy or literature or science by themselves, but we include all of these in one entity which we believe to be all important, the dharma, the national religion which we also believe to be universal. There is mighty law of life, a great principle of human evolution, a body of spiritual knowledge and experience of which India has always been destined to be guardian, exemplar and missionary. This is the Sanatana Dharma, the eternal religion.'[21]

In a world of darkness, confusion and a groping for Reality, Meaning and Purpose, India's destiny is self-evident. This, too, Tilak foresaw. This is the greatness of his vision of free India. This is the promise in which he believed. This is the legacy of the Lokmanya.

REFERENCES

1. Ghose, Aurobindo, *Bankim-Tilak-Dayananda* (Calcutta: Arya Publishing House), 1940, p. 16.
2. *Ibid.*, p. 18.
3. Saggi, P.D. (ed.), *Life and Work of Lal, Bal and Pal, op. cit.*, p. 124.
4. *Ibid.*, p. 126.
5. Ghose, Aurobindo, *Bankim-Tilak-Dayananda, op. cit.*, p. 25.
6. Athalye, D.V., *The Life of Lokmanya Tilak, op. cit.*, p. 120.
7. *Ibid.*, p. 168.
8. Ghose, Aurobindo, *Bankim-Tilak-Dayananda, op. cit.*, pp. 30-31.
9. Saggi, P.D. (ed.), *Life and Work of Lal, Bal and Pal, op. cit.*, p. 128.
10. Athalye, D.V., *The Life of Lokmanya Tilak, op. cit.*, p. 172.
11. Saggi, P.D. (ed.), *Life and Work of Lal, Bal and Pal, op. cit.*, p. 129.
12. *Ibid.*
13. *Samgra Tilak*, Vol. VI, *op. cit.*, p. 61.

14. Tilak, B.G., *His Writings and Speeches, op. cit.*, p. 164.
15. Shay, Theodore, *The Legacy of Lokmanya, op. cit.*, p. 189.
16. Ghose, Aurobindo, *Foundations of Indian Culture, op. cit.*, p. 386.
17. *Gleanings from Tilak Writings and Speeches, op. cit.*, p. 386.
18. *Selected Essays of Sister Nivedita* (Madras: Ganesan & Co.), 1911, p. 152.
19. Ghose, Aurobindo, *Speeches, op. cit.*
20. Tilak, B.G., *His Writings and Speeches, op. cit.*, p. 41.
21. Ghose, Aurobindo, *The Ideal of Karamyogin, op. cit.*, pp. 2-3.

BIBLIOGRAPHY

Ambirajan, S., *Political Economy and Monetary Management in India, 1766-1914* (Madras: Affiliated East West Press), 1984.

Athalye, D.V., *The Life of Lokmanya Tilak* (Poona: Annasahib Chiploonkar), 1921.

Azad, A.K., *India Wins Freedom* (New York: Longman), 1960.

Banerjea, S.N., *A Nation in Making, Being the Reminiscence of Fifty Years* of Puslic Life (London, Oxford University Press), 1925.

Banerji, A.K., *Aspects of Indo-British Economic Relations, 1858-1898* (Bombay: Oxford University Press), 1982.

Banerji, Arun, *Finances in the Early Raj: Investments and the External Sector* (New Delhi: Sage Publications), 1995.

Black, R.D., *Collison, Economic Thought and the Irish Question, 1817-1870* (Cambridge: Cambridge University Press),1960.

Bapat, S.V. (ed.), *Gleanings from Tilak's Writings and Speeches* (Poona: S.V. Bapat), 1926.

Bapat, S.V. (Ed.), *The Reminiscences and the Anecdotes of Lokmanya Tilak*, Vol. II (Poona: S.V. Bapat), 1925.

Blaug, Mark, "Kuhn versus Lakatos or Paradigms versus Research Programmes in the history of Economics" in *Method and Appraisal in Economics*, edited by Spiro J. Latsis (Cambridge: Cambridge University Press), 1976.

Blaug, Mark, *Economic Theory in Retrospect* (Cambridge: Cambridge University Press), 1978.

Bose, S.C., *The Indian Struggle (1920-34)* (Calcutta: Publications for Netaji Publishing Society), 1948.

Cashman, Richard I., *The Myth of Lokmanya* (Berkeley: University of California Press), 1975.

Central Statistical Organisation, *National Accounts Statistics: Sources and Methods* (New Delhi: Department of Statistics, Ministry of Planning, Government of India), 1989.

Chakarverty, S., "Drain Theory of Dadabhai Naoroji," a paper presented to the Indian Economic Association Conference, December 1968.

Chandra, Bipan, *The Rise and Growth of Economic Nationalism in India, Economic Policies of Indian National Leadership 1880-1905* (New Delhi: People's Publishing House), 1966.

Charlesworth, Neil, *British Rule and the Indian Economy, 1800-1914* (London: Macmillan), 1982.

Chatterjee, D.K., *C.R. Das and Indian National Movement: A Study in his Political Ideas* (Calcutta: Bhattachariya), 1965.

Chatterjee, R.N., *On Labour Capital* (Calcutta: Chatterjee & Co.), n.d.

Chaudhuri, K.N., "India's International Economy in the Nineteenth Century: An Historical Survey", *Modern Asian Studies*, Vol. 2, No.1 (January), 1968.

Chintamani, C.Y., *Indian Politics Since the Mutiny* (New Delhi: Rupa), 2002.

Chiplunkar, Vishnushastri, *Nibandh Mula* (Poona: S.V. Bapat), 1926.

Chirol, Valentine, *Indian Unrest* (London: Macmillan), 1910.

Coase, R.H., *Essays on Economics and Economists* (Chicago: The University of Chicago Press), 1994.

Clark, Colin, *Conditions of Economic Progress* (London: MacMillan and Co. Ltd.), 1949.

Dantwala, M.L., *Poverty in India, Then and Now, 1870-1970* (Delhi: MacMillan), 1973.

Das, C.R. and Bhagwan Das, *Outline Scheme of Swaraj* (Bombay: Swastik), 1923.

Das, M.N., *Indian National Congress Versus the British, Vol. 1, (1885-1918)*, Delhi, 1978.

Dasgupta, Ajit K., *A History of Indian Economic Thought* (London: Routledge), 1993.

Dasgupta, Hemendranath, *Deshbandhu Chittaranjan Das* (New Delhi: Publications Division, Ministry of Information and Broadcasting, Government of India), 1960.

Datta, Bhabatosh, *Indian Economic Thought – Twentieth Century Perspectives* (New Delhi: Tata McGraw Hill Publishing Company Ltd.), 1962.

Datta, Bhabatosh, *The Evolution of Economic Thinking in India* (Dr. P.N. Banerjea Memorial Lectures, 1961) (Calcutta: Federation Hall Society), 1962.

Desai, S.S.M., *Economic History of India* (New Delhi: Himalaya Publishing House), 1990.

Dimand, Robert W., "I have no Great Faith in Political Arithmetic: Adam Smith and Quantitative Political Economy" in *Measurement, Quantification and Economic Analysis: Numeracy in Economics* edited by Ingrid H. Rima (London: Routledge), 1995.

Dutt, R., Palme, *India Today* (Delhi: People's Publishing House), 1955.

Dutt, Romesh, *The Economic History of India Under the British Rule*, Vols. 1, 2 & 3 (New Delhi: Publications Division, Ministry of Information and Broadcasting, Government of India), 1963.

Dwyer, M.O., *India as I Knew It* (London: Seluryin Blornt), 1935.

Ganguli, B.N., *Dadabhai Naoroji and the Drain Theory* (New York: Asia Publishing House), 1965.

Ganguli, B.N., *Indian Economic Thought: Nineteenth Century Perspectives* (New Delhi: Tata McGraw-Hill Publishing Co. Ltd.), 1978.

Georgescu-Roegen, Nicholas, *Analytical Economics: Issues and Problems* (Cambridge, Massachusetts: Harvard University Press), 1966.

Ghose, Aurobindo, *Bankim-Tilak Dayananda* (Calcutta: Arya Publishing House), 1940.

Ghose, Aurobindo, *The Foundations of Indian Culture* (New York: The Sri Aurobindo Library), 1953.

Ghose, Aurobindo, *The Ideal of the Karmayogin* (Pondicherry: Sri Aurobindo Ashram), 1950.

Gopalakrishnan, P.K., *Development of Economic Ideas in India, 1880-1914* (Gravenhange: Institute of Social Studies), 1954.

Gupta, Ajit Das, *A History of Indian Economic Thought* (Madras: T.R. Publications Private Limited), 1990.

Ingrid, H. Rima (ed.), Measurement, Quantification and Economic Analysis: Numeracy in Economics (London: Routledge), 1995.

Iyer, C.S. Ranga, *India in the Crucible* (London: Seluryin Blornt), 1928.

Jenk, L.H., "British Experience with Foreign Investments," *Journal of Economic History*, 1944.

Jha, Shiva Chandra, *A History of Indian Economic Thought* (Calcutta: Firma K.L. Mukhopadhyay), 1981.

Jog, N.G., *Lokmanya Bal Gangadhar Tilak* (New Delhi: Publications Division, Ministry of Information and Broadcasting, Government of India), 1962.

Karmakar, A.D., *Economic Thought of Modern India* (Dharwar: J.S.S., Institute of Economic Research), 1974.

Karunakaran, K.P., *Indian Politics from Dadabhai Naoroji to Gandhi: A Study of the Political Ideas of Modern India* (New Delhi: Gitanjali Publishing House), 1988.

Kelkar, N.C., *Landmarks in Lokamanya's Life* (Madras: Ganesan & Co.), 1924.

Khan, Sir, Syed Ahmad, *The Complete Collection of Lectures and Speeches* (ed.) by M.I. Gujarati (Lahore: Nawal Kishore), n.d.

Knight, Robert, *India: A Review of England's Financial Relations Therewith* (London: W.J. Johnson), 1968.

Kulkarni, A.V., Lokmanya Tilak (Bombay: Inderprakash Steam Press), 1909.

Kurdas, Cigdern, "The Whig Historian on Adam Smith: Paul Samuelson's Canonical Model", *History of Economics Society Bulletin*, Vol. X, No. 1 (Spring), 1988.

Lakatos, Imre, "Falsification and the Methodology of Scientific Research Programmes" in *Criticism and the Growth of Knowledge* edited by Imre Lakatos and Alan Musgrave (Cambridge: Cambridge University Press), 1970.

Lipton, Michael and Ravallion, Martin, "Poverty and Policy", Policy Research Working Papers, No. WPS 1130 (Washington: The World Bank), 1993.

Loganathan, A., *History of Economic Thought* (New Delhi: S. Chand and Company Ltd.), 1987.

Madan, G.R., *Economic Thinking in India* (Madras: S. Chand & Co.), 1982.

Mahajan, O.P., *The Drain Theory: Fact and Fiction* (IEA), 1968.

Majumdar, Jatindra Kumar (ed.), *Indian Speeches and Documents on British Rule, 1821-1918* (London), 1937.

Masani, R.P., *Builders of Modern India—Dadabhai Naoroji* (New Delhi: Publications Division, Ministry of Information and Broadcasting, Government of India), 1960.

Masani, R.P., *Dadabhai Naoroji: The Grand Old Man of India* (London: George Allen and Unwin Ltd.), 1939.

Masani, R.P., *Dadabhai Naoroji* (New Delhi: Publications Division, Ministry of Information and Broadcasting, Government of India), 1960.

Marx, Karl and Fredrick, Engels, *On Colonialism* (Moscow: Progress Publishers), 1965.

Mill, John Stuart, *Principles of Political Economy*, edited by W.J. Ashley (London: Longmans, Green and Co.), 1909.

Morrison, Sir *Theodore Economic Transition in India* (London: London Press), 1916.

Mukherjee, M., *National Income of India: Trends and Structure* (Calcutta: Statistical Publishing Society), 1969.

Mukerjee, Tapan, "Theory of Economic Drain: Impact of British Rule on the Indian Economy: 1840-1900" in *Economic Imperialism: A Book of Readings*, edited by K.E. Boulding and Tapan Mukherjee (Ann Arbor: The University of Michigan Press), 1972.

Nabers, Lawrence, 'The Positive and Genetic Approaches' in *The Structure of Economic Science Essays on Methodology*, edited by Sherman Roy Krupp (Englewood Cliffs, N.J.: Prentice-Hall, Inc.), 1966.

Nanda, B.R., *Gokhale, Gandhi and the Nehru's Studies in Indian Nationalsim* (London: George Allen & Unwin Ltd.), 1990.

Naoroji, Dadabhai, *A Sketch of his Life and Career* (Madras: G. A. Natesan & Co.), 1920.

Naoroji, Dadabhai, *Speeches and Writings of Dadabhai Naoroji* (Madras: G.A. Natesan & Co.), n.d.

Naoroji, Dadabhai, *The Financial Administration of India* (London: W.J. Johnson), 1871.

Naoroji, Dadabhai, *Essays, Speeches, Addresses and Writings* (Bombay: Caxton Printing Works), 1899.

Naoroji, Dadabhai, *Poverty and Un-British Rule in India* (New Delhi: Publications Division, Government of India), 1962.

Naoroji, Dadabhai, *India's Wrongs and Remedy* (Madras: The Commonwealth Office), 1917.

Okakura, *Ideals of the East* (Calcutta: Edition Indian), 1973.

Pal, Bepin Chandra, *His Life and Utterances* (Madras: Ganesan & Co.), 1925.

Pandey, Shridhar, *Economic History of India* (Hindi) (Patna: Motilal Banarsidass), 1991.

Parekh C.L, *Essays, Speeches, Address and Writings (on Indian Politics) of the Hon'ble Dadabhai Naoroji* (Bombay: Asia Publishers), 1887.

Parliamentary Debates (House of Commons) Fourth Series, Vol. XI, 13th April 1893.

Parvate, T.V., *Bal Gangadhar Tilak* (Ahmedabad: Navajivan Publishing House), 1958.

Patwardhan, R.P. (ed.), *Dadabhai Naoroji Correspondence, Child and Youth Section*, Vol. II, Part I (Bombay: Allied Publishers), 1977.

Paul, R.R., *History of Economic Thought* (New Delhi: Kalyani Publishers), 1979.

Pradhan, G.P. and A.K. Bhagwat, *Lokmanya Tilak: A Biography* (Poona: J.S. Tilak), 1963.

Prasad, R., *At the Feet of Mahatma Gandhi* (Bombay: Asia Publishing House), 1961.

Price, Powell, *A History of India* (London: Thomas Nelson and Sons Limited), 1955.

Ranade, Mahadev Govind, *Ranade's Economic Writings* edited by Bipan Chandra (New Delhi: Gian Publishing House), 1990.

Rao, V.K.R.V., *An Essay on India's National Income, 1925-1929* (London: George Allen and Unwin), 1939.

Rashid, Salim, "Does a Famous Economist Deserve Special Standards? A Critical Note on Adam Smith Scholarship;"

History of Economics Society Bulletin, Vol. XI, No. 2 (Fall), 1989.

Ray, M.N., *India in Transition* (Bombay: Nachiketa), 1971.

Ray, P.C., *Life and Times of C.R. Das* (Calcutta: Orient Books), 1958.

Robinson, Joan, *An Essay on Marxian Economics* (London: Macmillan), 1966.

Rogin, Leo, *The Meaning and Validity of Economic Theory* (New York: Harper and Bros.), 1956.

Ronaldshay, Earl of the Heart of Aryavarta: *A Study of the Psychology of Indian Unrest* (London: Constable), 1925.

Saggi, P.D. (ed.), *Life and Work of Lal, Bal and Pal* (New Delhi: Overseas Publishing House), 1962.

Samuelson, Paul, "The Transfer Problem and Transport Costs: The Terms of Trade when Impediments are Absent," *Economic Journal*, Vol. LXII, No. 246 (June), 1952.

Samuelson, Paul, "Out of the Closet: A Program for the Whig History of Economic Science", *History of Economics Society Bulletin*, IKI (Fall), 1987.

Schumpeter, J.A., *History of Economic Analysis* (New York: Oxford University Press), 1954.

Scweinitz, Jr. Karl de, *The Rise and Fall of British India: Imperialism as Inequality* (London: Methuen & Co.), 1983.

Selected Essays of Sister Nivedita (Madras: Ganesan & Co.), 1911.

Sen, R.K. and Mandal, S.K., *Ranade's Analysis of India's Population Problem and The Views of Naoroji and Doskar, I.E.A.*, 75th Conference Volume, 1992.

Sen, Rathindra Nath, *Life and Times of Deshbandhu Chittranjan Das* (New Delhi: Northern Book Centre), 1989.

Sen, Sunanda, *Colonies and the Empire India, 1890-1914* (Hyderabad: Orient Longman), 1922.

Shanmugasundaram, V., *Indian Economic Thought and Policy* (New Delhi: S. Chand and Company Ltd.), 1981.

Sharma, Jai Narain, *Power, Politics and Corruption: A Gandhian Solution* (New Delhi: Deep and Deep), 2005.

Sharma, Jai Narain, "Gandhi and the Congress Presidents" in Malhotra, S.C. (ed.) *Gandhi and the Indian National Congress* (Chandigarh: Publications Bureau, Panjab University), 1988

Shay, Theodore, *The Legacy of Lokmanya* (London: Oxford University Press), 1956.

Singh, V.B., *From Naoroji to Nehru* (New Delhi: MacMillan), 1975.

Sitaramayya, Pattabhi, *History of Indian National Congress 1885-1935*, Vol. I (New Delhi: S. Chand & Co.), 1969.

Spear, T.G.P., *India* (London: Seluryin Blornt), 1935.

Stark, Werner, *The History of Economics in its Relation to Social Development* (London: Kegan Paul, Trench, Trubner & Co.), 1944.

Studenski, Paul, *The Income of Nations* (New York: New York University Press), 1958.

Tilak, B.G., *Gita Rahasya* (Poona: Tilak Brothers), 1925.

Tilak, B.G., *His Writings and Speeches* (Madras: Ganeshan & Co.), 1922.

Tilak, B.G., *Samagra Lokmanya Tilak*, Vol. IV (Pune: Kesari Prakashan), 1974.

Vaswani, T.L., *India in Chains* (Madras: Ganesan & Co.), 1920

Viner, Jacob, *Studies in the Theory of International Trade* (London: George Allen and Unwin), 1960.

World Bank, *World Development Report, 1990* (Oxford: Oxford University Press), 1990.

Zachaias, H.C.E., *Renaiscent India* (London: Allen), 1933.

Zaidi, A.M. and Others, *The Encycolpaedia of Indian National Congress* (New Delhi: S. Chand & Co.), 1980.

Zaidi, Moin A., *Dadabhai Naoroji, Speeches and Writings* (New Delhi: Indian Institute of Applied Political Research), Vol. 1, 1985.

Index